# The Complete Spanner's Worl

# Lambretta

# 'Slimstyle' Scooters

## by Martin 'Sticky' Round

Published by:

FINGERS IN PIES
PUBLICATIONS

ISBN 0-9548216-0-2

Distributed by:
**Scooter Products**
**10T, Elizabeth House**
**30-32 The Boulevard**
**Weston-super-Mare**
**Somerset, BS23 1NF**
**Tel/Fax: 01934 417834**
**www.scooterproducts.co.uk**
**www.lambrettabook.com**

# The Complete Spanner's Workshop Manual for:

# Lambretta

# 'Slimstyle' Scooters

# INTRODUCTION

The Lambretta scooter was born of post-war austerity, but grew to be so much more than basic transport for the Italian working class. It symbolised Italy of the 1950s and '60s, became an icon for the mod movement, spawned a fashion label, and mobilised another generation of scooterists through the '80s and '90s. Nowadays the name Lambretta means many things to many people, and like any fashion symbol, scooter prices have risen to reflect this status.

It is somewhat surprising then that there has never been a fully pictorial guide to stripping and rebuilding a Lambretta piece by piece. This is where the Complete Spanner's guide comes in. We like to think that a simple step-by-step approach will offer far better insight into working on your scooter and dealing with the problems thrown up by a vehicle which has design roots firmly based in the 1950s.

Where the Complete Spanner's guide scores over any previous publication on this subject is that it is written with the best information currently available. The book covers not just the accepted methods of nut and bolt restoration, but also shortcuts and modern methods of doing things that are often better and easier than the old ways.

The book also deals with the reality of running a machine for which new official spares are no longer freely available. Many companies produce pattern Lambretta spares, but not all of these are of sufficient quality. The Spanner's Manual will help you to find the best of what is available.

The other major problem encountered by people looking to build vintage scooters from items obtained at parts fairs is identifying the correct pieces. We will show the difference between late and early Special/TV-type headsets for instance. They may look the same at first glance, but important differences mean that the wrong one won't fit properly.

It should be remembered that nobody knows everything about Lambrettas: even the most respected restorer in Italy occasionally finds out something new. Certainly the author claims to be no world-class authority, and learned many things during the making of this book that he will probably forget in the course of time. With its publication though, a wealth of valuable information gathered from a range of experts will now be comfortably at hand, whenever it is required.

---

## The Future of this Book

The subject of Lambrettas is vast and complex. While we are certain that Complete Spanner's is the most comprehensive technical work ever produced on this subject, inaccuracies may have crept in. It is also inevitable that things will change after the book is published. As such whilst every care has been taken, the author, publisher and contributors can accept no responsibility for damage, loss or injury resulting from errors or omissions contained herein.

Our answer to the possibility of errors and future changes is to support the book with a web site www.lambrettabook.com where readers can notify us of any missing tips, figures or inaccuracies. These suggestions will be checked and then added to the web pages so that other Lambretta enthusiasts can benefit from the information supplied.

If and when we have enough extra information the book will be revised and updated for future editions. In this way we hope the guide will be organic and grow with your support. If there is something you feel should be added or corrected, please let us know via the web site. Do note though that we will not be able to enter into any correspondence about the contents of the book, or your submissions.

## Safety Warning

I'm not going to patronise you with endless DO and DON'T lists regarding workshop safety because it is really your responsibility to ensure that things are done to minimise risks. The three areas I really think you should be concerned about are eye protection, fumes and fire risk. Always use goggles when grinding or drilling, or even cleaning grit off a dirty scooter. Getting metal splinters in your eyes is no fun.

As someone who has had to push a flaming Lambretta from their burning garage into the street I think I can safely comment that flammable liquids and welders are not a good combination. The thought of losing all of my scooters to fire – let alone being burnt myself – has since made me a bit more careful. A dry powder fire extinguisher now hangs from the ceiling of my workshop.

Finally be aware of fume risk. Petrol, paint, running scooters and lots of other chemicals all give off nasty fumes which are best shared with the planet rather than kept selfishly enclosed with you in the shed.

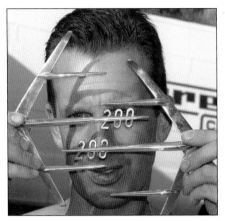
Dean

Mark

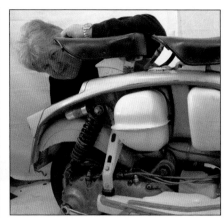
Nigel

## Acknowledgements

The original idea for doing a technical scooter book belongs to my wife Tracy, while specifically doing a Lambretta manual is down to former Scootering Magazine editor and publisher Stuart Lanning.

Thanks must go to Nigel Cox (Weston Scooter Parts) who both supplied the scooter used, and the parts to rebuild it. Much of the restoration information came from the vast experience of Dean Orton (Rimini Lambretta Centre) whilst the specific engineering and tuning info came mostly from Mark Broadhurst (MB Developments).

Alan (Speed Demons SC/Diablo Moto), Carl Newberry, Hippy Jerry and Ruggero Giusti provided the hands seen in many of the photographs.

The remaining information has either been gleaned from the current crop of Lambretta specialists around the world, Lambretta internet sites or from previous manuals or tuning books. Thanks should therefore go to: Mark Haines and Richard (Bedlam), Hippy Jerry (Scooter Surgery), Harry Barlow (Pro Porting/Grand Prix Scooters), Paul (Scooter Restorations), Pete Davies (LCGB), Paolo Catani (www.racinglambrettas.com), Dave Webster (Midland Scooter Centre), Terry and Ian Frankland (Taffspeed), Martin Lloyd (www.lloydy.org), Peter Bowden (Cambridge Lambretta Workshop), the contributors to www.lcgb.co.uk, Jerome Read (Readspeed), Ray Kemp and Paul Lazenby (AF Rayspeed), Vince Mross (Lambretta Works USA), Terry White (Rapid industrial Fasteners), Perry Lewis (Totally Scooters), Daniel (www.scooterhelp.com), Ian Hepworth (MBD), Ken Herlingshaw, Edward Stott and Arthur Francis.

A special thanks to those who helped to proof the final copy including Ben and Julie Round, Andy Gillard (Scootering), Adam Winstone and Jem Booth.

## Copyright

## About the Author

Sticky is the UK-based former editor of both Scootering and Twist & Go magazines, and now a freelance journalist specialising in scooters. He spent much of his youth breaking, rebuilding, tuning and occasionally racing Lambrettas, and riding them as far abroad as Athens. Sticky's respected technical articles in Scootering reflect his passionate belief that to go places on other brands of scooter means to get there, but to end a journey by Lambretta is *to arrive in style.*

## Dedication

This book is dedicated to the memory of Dave Fowler, my other club-mates from the Speed Demons Scooter Club, to all the good people I've met on the scooter scene, and also to Sam – so that one day he can fix his own scooter without nagging his dad for help.

I hope it also serves as an adequate memorial to scooter guru Terry Frankland of Taffspeed Racing who tragically passed away during final production of this book.

Alan

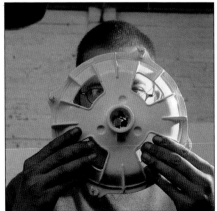
Carl

Ruggero

# CONTENTS OF THIS BOOK

## MODELS COVERED BY THIS BOOK

Terminology for Lambrettas within the scooter scene is fairly diverse and can get complicated. The models dealt with in this book are all derivatives of the Lambretta LI-series machines with chain-drive engines and fat tubular steel chassis. The Series 1 and Series 2 models were mechanically similar but considerably wider in their bodywork, hence when the Series 3 model was introduced in December 1961 the term 'Slimstyle' was coined for the sleeker 60s models. 'Slimstyle' has since stuck as a generic term for subsequent LI-based Lambretta production, and is often interchanged with the term 'Series 3' to mean post-1961 Lambretta production.

The specific Italian and Indian models covered by this term are as follows:

**LI 125 series 3**
**LI 150 series 3**
**TV 173 series 3**
**TV 200 (UK name 'GT 200')**
**LI 125 Special (not an official UK import)**
**LI 150 Special (also 'Silver Special', 'Golden Special' or 'Pacemaker')**
**SX 150**
**SX 200**
**GP 125 (Italian name '125 DL', also called 'Grand Prix')**
**GP 150 (Italian name '150 DL' also called 'Grand Prix')**
**GP 200 (Italian name '200 DL' also called 'Grand Prix')**

The majority of information in this book also applies to most Serveta (Eibar) models, though details of all Spanish bodywork modifications are not included.

## Lambretta LI SERIES 3

| Engine Size | Bore x Stroke | Power Output | Fuel Consumption | Max Speed | Gears | Tyre Size | Tank Capacity | Dry Weight | Overall Length | Overall Height | Overall Width |
|---|---|---|---|---|---|---|---|---|---|---|---|
| 125cc | 52x58mm | 5.5hp @5,200rpm) | 128mpg | 50mph | 4 | 3.50x10 | 8.5 L | 104 kg | 1800mm | 1030mm | 700mm |
| 150cc | 57x58mm | 6.6hp @ 5,300rpm | 124mpg | 55mph | 4 | 3.50x10 | 8.5 L | 105 kg | 1800mm | 1030mm | 700mm |

**LI 125 Series 3 (Innocenti)**
146,734 produced from December 1961 to November 1967

**LI 150 Series 3 (Innocenti)**
143,091 produced from January 1962 to May 1967

**Frame & Engine number identification**

| Model | Frame Prefix | Engine Prefix |
|---|---|---|
| LI 125 | 125LI | 125LI |
| LI 150 | 150LI | 150LI |

**Right: A mid-series LI 150. The very last LI models had no chrome ring under the headset.**

**Below: The LI 150 was offered in 2-tone paint schemes as standard while the LI 125 was only ever offered in single colours.**

## Lambretta TV SERIES 3

| Engine Size | Bore x Stroke | Power Output | Fuel Consumption | Max Speed | Gears | Tyre Size | Tank Capacity | Dry Weight | Overall Length | Overall Height | Overall Width |
|---|---|---|---|---|---|---|---|---|---|---|---|
| 175cc | 62x58mm | 8.75hp @5,300rpm | 118mpg | 64mph | 4 | 3.50x10 | 8.6 L | 110 kg | 1800mm | 1030mm | 700mm |
| 200cc | 66x58mm | 10.75hp @5,700rpm | 118mpg | 66mph | 4 | 3.50x10 | 8.6 L | 110 kg | 1800mm | 1030mm | 700mm |

**TV 175 Series 3 (Innocenti)**
37,794 produced from March 1962 to October 1965

**TV 200 (Innocenti)**
14,982 produced from April 1963 to October 1965

**Frame & Engine number identification**

| Model | Frame Prefix | Engine Prefix |
|---|---|---|
| TV 175 | 175TV3 | 175TV2 |
| TV 200 | TV3 | TV2 |

**Above: An early TV 200 with LI-style panels. Only the TV 200 used a fibreglass front mudguard as standard.**

**Right: A mid-series TV 175 as defined by the later panels with 'knuckleduster' badge, but also the chrome ring under the headset which was later abandoned.**

Lambretta 175tv

och enda scooter

# Lambretta LI SPECIAL ('PACEMAKER' in UK)

| Engine Size | Bore x Stroke | Power Output | Fuel Consumption | Max Speed | Gears | Tyre Size | Tank Capacity | Dry Weight | Overall Length | Overall Height | Overall Width |
|---|---|---|---|---|---|---|---|---|---|---|---|
| 125cc | 52x58mm | 7.12hp @5,200rpm | 122mpg | 53mph | 4 | 3.50x10 | 8.1 L | 118 kg | 1800mm | 1030mm | 700mm |
| 150cc | 57x58mm | 8.25hp @5,590rpm | 107mpg | 59mph | 4 | 3.50x10 | 8.3 L | 120 kg | 1800mm | 1030mm | 700mm |

**LI 125 Special (Innocenti)**
29,841 produced from October 1965 to Jan 1969

**LI 150 Special (Innocenti)**
68,829 produced from September 1963 to October 1966

### Frame & Engine number identification

| Model | Frame Prefix | Engine Prefix |
|---|---|---|
| Li 125 S | 125LIS | 125LIS |
| Li 150 S | 150LIS | 150LI |

The limited edition LI 150 'Golden' Special was exactly what it said on the tin: painted almost totally gold with a unique gold rear frame badge and a metal 'GOLDEN' badge on the legshields. Ideal transport for the A-Team's Mr T, maybe. . .

An Innocenti brochure for the LI 125 Special. Either the photo was flipped by a dope in the advertising department or the factory went to the expense of producing a mirror-image Lambretta with a kickstart on the left. Probably the former . . .

# Lambretta SX (SPECIAL X) SERIES

| Engine Size | Bore x Stroke | Power Output | Fuel Consumption | Max Speed | Gears | Tyre Size | Tank Capacity | Dry Weight | Overall Length | Overall Height | Overall Width |
|---|---|---|---|---|---|---|---|---|---|---|---|
| 150cc | 62x58mm | 9.38hp @5,600rpm | 118mpg | 56mph | 4 | 3.50x10 | 8.3 L | 120 kg | 1800mm | 1030mm | 700mm |
| 200cc | 66x58mm | 11.00hp @5,500rpm | 93mpg | 66mph | 4 | 3.50x10 | 8.3 L | 123 kg | 1800mm | 1030mm | 700mm |

**SX 150 (Innocenti)**
31,238 produced from October 1966 to January 1969

**SX 200 (Innocenti)**
20,783 produced from January 1966 to January 1969

### Frame & Engine number identification

| Model | Frame Prefix | Engine Prefix |
|---|---|---|
| SX 150 | SX150 | SX150 |
| SX 200 | SX200 | SX200 |

An early SX 150 as denoted by the shield-type badge on the horncasting. This model is most easily identified by a chrome crest on the front mudguard.

In Italy the SX 200 was only offered in white with an oxblood red seat. In the UK it was more commonly sold with coloured panel flashes and a black seat.

## **lambretta** GP 'GRAND PRIX' SERIES (DL in Italy)

| Engine Size | Bore x Stroke | Power Output | Fuel Consumption | Max Speed | Gears | Tyre Size | Tank Capacity | Dry Weight | Overall Length | Overall Height | Overall Width |
|---|---|---|---|---|---|---|---|---|---|---|---|
| 125cc | 52x58mm | 7.4hp @6,400rpm | 112mpg | 57mph | 4 | 350x10 | 8.1 L | 118 kg | 1800mm | 1012mm | 680mm |
| 150cc | 57x58mm | 9.40hp @ 6,300rpm | 82mpg | 64mph | 4 | 350x10 | 8.1 L | 120 kg | 1800mm | 1012mm | 680mm |
| 200cc | 66x58mm | 11.74hp @ 6,200rpm | 70mpg | 68mph | 4 | 350x10 | 8.1 L | 123 kg | 1800mm | 1012mm | 680mm |

**GP 125 (Innocenti)**
15,300 produced from January 1969 to April 1971

**GP 150 (Innocenti)**
20,048 produced from January 1969 to April 1971

**GP 200 & GP 200 Electronic (Innocenti)**
9,350 produced from January 1969 to April 1971

### Frame & Engine number identification

| Model | Frame Prefix | Engine Prefix |
|---|---|---|
| GP 125 | 22/1 | 125LIS |
| GP 150 | 22/0 | SX150 |
| GP 200 | 22/2 | SX200 |

The ink-splat legshield logo was used for the Italian market where this model was sold a DL 125. In the UK a chequered flag sticker was used instead.

An Innocenti GP 200 Electronic for the British market. In the UK these machines were fitted with an 'Electronic' sticker on the legshields and this unique seat.

## **lambretta SERVETA** SPANISH SERVETA ('EIBAR') MODELS

| Model | Bore x Stroke | Power Output | Max Speed | Gears | Tyre Size | Tank Capacity | Length | Height | Width |
|---|---|---|---|---|---|---|---|---|---|
| Scooterlinea 125 (LI) | 52x58mm | 5.5hp | 50mph | 4 | 3.50x10 | 8.5 L | 1800mm | 1030mm | 700mm |
| Scooterlinea 150 (LI) | 57x58mm | 6.6hp | 56mph | 4 | 3.50x10 | 8.5 L | 1800mm | 1030mm | 700mm |
| Special 150 | 57x58mm | 7.6hp | 60mph | 4 | 3.50x10 | 8.5 L | 1800mm | 1030mm | 700mm |
| TV 175 S.3 | 62x58mm | 8.75 | 64mph | 4 | 3.50x10 | 8.5 L | 1800mm | 1030mm | 700mm |
| Jet 200 | 66x58mm | 9.75hp | 66mph | 4 | 3.50x10 | 8.5 L | 1800mm | 1030mm | 700mm |
| Lince 125 (Lynx) | 52x58mm | 6.0hp | 54mph | 4 | 3.50x10 | 8.5 L | 1800mm | 1030mm | 700mm |
| Lince 150 (Lynx) | 57x58mm | 7.6hp | 60mph | 4 | 3.50x10 | 8.5 L | 1800mm | 1030mm | 700mm |
| Lince 200 (Lynx) | 66x58mm | 9.75hp | 68mph | 4 | 3.50x10 | 8.5 L | 1800mm | 1030mm | 700mm |

**Left:** The early Serveta Slimstyles - even with disc brakes on the Jet 200.

**Right:** In the 1970s an ugly back light and speed stripes were added.

**Centre:** For 1983 Serveta introduced the Lince (Lynx) range with a revised headset, horncasting and mudguard made from fibreglass.

# Lambretta INDIAN SIL GRAND PRIX MODELS

| MODEL | Bore x stroke | Power Output | Max Speed | Gears | Tyre Size | Tank Capacity | Length | Height | Width |
|---|---|---|---|---|---|---|---|---|---|
| Grand Prix 125cc | 52x58mm | 7.3hp @ 6,400rpm | 58mph | 4 | 350x10 | 8.1 L | 1800mm | 1012mm | 680mm |
| Grand Prix 150cc | 57x58mm | 9.60hp @ 6,300rpm | 64mph | 4 | 350x10 | 8.1 L | 1800mm | 1012mm | 680mm |
| Grand Prix 200cc | 66x58mm | 11.9hp @ 6,200rpm | 74mph | 4 | 350x10 | 8.1 L | 1800mm | 1012mm | 680mm |

**Right: Over the years Scooters India Limited (SIL) made numerous changes to the Innocenti GP specification. Modifications included the use of turning front mudguards, different forks, and various types of indicators. Never once did they manage to improve Bertone's original styling.**

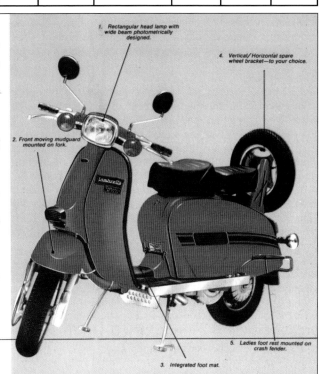

The safe and sturdy Lambretta Grand Prix is elegantly styled and superbly crafted. It has been continuously upgraded to give the utmost economy, power and safety. It's normal speed makes it eligible to run on highways in many countries. When it comes to racing—it has outperformed all other scooters on the tracks. Establishing many glorious records the world over.

The legendary Lambretta has technological inputs from three continents—America, Asia and Europe. It has a feather kick start in all weather and a lightning acceleration yet the fuel economy is fantastic. The four speed gear box gives driving flexibility all along the power curve. Whether idling or at top speed, it always leaves the environment clean. It has already passed emission control tests in many countries including EPA regulation of USA.

Available in eye catching colours, the Grand Prix has girdled the globe since its inception. The difference between then and now is that the Innocenti plant has shifted from Italy to India.

1. Rectangular head lamp with wide beam photometrically designed.

4. Vertical/ Horizontal spare wheel bracket—to your choice.

2. Front moving mudguard mounted on fork.

5. Ladies foot rest mounted on crash fender.

3. Integrated foot mat.

# LAMBRETTA HISTORY – EVOLUTION NOT REVOLUTION

## In The Beginning

The problem with working on Lambrettas and trying to produce an exact book like this is that Lambrettas themselves were never an exact vehicle. The different models evolved from one series to the next, but because of the slow process of change – and the nature of mass production – parts for old series machines were often used on new models until stocks were exhausted. There's no point throwing away old components if they will still fit on the new bikes, eh Luigi?

Whilst the chassis number gives an indication of the period of manufacture of the model, records of exactly which parts were fitted and when they were changed over are sketchy. For instance LI 125 series 3 production started with 'chrome ring' type frames and headsets, and handle-type panels. They ended up with totally different headsets, horncastings, engine internals and clip-on panels, but essentially were still sold as LI 125s. Many components were changed mid-run of a particular model, either to solve a specific problem, as part of a restyle, or simply to economise. This presents some difficulty for Lambretta enthusiasts looking to restore a bare frame to its original state.

Where possible we have used the extensive knowledge of our chosen experts to identify which major components have been found on which models. This will help when trying to sift through parts at a fair in order to find a specific piece to fit your machine. To our knowledge such a task has never been undertaken before, but even this is only a starting point. As such we make no claim to cover every mid-series change.

Equally, this book concentrates mainly on Italian Innocenti-produced Lambretta models rather than those produced in Spain by Serveta (originally 'Lambretta Locomociones') or in India by Scooters India Limited (SIL). Mechanically they are largely similar to Italian production, but differ particularly in electrical components and body detail. Where reasonably possible we have included data applicable to these machines, but not in every case. For more detailed descriptions of the changes found on these models may I recommend The Unofficial Lambretta Manual Update by Mark Haines.

## The Layout of the Book

Originally this book was intended to be a pictorial workshop manual which showed you how to assemble and disassemble a scooter step by step. Typically we started with a simple plan, but this snowballed into a bigger and more thorough project as it went along. The initial idea was to take an unrestored scooter, strip it down to its component parts and reassemble it. To that end Nigel Cox of Weston Scooter Parts was kind enough to lend us a totally original, 5,000 km old, 1961 LI 125 from his unique Lambretta museum. The idea of using such a low mileage scooter was that we would get to see how it was assembled as it came out of the factory. Our 'donor' was so 'new' that it is unlikely to have had more than a couple of services. We doubt it had barely met a spanner before Alan and I started hacking at it with bolt croppers. *Forgive us Lord, for we are sinners.*

During the course of our rebuild we did locate some things that were mechanically wrong with the LI, which were fixed along the way. We ended up leaving it running sweetly for the first time in many years. The two weeks spent working on the LI – and rebuilding an SX 200 engine – were to be the basis for most of the book, but there was still a lot more to add.

With respect to Lambretta engines the LI 125 is the least powerful Slimstyle you can get, but there are those of us who like to have a lot more power than even the GP 200 can

supply. For advice on advanced engine building – which should be the basis for any tuned scooter – we went to Mark Broadhurst of MB Developments. He took us through all the modifications that can be done to improve on Innocenti's engine design. A massive amount has changed in the 30-odd years since the Italian firm ceased development.

At the time of writing (2004) we seem to have hit a fork in the road with the Lambretta where the scarcity of original parts – and their subsequent value – has caused many firms to start remaking components. The range in quality of these parts is enormous; from those British firms like MB Developments who are improving on the quality of Innocenti components by making them in long-lasting stainless steel, to the backstreet firms in India and the Far East producing parts that not only fail to meet Innocenti's standards but can actually be dangerously defective. The problem is that you can't generalise about Asian production because in some cases they have improved on anything the Italians ever did.

**Above: At the time of writing the last Lambretta factory (Scooters India Limited) is still producing 'original' spare parts, if no longer making new machines. Unfortunately manufacturers of vastly inferior pattern components – such as the top two kickstart shafts – have no scruples about copying the original SIL packaging, making it very difficult to tell good spares from bad. SIL have recently started attaching hologram stickers to their parts (bottom) in a bid to clearly identify genuine components, but it is unlikely to be too long before these stickers are also copied and found on poor quality pattern parts. Your only defence against this bootlegging is to take the advice of a reputable dealer.**

The whole question of spare part quality is a minefield, and one that I was happy to be lead through, not only by Mark, but also by Dean Orton of Rimini Lambretta Centre. Dean lived in Italy right through the 1990s, when nobody there – not even the Lambretta Club – held the Slimstyle range in high regard. His specialisation in these models at a time when vintage machines were truly abundant meant he has learned more about the nuances of Innocenti Slimstyles than anyone I know. As a result his restorations are first class. Dean and several other people persuaded me that we needed to go deeper into the differences between models. After all, not every Slimstyle Lambretta is an LI 125.

In an effort not to let those simply looking for fitting instructions get bogged down in details, the chapters on stripping and rebuilding the engine and chassis have been kept as originally intended; quick, simple and easy to follow. If you want to know what fits where, then hopefully the pictures and captions have all the answers.

Between each of the strip-and-rebuild sections are chapters that deal with the nitty gritty of deciding whether the parts you have are correct, useable, repairable or replaceable.

These chapters are written with all sorts of scooterists in mind. There is information for restoration enthusiasts as well as tuning freaks, but mostly for the middle ground of owners who just want a decent, reliable scooter to ride and aren't fussed if it will break the sound barrier, or has the original colour nylon in the wheel nuts. I make no judgement on what style your Lambretta should be, as long it is a source of enjoyment to you.

## What Are These Icons All About?

Throughout the book you will notice various sections of text are highlighted and marked with an icon for ease of digestion:

 These sections point to areas of potential damage, danger or confusion, so it is important to take heed of them.

 These sections simply point to an alternative technique or part that may be employed to solve a particular issue.

 These sections offer useful advice on parts, tools, methods, and even a glimpse at the meaning of life. Well almost.

## The Future of Lambretta

At the time of writing the value of Lambretta scooters has never been higher, with certain dealers charging as much as £8,000 for a restored SX 200. Consequently, there are currently rumours circulating of several firms looking to restart the production of 'Lambretta' scooters in one form or another. A further result of these high prices is an increase in crime relating to Lambrettas, whether that is the theft of scooters themselves or the falsification of machine identities to raise their value. The current state of play is that you could get an imported 150 Special, and restore it using SX 200 panels, badges, forks and a 200cc engine. The result would be essentially indistinguishable from an SX 200 and the machine would be worth several thousand pounds. If it had the correct SX 200 chassis numbers however, it would be valued several thousand pounds higher. Since there is quick money to be made simply by changing a few numbers then I'm sure there are plenty of unscrupulous people out there willing to risk it.

Personally, I think a nice Lambretta is a nice Lambretta and that a few stamped numbers simply don't justify massive price differences. Those of you that do care about such things however should be very scrupulous about checking the identity of any machine you are looking to buy. If the numbers look like they have been tampered with – or even if whole section of frame tube with the numbers on looks like it has been freshly welded in – then just walk away. If you don't, then you may end up paying considerably over the odds for something that isn't what it purports to be. Anyone who profits from selling a scooter as one thing in the knowledge that it is actually something else is little more than a thief.

## Chassis Number Location

A Lambretta chassis number is the figure between the two stars to the rear of the engine mount on the kickstart side of the frame. The figures preceding this are the machine model prefix.

 The chassis number should be in a similar condition to that shown below on Italian machines, with no signs of stamping, filing or welding in this vicinity.

 Do not panic if the numbers (and particularly the stars) on an Indian machine look like they have been produced by a toddler wielding a chisel. *They're all like that guv'nor.*

 Indian GPs produced during the early-mid 1980s often have no number stamping on the frame and instead have a VIN plate mounted on the seat arch between choke and fuel taps.

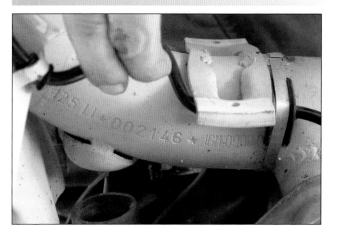

## Engine Number Location

The engine number can be found (between two stars) on the flat area of the casing behind the clutch arm.

 Don't worry if the chassis and engine number do not match up. During Italian production they were never intended to, though Spanish machines usually had matching frame/engine numbers.

 Do not be surprised if your GP 200 has an engine prefix 'SX 200' because they all do. Some models used engines with different prefixes, and this explained in chapter 6.2.

 On some Innocenti GP 125s, the '125 LIS' engine number prefix may appear to have been re-stamped. It has been - in the factory! It's not uncommon to find badly re-stamped prefixes where you can still make out '125 LI' underneath the new '125 LIS' stamp. Innocenti were basically using up the LI casings they had lying around. This factory bodging can be found ONLY on Italian GP 125's.

# TOOLS FOR THE JOB

Your ability to deal with breakdowns on the road or jobs in the garage is entirely dependent on the quality and selection of tools you have to work with. The better prepared your tool-box then the easier all the jobs in this manual will become. With quality tools you have a much better chance of undoing nuts rather than simply rounding them off. Likewise, using the correct workshop tool rather than 'making do' reduces the chances of damaging vital, and sometimes irreplaceable components.

## Minimum You Should Carry On Your Scooter

- Combined spark plug and wheel nut tool. (13mm or 14mm to suit your wheelnuts).
- 3.5mm Allen key – or the correct key/spanner to fit your trunnions ('adjustable nipples').
- Compact open/ring spanner set (8mm-19mm).
- Screwdrivers.
- Vice ('Mole') Grips.

## Also In Your Toolbox:

- Bottle of two-stroke oil.
- Oil measuring jug.
- Spare spark plug (pre-gapped).
- Spare gear inner cables (and spare trunnion).
- Spare long throttle inner cable with fixed nipple at carb end.
- Small round solder-less nipple which fits handlebar pulley (for throttle use).
- Spare clutch inner cable (can also be used as front brake cable) and lever ferrule.
- Spare inner tube and $CO_2$ gas cartridges (if no spare wheel is carried).
- Rear wheel prop-stand for easy wheel changes.

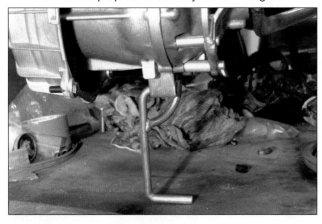

## Preferable Scooter Tools

- Allen key set.
- Feeler gauge.
- Compact flywheel holding tool.
- Compact 3/8 drive socket set.
- Tube or stick of low-strength Loctite .
- Lambretta flywheel puller (the type shown fits both Italian and Spanish flywheels).

## Minimum Workshop Tools

- Comprehensive 3/8 or 1/2 inch drive deep socket set (preferably 6-sided rather than 12-point sockets).
- Soldering iron.
- Selection of hammers (inc. a copper or nylon faced one).
- Circlip pliers.
- Lambretta clutch compressor.

- Flywheel holding tool.

- Clutch holding tool.

- Rear hub puller.

## Optimum Workshop Tools

- Drift set. (Specific ones for Lambrettas now available)
- Tap and die set.
- Angle grinder.
- Blowtorch or electric heat gun.
- Impact screwdriver set.
- Electrical contact cleaner spray/brake cleaner spray.
- T-handle Allen key set.
- Various strengths of Loctite.
- Electrical multimeter.

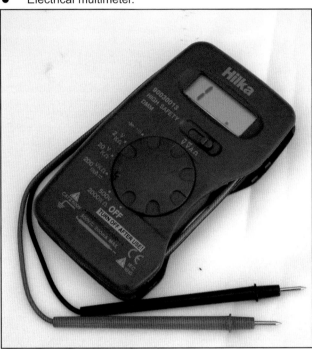

- Fork spring compressor/rear shock compressor.

- Rear hub holding tool (home-made as below is fine).

- Layshaft puller tube.

- Con-rod holding tool (various types).

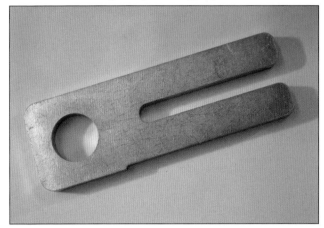

- Crankshaft puller sleeve.

- Steering bearing spanners .

- Degree disc.

- Thread file.

- Electric impact gun (powerful 12v ones from as little as £20).

- High rpm grinder (e.g. Dremel Multi or similar).

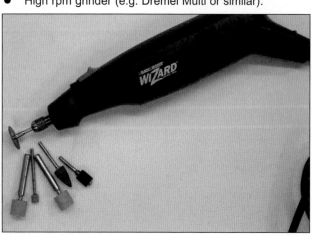

## Specialist Dealer Tools

- Gudgeon pin removal tool.

- Engine mount 'silent block' removal/fitting tool.

- Workshop-type hub puller.

- Brake shoe skimming tool.

● Front sprocket sleeve puller.

● Workshop-type crank holding tool.

● Workshop M6 T-handle extractors.

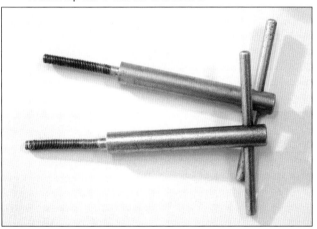

● Gear selector bush tool.

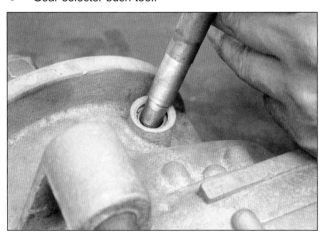

● Oil seal fitting tools.

● Grease gun.

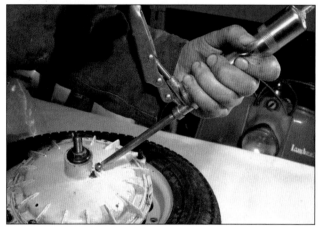

● Timing tools (battery & bulb, dial gauge and support bracket).

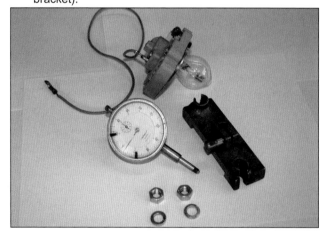

● Flywheel re-magnetiser & flux meter.

# RUNNING A LAMBRETTA IN THE 21st CENTURY

## Fuel

The Lambretta's roots in the 1950s as a utility vehicle mean that it was designed to run on fuel of variable quality. In the UK, it was possible to buy high octane 4-Star or even 5-star leaded fuel, but in other scooter markets fuel will have been much lower quality.

As a result of this, there should not be a problem running a healthy standard machine on modern unleaded fuel of 95 RON (octane rating) provided you use suitable quality two-stroke oil. The lead in old fuels served two purposes; to act as a lubricant on the valve seats of early 4-stroke cars with primitive metallurgy, and also to increase the octane rating and the fuel's resistance to 'knock' (also known variously as 'detonation', 'pinking' or 'pre-ignition'), which allows engines to run higher compression ratios and more advanced ignition timing without damage.

According to sources within the fuel industry, the lead element of fuel (for lubrication purposes) should not be important to modern two-stroke engines - including the Lambretta Slimstyles - since the two-stroke oil should be taking care of all the lubrication issues.

Problems are more likely to arrive as the result of a reduced octane rating, particularly with engines that may have been tuned or set-up in the '80s or early '90s with the high compression ratios used at the time. In order to avoid problems with such engines, they should either be run on the highest octane fuel available (i.e. 98 RON Super-Plus unleaded) or have their timing, jetting or compression ratios modified to be safe on 95 RON fuel. If in doubt contact a reputable scooter tuner.

It is wise to run on the highest octane fuel you can afford, if only to give any engine the biggest possible safety margin against fuel-related problems.

## Two-stroke Oil

Oil technology is one of the areas of greatest advances since Innocenti wrote their Lambretta owner's manuals. These were produced at a time when it was possible to go to petrol stations in Europe and buy pump fuel already mixed with oil at different ratios. As you may expect, this will have been with basic mineral oil, so Innocenti specified a quite high ratio for larger capacity models of 4% (25:1).

Modern two-stroke oils are available in three rough grades; mineral, semi-synthetic and fully-synthetic. Ideally you should run fully-synthetic oil if you can afford it, and use quality semi-synthetic as a minimum.

For original 125/150/175 engines using quality synthetic oil, 3% (33:1) oil in your fuel should be sufficient, with the improved anti-wear properties of modern oil making up for the reduced quantity required. Using less oil will result in a cleaner engine, producing less carbon build-up and thus keeping its best performance for longer. None of the people I consulted suggested going as low as 2% even for standard GP engines. If you run cheaper oils then 4% would be better.

On larger capacity and tuned engines then you really should be running the very best synthetic oils available at a minimum of 3% (33:1) mixture for round town riding, and putting this up to 4% (25:1) for sustained high speed use. With mid-quality semi-synthetic oils a 4% mixture is still preferable for general use. For best results consult the tuner of your engine.

If you must run a tuned Lambretta engine on cheaper mineral oil, then you could use as high as 5% (20:1) for high speed use, but this is really best avoided due to the increased coking and plug fouling that will result.

Try to stick to one brand and use that all the time. Not all oils mix well with one another.

MB Developments specify using the 'injector' versions of some of the top brand oils rather than the 'pre-mix' versions. This is because the injector versions are less viscous (thinner) to make it easy for oil pumps to shift them. These thinner oils actually mix better with petrol in a Lambretta than some of the thicker racing 'pre-mix' oils which can sink to the bottom of the tank giving you a rich, smoky mixture with too much oil at first and not enough oil as the tank runs low. Very viscous pre-mix racing oils of SAE 50 are really intended to be mixed thoroughly in fuel cans before adding to the machine, which is why the injector oils often mix better. Innocenti never specified two-stroke oils thicker than SAE 40.

> **Remember to turn off your fuel tap when adding oil to your fuel or you can end up with oil sinking to the bottom of the tank and filling the carb bowl.**

Popular quality synthetic 2-stroke oils in the UK are produced by Putoline, Castrol, Rock Oil, Silkolene and Motul, though there are other good makes to choose from. Of the oils available in petrol stations Shell is probably the favourite of most British scooterists. Agip and Repsol are reliable brands found on the continent. Oil is very much a matter of personal preference so simply ask advice and stick with something you like.

> **The last few years have seen many of the famous brands introduce specific 'scooter' oils, often in a range of low, medium and high quality versions. In our experience the top-quality synthetic versions of these 'scooter' oils are perfectly good, and often cheaper than dedicated fully-synthetic motorcycle oils.**

| OIL PERCENTAGE | OIL RATIO | CC (ml) of oil per litre of fuel |
|---|---|---|
| 2% | 50:1 | 20cc |
| 3% | 33:1 | 30cc |
| 4% | 25:1 | 40cc |
| 5% | 20:1 | 50cc |

## Good Habits

To keep your Lambretta in good condition and starting well, always:

- Turn the fuel off when you stop the engine to prevent carb flooding.

- Kickstart at the side of the scooter when it is on the centre stand, or if your legs are long enough kickstart it with the scooter off the stand and you astride the machine. This method will turn the engine over more times per kick. Do not 'stab' at the kickstart but use long swings.

- A properly set-up machine should be started from cold with the choke on and the throttle closed. The choke may not be required when the engine is warm.

- Avoid sitting on your Lambretta when it is on the centre stand, and NEVER ride your scooter off the stand. This will bend the frame struts and stand brackets.

## ORIGINAL RECOMMENDED LAMBRETTA SERVICE SCHEDULE

### Every 250 miles

- Check and adjust tyre pressures. Look for tyre wear or damage.
- Check operation of electrical items (horn, lights, and indicators).
- Top up battery level (if fitted).
- Clean and re-set spark plug gap. *[not really required so often - see notes]*
- Check oil level in chain case.
- Check tightness of wheels and hubs.

### First 500 miles after rebuild or Restoration

- Change gearbox oil.
- Check and adjust carb settings.
- Check and adjust control cable tension.
- Check & tighten ALL nuts and bolts etc. as paintwork & bodywork can 'settle' causing the fasteners to come loose - particularly on powder-coated wheel rims!

### First 1500 miles after rebuild or Restoration

- As above plus:
- Lubricate all control cables as required.
- Lubricate all greasing/oiling points.

### Every 3,000 miles

- Lubricate and adjust all control cables.
- Lubricate all greasing/oiling points.
- Change gearbox oil.
- Strip, clean and re-set carb.
- Clean and re-set contact breaker points and lubricate felt pad  (if fitted).
- Strip and clean brakes and drums, and sparingly grease brake pivot pins.
- Clean air filter with compressed air.
- Fit new spark plug.

### Every 6,000 miles

- As 3,000 miles service plus:
- Fit new air filter and check hose condition.
- Fit new contact breaker points (where fitted)
- Re-pack front wheel bearings with grease.

### Every 12,000 miles

- As 6,000 miles service plus:
- De-coke cylinder/head/piston and fit new silencer.
- Fit new piston rings.
- Replace brake shoes (unless done previously).
- Check and adjust chain tensioners.

### Every 25,000 miles

- As 12,000 miles service plus:
- Re-bore cylinder and fit new oversize piston assembly.
- Strip and re-pack mag side main bearing with grease.
- Check both main bearings for wear.

The service schedule above says a lot about when Lambrettas were made and how diligent their owners and service engineers were expected to be. In these days with car manufacturers setting 20,000 mile service intervals, having to clean and reset your spark plug every 250 miles or strip your vehicle to lubricate the cables every 3,000 miles seems rather extreme. In reality this schedule was based on sound principles for the build quality of the machine as it left the factory. If you were to adhere to this schedule – and used quality spares – then a standard Lambretta would probably serve you reliably for many thousands of miles. In the real world however – with scooterists undertaking journeys of over 250 miles in a day on tuned Lambrettas – the standard service schedule needs some qualification.

- **Gearbox oil** – on highly tuned engines it won't hurt to change more frequently than 3,000 miles.
- **Open mouthed carbs** – every few thousand miles check for throttle slide wear and change piston rings. Also check for bore wear more frequently.
- **Clutch plates** – cork plates will need to be replaced regularly on highly stressed engines.
- **Spark plugs** – you should not need to clean and reset your plug gap every 250 miles unless you have a problem. The wear rate for a plug in a modern 2-stroke is around 0,03mm per 1,000km so gaps will occasionally need to be re-set. If you accept we live in a wasteful, disposable society then simply fit a new one occasionally rather than cleaning cruddy old plugs.
- **Hydraulic brake conversions** – you should change the fluid every year. Also regularly clean and apply copper grease to hydraulic slave/caliper pistons particularly after use in salted conditions. Also watch for pad wear/disc squeal since front pads are unlikely to last 12,000 miles.
- **Cables** – fit quality nylon/Teflon lined cables and they should not need such regular replacement or lubrication. Do not grease nylon/Teflon lined cables!
- **Electronic Ignition** – fit one and forget about points adjustment and replacement forever!
- **De-coke and new silencer** – modern two-stroke oils should lead to much slower carbon build-up so hopefully you won't need to throw your exhaust away so often, unless it is broken.
- **Tuned cylinders/kits** – are likely to need new pistons and rebores more often than standard, particularly if run without air filters. Plated alloy cylinders will probably need to be re-plated or replaced before 25,000 miles. Also expect more regular bearing checks or replacement with high performance motors.
- **Fork link pivot bushes** – the early brass type might last 25,000 miles with proper lubrication, but the plastic sort will almost certainly be worn out before then.
- **Chain guides.** The modern nylon-type chain guides are much more reliable than the old sort, but should still be regularly adjusted unless of the self-adjusting type.

## Gearbox Oil

The vast majority of dealers and tuners continue to recommend the same oil that Innocenti did; straight SAE 90 grade (e.g. Castrol ST90), but not Hypoid or EP90 which contain additives harmful to the clutch. Gearbox oil should be changed 500 miles after a rebuild (when you will most likely find some metallic particles on your drain plug magnet) again at 1,500 miles and then every 3,000 miles thereafter. Oil changes are best done when the engine is warm after a run.

If your oil is black and smells burnt, this is usually an indicator of a burned-out clutch. If there seems to be less oil in the gearbox than you expect, but you've never seen it drip, then there is a good chance that your drive-side crankshaft oil seal is damaged and the engine is consuming gearbox oil. This can be a pointer to a blocked breather in the filler bolt, so it is important to check this.

The recommended oil level from the manual is 0.7 litres, but for a quick oil change where the parts remain 'wet' it is normally sufficient to refill with 0.5 litres of oil. At any rate you can set the correct level by removing the front level plug

(10mm Allen key) with the machine level on the stand, and letting any excess drain out.

Replace the oil drain plugs in the correct position (magnetic one at the bottom) and renew the fibre washers if required. Do not over-tighten.

It is normal for the magnets on the drain plug to pick up this amount of metal filings between oil changes, but if it looks like a big furry thing then it indicates something may be wrong inside the transmission.

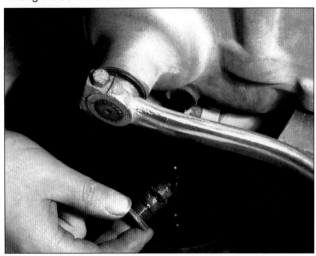

 **Most Spanish machines were never fitted with a magnetic oil drain plug, but considering the amount of metallic particles these devices attract it would probably do no harm to fit one to any Serveta.**

## Greasing

On very early Slimstyle machines you may find grease nipples on items such as the brake pedal, brake cam, fork links and front hub. On later machines Innocenti abandoned this idea, presumably not only to save money but because so few people actually used greasing points correctly. Grease nipples tend to be neglected entirely, or over-filled.

If you have a grease gun, then fill it with multi-purpose grease and it can be used on most grease nipples of an early machine. It can be used freely and liberally on any fork link or brake pedal grease nipples (which are absent on later models where plastic bushes were used instead), but only sparingly on the rear brake camshaft, speedo drive or front hub bearings for fear of spreading grease into the brake linings. It may be better to dismantle these components occasionally and grease them by hand. Those in the front hub can be manually greased by removing the spindle and spacers and using a thin strip of metal to place grease around the bearings.

 **Your front hub and flywheel bearings should be lubricated with High Melting Point grease. Do not use LM (Low Melting Point) grease on these points because it can turn liquid and ooze past the seals when hot.**

## Spark Plugs and HT Caps

These should be changed periodically, depending on condition and wear. Every Lambretta rider should keep a new plug and plug spanner in their toolbox for emergencies.

Based purely on personal experience, I prefer NGK plugs and caps, which are the most commonly available ones in the UK. Other people have recommended expensive platinum racing plugs, but for road use I've never found anything that lasts as long or is as reliable as a bog standard BxES (where 'x' denotes the heat range of the plug). If you want to use another brand then the most common (now that Champion plugs have become increasingly hard to find) and increasingly popular is Nippon Denso.

 **The heat range of a compatible Nippon Denso plug can be calculated by multiplying the NGK heat range figure by three and selecting the closest match. In other words an NGK B8ES is equivalent to a Nippon Denso W24ES.**

 **Bedlam Scooters suggest that Champion plugs work better with the ignitions of early 6-volt Indian Lambrettas than NGK.**

 **The screw-on spark plug nipple used with some HT caps must be done up tight to avoid ignition problems.**

With the high temperatures experienced under Lambretta panels and the proximity to rubbing elements such as the rear brake cable, a very good HT plug cap is required. Commonly recommended are the red rubber waterproof NGK models (LB05EMH) which are worth paying extra for.

Plugs are graded by heat range. A hot plug (e.g. NGK B7ES) is not for hot engines – 'hot' means that the plug tip is kept at a high temperature to burn off the carbon deposits which build-up due to regular starting and town use. A cold plug (e.g. NGK B10ES) has a cooler running tip to prevent the electrode overheating – and any subsequent engine damage as a result – when an engine is held at high revs for a long time.

Most Lambretta Slimstyles will run fine on a B7ES (standard) or B8ES (lightly tuned) around town, and maybe require a B9ES for motorway use. If you have problems with plug fouling round town, then consider a B7ES or even B6ES. Only racers should ever find need of a B10ES.

The recommended plug gaps are: 0.5 – 0.6mm (0.020-0.024 in.) for early 4-pole points and electronic ignitions, and 0.45 – 0.5mm (0.018-0.020 in.) for 6-pole points systems. Points-type Indian models specify a plug gap of 0.35mm (0.015 in.).

## SPARK PLUG EQUIVALENTS

| NGK | NIPPON DENSO | CHAMPION |
|-----|--------------|----------|
| B7ES | W22ES | N4 |
| B8ES | W24ES | N3 |
| B9ES | W27ES | N2 |
| B10ES | W31ES | N1 |

# Ignition Adjustment

If you have any intention to seriously use your Lambretta then the benefits of a good quality electronic ignition system with 12-Volt lighting cannot be underestimated, though nowadays with most production confined to India the quality of these systems varies enormously. Currently the best Indian ones are those that have been reworked and rewired in the UK.

**If you purchase an Indian electronic ignition as a spare part, make sure you tighten up the rivets holding the earth tags for the stator plate wires. Coating these earthed wires in Araldite or equivalent epoxy will support and prevent them from coming loose due to vibration.**

Conversion flywheels are available to fit electronic ignition systems onto 'thin-taper' LI/SX/TV crankshafts, but it is often better to convert to a GP crankshaft with its stronger taper and use the GP electronic ignition flywheel. The beauty of an electronic ignition is zero maintenance once set- up.

If you use points ignition, then you will have to adjust your points occasionally due to wear.

**Before attempting to set a points gap, first remove the flywheel cowling, hold your flywheel by the fins and check for any up and down movement. If there is noticeable play or you can hear knocking, then points adjustment is basically a waste of time, and you will first need to renew your flywheel-side (and possibly drive-side) main bearing.**

Lambretta points gap should be set between 0.35-0.45 mm (0.014-0.018 in.) using a feeler gauge. Select the correct gauges, insert when the points are fully open, loosen the points screw and the re-tighten. There is a cam screw or notched V-shape machined into the points which can be moved using a flat screwdriver to aid adjustment. The gap variation offered allows some possibility to tailor your ignition timing to suit your machine, but it is best to start with the points set to 0.4mm (0.015 in.) and work from there.

Your points should be cleaned with a strip of petrol-soaked (not oiled!) card or a light spray with electrical contact cleaner. If the points are misaligned or pitted it is better to replace both them and the condenser, but you will need a soldering iron to do this. Whenever your flywheel is off, put a few drops of gearbox oil or light grease onto the felt lubrication pad on the stator plate to prevent points heel wear.

For more details on ignition systems and timing see the relevant chapters.

**Vespa PX points are sold by some dealers as Lambretta points. These are slightly different and will upset your timing as the 'fibre' cam heel is shorter.**

# Battery

If fitted, original lead-acid type batteries should be kept topped up so the acid stays within the level marks. Only top up with distilled water and be careful not to over-fill. Also make sure that the breather pipe from the battery is clear and unblocked.

**If a battery-fitted machine is to be laid up for a long time it is a good idea to keep the battery maintained by attaching an intelligent trickle charger such as Optimate or Accumate. These can be left permanently attached while parked and will monitor the battery to keep it in tip-top condition.**

# Carburettor

It is worth removing your carb periodically to clean out any deposits that may have built up through impurities in the fuel.

**Open-mouthed carbs are very prone to wear around the slide as well as suffering from water ingress, both of which can cause poor running. They are also prone to carb icing on very cold days, which is dangerous as it can cause the throttle slide to stick open.**

**If your fuel tank has just been repainted (particularly if it was sand blasted) or has been sat for a long time and your engine starts to misbehave, one of the first places to check is your fuel filter. Loose grit, rust or paint particles will quickly clog a carb and may cause a lean fuel mixture that can damage your engine. Rusty fuel tanks can be treated with sealing agents such as 'Petseal'.**

Most types of carb that fit a Lambretta will have an internal fuel filter that can be cleaned out. You should also blow through the jets and clean the carb bowl. Original Lambretta carbs have their own chapter later in the book which covers this process in more detail.

# Fuel Tap

The fuel tap can be removed and the filter checked for blockages. The 19mm nut that secures the tank to the tap has both left and right hand threads. When refitting the nut you should start both tank and tap threads at once. The fibre washer for the tap on early models has now been superseded by a plastic flange as part of the tap's mesh filter, so there are no service parts to change.

If you do not wish to strip your fuel tap during a service it may be sufficient simply to check the fuel flow available. Fast-flow fuel taps have been available for some time now and these are viewed as essential on any tuned engine and advisable on all other machines. Ideally you should be looking for the tap to flow around half a litre per minute, but original taps will flow much less. If your tap only allows through a trickle, then clean or replace it. If the flow rate changes when you remove the filler cap then it could be that the breather hole in the cap is blocked and must be cleared.

# Air Filter

Use of the correct air filter is important for the smooth running of engines with original carbs and jetting. These paper elements can be cleaned by blowing through with a high-pressure air-line, but it is better simply to buy a new one if yours is very dirty.

Most tuners now recommend the use of foam air filters – such as Ram Air – on all reedvalve engines (TS1, Imola etc) but these can quickly flood with fuel if used with a tuned original cylinder and large carb. Fitting such filters to traditional engines may best be achieved by mounting them remotely at the end of some form of air hose.

Air filters enhance engine life – which would be drastically reduced by the sandblasting effect of unfiltered air. Foam filters can be cleaned in petrol or specific cleaning agents, and may be lightly oiled to improve performance when re-fitted.

**Spanish models use different air filter systems depending on model. Spare filters for these Servetas have recently been remade by Casa Lambretta.**

Unhook the spring clip and loosen the carb hose clip to remove the air filter.

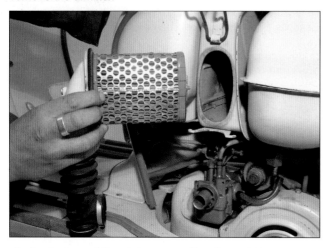

In the bottom of the air hose on all early models is a metal one-way valve and it is important for this to be in good condition to prevent dirt being sucked up the drain hose.

 **Unless you are looking for total originality, use the simpler GP 125 air hose set-up (which has a closed bottom with no valve) on machines with 18 or 20mm carbs. This will reduce muck build-up around your footboard & flywheel cowling.**

If you use an air hose it is important to check for splits in the rubber as this can drastically affect your engine's carburation and reliability.

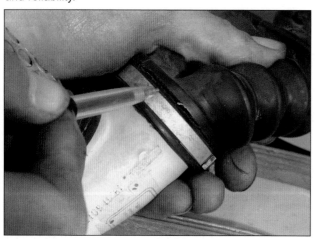

# Exhaust System

One of the benefits of clean-burning modern synthetic 2-stroke oils is that deposits are dramatically reduced, so exhausts no longer need be thrown-away after 12,000 miles use.

The main thing to check on your exhaust during a service is its structural integrity, and how well it fits. Any leaks or cracks in the downpipe can let air get into the cylinder. This can cause a weak mixture and harm your engine.

 **Switching to modern synthetic oils will drastically reduce the carbon build up in your exhaust. Any carbon that does appear in your exhaust should be scraped out. Polishing the metal inside will not give a big performance advantage but it will help prevent the carbon deposits from reforming.**

# Cables

Cables are another item that really varies in quality depending on who made them. In recent times Taffspeed and other dealers popularised the use of nylon/Teflon-lined outer cables and fine wire multi-strand inner cables. These give a much smoother and easier action than traditional cables while at the same time requiring minimal maintenance. Nylon or Teflon-lined cables are thoroughly recommended in any scooter application, and are available in either grey or black to suit any machine. These can be run dry or lightly oiled top and bottom.

It is really very hard to lubricate conventional cables when they are in place. You can use the nozzle of a tin of WD40 to spray down inside the outer gear and throttle cables with the headset top removed, or drip thin oil like 3-in-1 down the inner cable, but this won't treat the whole cable. You can release the inner cables from their trunnions and pull them up to oil the outers. In practice this isn't good advice because it can lead to the outer gear and clutch cables falling out of position in the headset and you may also find it impossible to re-thread the inners if they have been previously squashed by the trunnions. If any of your cables are feeling stiff or look visibly frayed then it makes more sense to simply replace the inners.

**TOP TIP** Cable oilers can come in handy for non-lined cables since they allow for full lubrication even from the lower end. To use insert the cable with the inner poking through and wind the nut tight to seal the rubber part around both inner and outer cable.

 **TOP TIP** The Bedlam tip for placing gear cables is 'Front to Back, and Back to Front' – i.e. The cable at the FRONT of the machine in the headset (nearest the headlight) connects to the BACK position (next to the tyre) as you look at the engine, and vice versa.

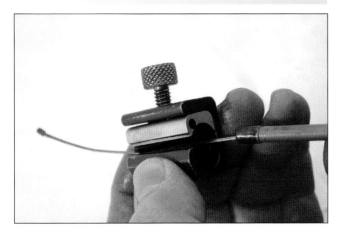

Using an oil can pressed to the filling hole it is possible to force oil into the cable.

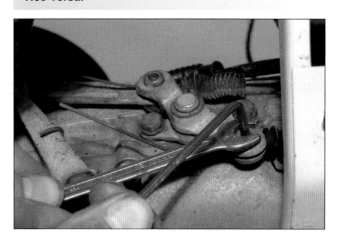

## Correct Control Adjustment

A set of correctly adjusted cables can make a scooter a pleasure to ride, but there is a lot more to it these days. With over 40 years of wear on some components, you can adjust your cables to perfection and still have several degrees of unwanted slop in your gearchange due to component wear in the headset or engine linkages.

**GEAR CABLES:** These should be adjusted so that the neutral marking on the headset does actually equate to neutral in the gearbox. The adjuster block fitted to the engine is where you should look to remove any unwanted slack. Wind the adjuster out from the block to tighten a specific cable, and vice versa. If the adjusters are at their limit and the cables still slack, then the only solution is to wind them back to a central position, loosen the cable trunnion and pull the inner cable through the trunnion before locking it back up. If this condition of slackness has recently developed, then it is usually an indication that the inner cable is about to fail and needs replacement anyway.

It is worth greasing your levers occasionally, particularly in the pivot points. Use a spanner or Mole grips to move the clutch arm on the engine forward enough to unhook the clutch inner, and undo the adjuster on a Lambretta front brake. This loosens both the inner cables, so you can remove the handlebar levers and have access to grease all around the cable ferrules and pivots.

With the gear cables adjusted so that neutral is in the correct position, check that the two gear cables are not too taught by trying to squeeze them together between thumb and forefinger. If they are tight like piano wire, slacken both adjusters off a little and re-tighten the locknuts. Gear cables are often over-tightened when someone is trying to remove unwanted slop in the gearchange, but if this is due to wear in the mechanical components no amount of cable tightening will remove it. In fact the added friction of over-tight cables will only make things worse.

 **ONE TO WATCH** Be wary of the anti-rattle spring and pressure cap fitted into the lever. If you aren't ready to catch them when the lever is withdrawn, they will fly off into the distance.

 **ONE TO WATCH** Original Italian trunnions 'adjustable nipples' are tightened with a 3.5mm Allen key which is an unusual size and hard to get hold of. Recent pattern trunnions have a common 3mm Allen key head, or a hex bolt head. Whichever sort you have, make sure your toolkit contains the correct one.

 **TOP TIP** Always hold the outer part of the trunnion with a spanner when tightening or loosening. If not you will kink and weaken the cable, causing it to fail prematurely.

Adjusting Lambretta gear cables is not easy at the best of times because the adjuster block was designed in such a way that the clutch adjuster limits access to one of the gear adjusters. MB Developments produce an alternative cable adjuster block (below) with the clutch adjuster in a slightly different place, thus offering improved access. Note the frayed gear cable which requires urgent replacement.

**CLUTCH ADJUSTMENT:** Lambretta designed their clutch set-up so that there should be a tiny amount of free play at the lever when correctly adjusted. This amounts to a 1.5mm gap between the front of the lever and the handlebar housing before you feel tension on the cable. If the cable is too tight and there is no free play then the clutch will tend to slip. Too loose and the clutch will drag, with the symptoms of the scooter trying to creep forward while in gear with the clutch pulled in.

**THROTTLE ADJUSTMENT:** This is taken care of by a screw adjuster on the carb. It is best to leave the tiniest bit of free play so that the throttle slide closes fully and your idling speed is set by the tick-over screw, not by cable tension. You can check that you have enough free play by trying to lift the outer cable out of the adjuster at the carb end. If you can pull the outer by 1mm without the slide moving, then you have sufficient play.

 To prevent your throttle cable popping out if it gets slack, use a pair of thin-nosed pliers to gently grip the fingers of the lever together. These can easily be levered apart with a screwdriver to release the cable again.

**DRUM BRAKE ADJUSTMENT:** On a healthy brake, it should be possible to do up the thumbwheel adjuster by the wheel to the point where the brake is locked on. Then back if off a turn or two until the wheel is free. If the brake still binds at some points but is free on others, then the hub (or wheelrim) is warped and replacement is the only viable option. If the thumbwheel bottoms out on the adjuster thread, it is possible to loosen the cable clamp and pull the inner cable through a little to get the adjuster back into range, but needing to do this (or the brakes sticking on) is often a sign of worn brake shoes which need replacement anyway. A correctly set up brake should be on hard before the pedal or lever has covered half of its travel.

**LAMBRETTA DISC BRAKE ADJUSTMENT:** Many of the original cable disc brakes in the UK have already been converted to hydraulic actuation by tuning shops for owners who are keen on stopping before they hit things. Adjustment of a cable disc is the same as a cable drum, except when the arm moves so far forward that the angle between it and the cable exceeds 90 degrees. In that instance you need to adjust the seating of the static brake pad inside the hub, which is done through one of the disc brake windows. You will probably need to do this more often with a hydraulic-converted standard Lambretta disc brake.

To adjust the static pad, undo the brake adjuster from the brake arm so it is in its rest position. Remove one of the disc brake windows, flatten the tab washer if fitted holding the adjuster nut and loosen it with a cranked 13 or 14mm ring spanner. Do up the Allen screw until the pad is hard pressed against the disc, then back the Allen screw off half a turn. Hold the screw in position and tighten the lock-nut and tab washer. Reconnect the cable adjuster to the lever and re-adjust. This operation ensures that the floating disc is evenly located between both brake pads.

 If you do not have access to the correct spanner it is possible to tighten the locknut on the disc brake static pad using a deep socket held by mole grips. An Allen key through the middle of the socket will ensure that the adjustment does not alter while the nut is being tightened.

## Tyres

The biggest and best leap forward in scooter riding since the 1960s has been in tyre technology. The additional grip available from a modern compound Michelin sports tyre (e.g. S1) compared to their old ACS pattern is amazing. Any scooter will be safer and more fun to ride with modern tyres, but it is also important to monitor your tyre pressures.

| RECOMMENDED TYRE PRESSURES in PSI (Bar in brackets) | NORMAL USE | MOTORWAY USE |
|---|---|---|
| FRONT | 18 (1.2) | 20 (1.3) |
| REAR | 28 (2.0) | 30 (2.1) |
| REAR + PILLION | 34 (2.4) | 36 (2.5) |

The above pressures are for an average weight rider without luggage. If additional weight is being carried, the tyre pressured should be increased to suit: for example if a front carrier is loaded then the front tyre should be given an extra couple of PSI.

The original specified tyres for all Slimstyle models is 3.50x10 but other tyres may be fitted and these will have an effect on handling and gearing. The circumference and % gearing change figures listed below are approximate and depend on the width of the rim used. Wide wheel rims are available for use with wider than standard tyres.

| TYRE SIZE | WIDTH (mm) | HEIGHT (mm) | CIRCUMFERENCE (approx. mm) | % GEARING CHANGE (approx.) |
|---|---|---|---|---|
| 3.50x10 | 89 | 89 | 1357 | 0% |
| 90/90x10 | 90 | 81 | 1307 | -4% |
| 100/80x10 | 100 | 80 | 1300 | -4% |
| 100/90x10 | 100 | 90 | 1363 | 0% |
| 110/90x10** | 110 | 99 | 1420 | +4.5% |
| 4.00x10* | 101.5 | 101.5 | 1435 | +6% |

*requires grinding of bump stop **may be too wide for rear fitment

 **The ability to carry a spare wheel is a great advantage on a Lambretta, but if you do so, also to carry a rear wheel prop stand, and make sure that the spare is pumped up to the highest pressure you are ever likely to need (e.g. 36 psi). It is a lot easier to let air out at the side of the road than add more without a pump!**

 **Tyres that run inner tubes deflate very quickly when punctured. To avoid accidents make sure that your wheels are assembled properly (without pinching the tubes between the rims) and using only the best components such as non-rusty rims and quality inner tubes.**

 **I tested the anti-puncture compound Ultraseal in a tubed 10" tyre and it successfully prevented a puncture when a small nail was hammered into the tyre and removed. Ultraseal – and similar compounds – can't guarantee to prevent a puncture if your inner tube becomes torn by a metallic intrusion, but if it prevents a high speed blow out long enough for you to examine your tyre and find a nail in it then the protection was priceless.**

 **Certain brands of inner tube have valves that are too long for use in Lambretta front wheels and can catch on the fork link bolts – particularly when used with non-Innocenti wheel rims which have a slightly different valve hole position. Check that there is at least 5mm of clearance every time you fit a wheel, as a front wheel puncture is unpleasant at best.**

## General Assembly

Lambrettas vibrate, and this causes things to come loose. For you to arrive anywhere with the same number of components as you left, it is wise to periodically check the tightness of all the fasteners on your machine.

Important nuts like those holding on the rear hub and the wheels themselves should ideally be torqued to the correct settings listed in the appendix of this book.

All other nuts and screws should be regularly checked for tightness. If you ride along with one part loose and rattling, you'd be amazed at how quickly other pieces around it join the party.

 **Another essential for the toolkit of any Lambretta - and particularly a tuned one - is a small tube of Loctite thread lock. The smallest dab of this is ideal to keep the tiny flywheel and cylinder cowling screws in place.**

# FAULT DIAGNOSIS – WHAT'S UP DOC?

## The Engine Won't Start!

Ah, a classic, but one that has been made much rarer by the introduction of electronic ignition systems. In theory your engine needs four things to start:

1. **Enough compression to squeeze the fuel/air mixture into an easily combustible pocket of gas.**
2. **A healthy spark jumping the plug gap at the right moment.**
3. **The correct fuel/air mixture trapped in the combustion chamber.**
4. **A hefty enough force to turn the engine a few times.**

If you have all the above things in place then there's no reason why the engine shouldn't start, but if it doesn't you need to explore the potential problems one at a time, in a methodical manner. Check the fuel tank first though!

## 1. Compression Problems

Try turning your engine over slowly using the kickstart. If your engine feels easier to turn over than it should, then it may simply be that your rings are worn and in need of replacement. Alternatively a rebore and new piston may be required. If after a seizure the motor turns over with little or no resistance then the scooter probably has a holed piston – or rings that have been seized into the piston – both of which require major surgery.

Reluctant starting on rattling piston-ported cylinders – particularly tuned ones – can indicate a poor seal between the skirt of the piston and the cylinder which requires a rebore and new piston.

An audible 'squeak' or lots of fuel spit-back from the carb mouth on reedvalve engines can indicate a problem with the reed petals being damaged or not sealing properly.

If the compression of your engine feels fine then move on to check the spark plug.

## 2. Spark Problems

The first step is to check the quality of the spark because the majority of starting problems are plug, HT cap or coil related.

First check that the HT cap is fitted securely. If so then remove the spark plug and examine it.

### Is the plug worn out or coked up?

It could simply be that your plug is in need of replacement. In which case fit the spare pre-gapped one that you keep in your toolbox. You do have one in your toolbox don't you? If not, adjust the spark plug to the specified gap again and wire brush it to get going again.

### What is the plug colour like?

Check the firing end of the plug nose. On a healthy engine the metal parts of the plug should be chocolate brown and the insulator around the plug nose should be light brown (if the plug isn't brand new). If the plug colour is much lighter or greyer than expected, this can be a sign of a lean carburation, an air leak or insufficient fuel supply.

### Does the plug look wet?

This is a positive sign that at least some petrol is getting through but possibly too much to burn. Suspect either an ignition problem, 'flooding' which can occur due to seepage of fuel from the carb into the engine (particularly if the fuel tap has been left on when parked), or over-use of the choke on an engine which didn't need the extra fuel. Kick the engine over a few times with the plug out (and well out of the way) and the fuel and choke turned off. If you can smell or

see fuel vapour coming from the plug hole then keep kicking the engine over until it clears. Then try a new plug, but if the problem reoccurs suspect an ignition or carburettor fault.

### Is the plug black and oily?

If the engine was smoking heavily last time it ran, this is an indicator of either too much two-stroke oil in the fuel or possibly a blown drive-side crankshaft seal allowing the engine to burn your gearbox oil. If so then inserting a fresh plug should get the engine running until that too becomes oiled.

A blown drive-side crankshaft seal can usually be defined by billowing white smoke from the exhaust which has a different smell to two-stroke smoke. Test for this by blocking the tailpipe. If the oil seal is good (and the exhaust has no leaks) then the engine should quickly stop. If it continues to run then the oil seal has failed.

Another test for a suspected blown drive-side oil seal is by running the engine on steady tick-over and draining the gearbox oil. If the engine rpm starts to rise as the oil drains it is a sure sign that the seal has failed. Often this is caused by a blocked breather hole in the gearbox oil filler bolt.

If your drive-side crankshaft seal has failed it will allow the engine to consume your gearbox oil. If you need to get home a short distance then you should be safe to carry on, but doing so over a long distance will allow the gearbox to run dry and damage your transmission parts. Top up as required to get you home, even with two-stroke oil if you are desperate.

### Is the plug gap bridged?

On rare occasions small pieces of metal or carbon will bridge the gap of the plug preventing a spark. You may be able to remove these deposits and get going again but usually they are a sign of overheating indicating a more serious problem somewhere else in the engine.

### Does it have aluminium or steel speckles on it?

If so, this is an indicator of more serious engine damage that is occurring possibly due to incorrect timing, carburation or a piston or crankshaft failure. It is best to stop riding until the engine can be stripped and examined.

Next fit the plug into the HT cap and rest it against one of the metal parts of the engine. Kick the engine over. You should be able to see a healthy, fat spark jump the gap on the plug each time you hear the piston coming up the barrel. Spark colour is not too important since it will appear different according to the ambient light conditions, but visible intensity and regularity are important. Be aware that seeing a decent spark outside the engine is not proof of a good plug, as it may not spark so well under compression.

If the spark is missing or intermittent then try tracing it back down its route from the stator plate. First unscrew the HT cap, hold the lead close to the engine and see if you get a healthy spark that can jump a gap of at least 5mm. If the spark looks much healthier than it did at the plug then suspect a faulty cap or spark plug and renew them. If the spark is still not strong then work further back.

 **Make sure you are testing with the ignition switched on! Ignition faults can sometimes be due to problems with cut-out switches on early models, or ignition switches on later types. Also check the green wire connections in the headset for short circuits.**

**POINTS SYSTEMS:** Remove the green stator wire from the junction box, hold it against a metal part of the engine and kick the motor. If you see a regular spark here (it will be less intense) but not at the HT lead then the coil – or wiring to it – is most likely your problem. If there is no visible spark (or it is weak) then suspect a points or condenser problem.

**ELECTRONIC IGNITION SYSTEMS:** Remove the ignition cut-out wire (usually green) from CDI box so that only the wires from the stator are attached. If there is now a spark it indicates that you have a problem with your ignition switch. There is no easy way to check the wires coming out of the stator for signal, but you can measure the resistance readings of the coils if you have access to a multimeter. Details of how to do this are in the Electrical System chapter.

 **Most Indian electronic stators supplied by UK dealers have been rewired to conform to the AF/Vespa colour coding, but original ones often aren't. On Indian stators particularly, check for loosely riveted earth tags.**

 **A digital rev counter (single cylinder two-stroke versions only) which counts spark signals from a wire wrapped round your HT lead can be useful when trying to pinpoint intermittent problems on electronic ignitions. If the rpm reading suddenly doubles unexpectedly as the engine revs rise, this is usually a pointer to problems with the black pick-up ('trigger') coil on the stator plate.**

## 3. Fuelling Problems

It should go without saying that the first thing you should do is look in the tank to make sure you have enough fuel, and turn onto reserve if required. You wouldn't be the first person to start stripping down a scooter when you just have an empty tank though!

 **One of the best ways of diagnosing if you have a fuel problem is to remove the air hose and spray Easy Start into the engine through the carburettor. If the motor starts briefly and then stops again it is almost certainly a fuel supply problem. At least if it runs on Easy Start you know your compression is fine and the ignition system is functioning.**

If you have been kicking the engine for a while with the choke on and the engine hasn't started, then the plug should be wet. If it is then follow the advice in the Spark Problems section. If the plug still looks dry then suspect a fuel blockage somewhere or a malfunctioning choke. If there is a lot of play in the choke cable then it could be that the choke isn't opening properly and the cable may require adjustment.

 **One way to test for a carburettor jet blockage is to remove any air hose or filter fitted and kick the engine a few times with your hand over the carb (until the engine fires) and the throttle open. If the engine starts like that and runs fine, then your choke may not be working. If the engine dies soon-after then you probably do have a blocked jet or fuel pipe. If your engine does not start and there is no sign of petrol on your hand then something is definitely blocked.**

 **If the engine starts fine from cold but is reluctant to start once hot, check that the float needle seats properly.**

Remove your fuel pipe and turn on the tap to check for flow problems. These are sometimes caused by improper fitting of the rubber gasket inside the tap. A blocked tap can usually be dismantled and cleared. If the pipe flows fine then remove the fuel banjo from the carb and check the filter. Clear if blocked.

If fuel flow to the carb seems fine then take the carb off the manifold and remove the float bowl. Before draining it, look inside for impurities such as grit or water (which forms visible globules below the fuel).

With the pipe and banjo attached to the carb, turn on the tap. Fuel should flow out through the float needle valve unless you lift the float with your finger, whereupon flow should stop completely. If fuel flow does not stop when the float is lifted then the valve needle must be cleaned or renewed. If the float needle valve does not flow properly then strip and clean as best you can, and blow through with a high pressure air line.

If everything else flows fine, then the problem is possibly a blocked jet. Unscrew all of them and blow them through with air.

## 4. Kickstart Problems

The Lambretta kickstart mechanism is a very poor design because you have to turn the entire transmission with each kick, and doing so only turns the crank a few revolutions. If you have long enough legs, maximise the effect of your kick by doing so astride the machine with it off the stand.

The last resort when kick-starting fails is to try bump-starting, but be careful because this is a dangerous procedure if the engine fires and you aren't swift enough at pulling the clutch in or jumping on.

## The Engine Stops Running or Misfires

For engines that do start but then run badly, first check the items previously suggested, but also consider:

- If the engine only ticks over with the choke on then the pilot jet or passage in the carb may be blocked, the slide may be worn or the mixture screw improperly adjusted.
- If there is a knocking sound from the flywheel side of your engine and it misfires at high rpm this could indicate a loose or failing flywheel, or a worn out flywheel bearing. On points systems also check the insulation on the condenser wire is not breaking down.
- If the engine splutters (4-strokes) check if the choke is stuck on, any of the jets have come loose, the choke cable is too tight or if something has obstructed the air scoop under the seat.

- On points systems, if the engine cuts out when the lights are switched on suspect a demagnetised flywheel, failing coil, or a plug or points problem. This symptom can sometimes be relieved by making the plug gap smaller.
- If the engine won't hold a steady tick over it could be that the carburettor air-screw is not set correctly.
- If the engine cuts out when you brake on very early 4-pole machines, this can indicate a blown brake light bulb which forms part of the ignition circuit in the strange wiring system used.
- If it has been raining heavily suspect water ingress into the electrics. Liberally spray the whole electrical system with WD40 or similar water dispersant.

## Engine Lacks Power

- Possible blocked silencer.
- Possible rich mixture due to blocked air filter. Renew filter.
- Possible worn piston/rings/bore. Check and renew as necessary.
- Drive side oil seal failed.
- Obstruction to air scoop intake under seat.
- Overweight pillion passenger fitted.

## Engine Overheats

- If the engine still runs when switched off then this is a serious problem called pre-ignition which is caused by the engine overheating. Check that the spark plug is a suitable grade, the timing is correct and the carburation is properly set.
- An overly lean mixture caused by incorrect carburettor jetting, a missing air filter or split air hose can cause engine overheating.
- Check for obstructions under the cylinder cowling. It is possible for a 'birds nest' to form near the head if you have ridden over long grass or litter which has been sucked into the flywheel and blocked the cylinder fins.
- De-coke your cylinder head, piston and ports to improve cooling efficiency.

## Engine Revs Higher Than Normal At a Given Road Speed

- Suspect a slipping clutch due to an over-tight cable or worn out cork clutch plates. Adjust the cable or replace clutch plates as required.

## Engine Tries To Pull Away When Gear Is Selected, Even With Clutch Pulled In

- This symptom is known as clutch drag and is caused by an overly loose clutch cable or a poorly assembled or worn clutch. Adjust the cable or rebuild the clutch as required.
- Loose rivets in the clutch spider may also cause clutch drag. Either renew the part, tighten the rivets and weld the two parts together as shown in the Advanced Engine Building chapter.

## Dim Lights

This is most likely to be a problem on early non-battery points systems. Later electronic ignition systems have much brighter lights that should only dim at very low tick-over.

- Check bulbs fitted are of the correct voltage and wattage. If your stator has a poor output it is possible to fit lower wattage bulbs e.g. 20/20W or 15/15W to get a bright white light.
- Check that the rear light unit is wired correctly and that the powerful brake light bulb is not on all the time.
- Suspect a demagnetised flywheel, or engine-to-chassis earth wire problem.

## Frequent Bulb Blowing

- The correct 12-volt (2.5W – 4W) speedo bulb must be fitted and working on all 6-volt models as this acts as a buffer to prevent bulb blowing. Fit an earth wire to the speedo bulb holder as described in the chassis check chapter.
- Check bulbs fitted are of the correct voltage and wattage. Note that some Indian machines used a 12-volt headlight but all the remaining bulbs were 6-volt!
- Tail-light bulb blowing can be caused by faulty headlight dip switches which are supposed to illuminate both headlight bulb filaments when switching between the two settings. Some switches momentarily turn both filaments off, which puts too much power to the rear light bulb and this can blow as a result.
- Ensure a good chassis to engine earth wire connection, and that all the connections in the headset are in good order.
- On 12-volt AC systems (e.g. AF, Vespa conversion or recent Indian) suspect a failing AC regulator.

## Poor Handling

- First check your tyre pressures.
- If the back end of the scooter bounces up and down when you kickstart it – or after riding over a pot-hole – then the rear damper has gone. Complete rear shock replacement is the only cure.
- Check if the rubber in the engine mount silent block has collapsed; particularly on all later machines with 'wide'-type engine mounts. If the engine pin nut sits anywhere other than central to the mount, then both silent blocks need to be renewed.
- Support the rear of the machine off the ground, hold the back wheel top and bottom and try to rock it. Unlike a Vespa there should be virtually no play. Slight movement could be a loose wheel, loose hub nut or failing layshaft bearing. Excessive movement could be a loose gearbox endplate. All of these require urgent attention. Try the same with the front wheel. Any noticeable movement at the edge of the wheel rim indicates a loose wheel or failing wheel bearings.
- With the machine head on to you, see if the top of the front wheel sits centrally to the forks, and stays central if someone puts the front brake on and pushes the machine forward. If the wheel tips to one side then the fork buffers, fork springs and/or fork link bushes need to be renewed.
- Put the machine on the centre stand and tip it sideways to get the front wheel off the floor. Turn the headset slowly and gently. If it feels notchy in any way then the fork bearings are over-tight or damaged and should be greased or renewed.

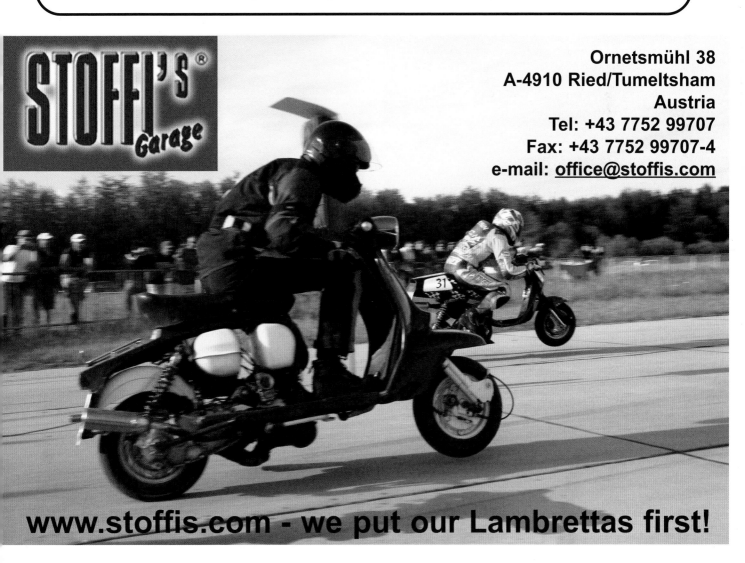

# COMMON REPAIR WORK

## Cables

If your cables are correctly lubricated and routed then the inners should last a very long time, but occasionally they will fray or snap. For gear, clutch and front brake cables replacement often means removal of the headset top first.

## Headset Top Removal

Undo the screws securing your headlight rim, and once off, unclip the bulb holder. Depending on model you may also need to remove two of the headlight rim screws. On Special/SX/TV-type it is sufficient to remove only the top two screws and slacken the bottom two a couple of turns. Next undo the two screws under the headset which secure its top. Push up the speedo outer cable until there is enough slack to reach under the speedo and unscrew the knurled cable nut.

 **Tape the nut to the top of the speedo cable to prevent it sliding down inside the fork tube. If you don't they can be difficult to retrieve. Should the nut drop down then one solution is to remove the speedo cable completely and use an air line to blow into the speedo cable hole at the bottom of the fork. Hey presto - out shoots the knurled nut!**

Disconnect the bulb holder from the headlight, and unplug the white earth wire from the bulb holder. Unplug the speedo light bulb. The headset top should now be free to be removed.

## Gearchange Cable Replacement

 **To prevent your outer gear cables dropping down when the inners are removed add a plastic tie around the frame tube and cables just behind the forks, if one is not already fitted.**

 **If a tie is fitted behind the forks and none is used on the headstock ('steering column') then it is possible to change outer cables without the need to remove your horncasting.**

Use an Allen key and spanner to undo the cable trunnion and withdraw the broken inner cable.

Pull out the remaining inner cable, oil a new one (two-stroke will do if you are at the side of the road) and then thread it into place. Hook it into the gear pulley. Check that the outer cable is seated properly before refitting the trunnion at the engine end and re-adjusting.

 **Nylon-lined cables do not require oiling or greasing along their full length and may be used dry. A coating of oil or grease on the exposed part of the inners can prevent water ingress and frozen cables in the winter though.**

There are two different standard sizes of gear cable trunnion. The longer one is used nearest the wheel since it is also used to locate the gearchange tie rod.

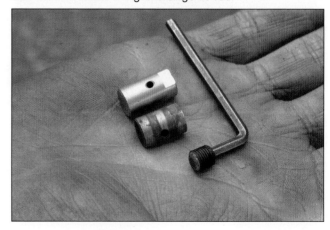

## Clutch and Front Brake Cable Replacement

It is sometimes possible to change a broken Lambretta clutch cable without first removing the headset top. If the outer cable moves out of position then the headset top must be removed. Undo the lever pivot bolt and withdraw the broken cable from both ends. Front brake cable replacement follows broadly the same process.

Slide a freshly lubricated cable through the lever housing, attach the loose ferrule (if required) and fit the lever to the end of the cable. Now thread the inner down through the outer cable.

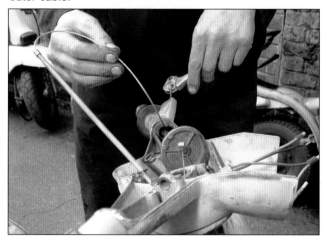

Ensure that where they cross the clutch cable runs nearest to the headlight and the front brake cable nearest to the rider.

Check that the outer cable and lever are fully seated before attempting to fit a trunnion and adjust the cable.

Lots of inner cable problems at the engine end occur because the small protective pads in the trunnion have been omitted, allowing the grub screw to cut the cable. In most trunnions a single pad is fitted between the cable and the screw, but in these stainless versions there should be a pad either side of the inner cable.

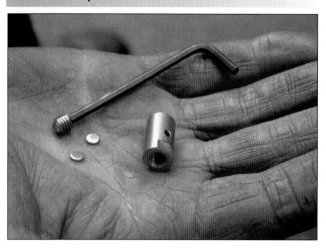

Though rare, original type trunnion tools make adjustment a cinch.

## Choke Cable

The inner and outer choke cable must be replaced as a complete unit. This cable is released by first unscrewing and removing the connection to the carb and removing the brass plunger. Then the 'lever' end of the cable can be removed.

## Back Brake Cable

Undo the inner cable at the pedal end, straighten it as much as possible and withdraw it completely by pulling the adjuster at the wheel end. If the inner cable is in good condition it can be greased and replaced, otherwise renew it.

# Tyre or Inner Tube Replacement

Any work you do regarding your wheels, tyres or inner tubes must be carried out to a very high standard because your life is at risk. Two things to be particularly careful of are not to pinch the inner tube between the rims when a wheel is being rebuilt, and to always check that you have adequate clearance between the tyre valve and the fork link bolt on the front wheel. Failures to do either of these things can lead to sudden tyre deflation with potentially dire consequences. Despite their undoubted quality Michelin Airstop tubes are one of the worst culprits for touching the fork link bolt, particularly when used with non–Innocenti rims because the valves are so long. Michelin do produce a tube with an almost straight valve that is suitable. These are available from Casa Lambretta outlets on request.

Always deflate your inner tube before undoing the wheel rim nuts. Carefully push in the valve centre with a Phillips screwdriver.

Some valve caps can be turned around and used to unscrew and remove the valve core for complete deflation.

Undo the four wheel rim nuts. Some lubrication can be useful to remove the rims. Brake cleaner works and evaporates quickly leaving no residue. Never use grease or oil.

Some dealers use washing up liquid or even KY Jelly to help ease tyres off and on to rims, but be careful because both of these have some water content that can rust rims if left inside. Specific tyre-fitting lubricant is obviously the best stuff to use.

If your rims are in good condition the tyre should separate quite easily from the rim with the help of a tyre lever (or a large flat-bladed screwdriver when at the side of the road).

For simple puncture repair then it is often sufficient to remove only one half of the rim – or even just pull the rims apart to change the tube – but do not fit a new tube without first finding the cause of the puncture.

Mark the position of your valve against the tyre before you remove the tube. Then you can re-inflate the tube to find the hole and line the tube up in its previous position to help find the cause of the puncture.

Never patch inner tubes unless you are really desperate because if they leak they tend to deflate rapidly and dangerously. For the modest cost of a replacement it is far better to fit a new tube.

If your rims are rusty then the tyre may need some more encouragement to make it move. Space the rims apart with a block of wood or a socket and then clamp the tyre in a vice as close as possible to the rim. This will unseat all but the most stubborn tyres.

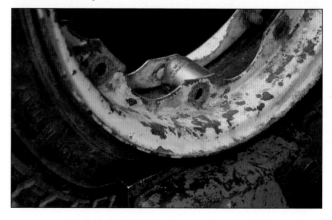

**Badly flaking rusty rims can cause punctures. If they are too bad to wire brush, rust treat and paint then they are probably best off in the bin.**

Lever off other rim half with the tyre clamped firmly in the vice.

When rebuilding a wheel always put a little air into the tube first as this minimises the chances of it getting pinched between the wheel rims.

Many modern tyres are directional with the arrow representing the rotation of the wheel. Make sure you assemble the wheel with the valve facing the correct way.

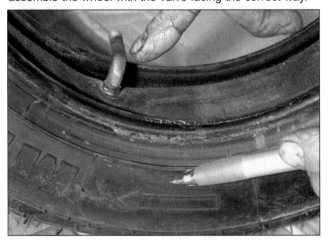

 **One good test for a trapped tube is to stand on the rims before the nuts are fitted. If both sides of the rim touch evenly all the way round then the tube isn't trapped, if there is a gap in one place then either the tube is trapped or your rims are bent!**

Make sure that the tube does not get pinched when the rims are bolted together. Sometimes a pinched tube is visible through the holes for the wheel studs.

Pull the valve up into position while the tyre is being inflated.

**The small $CO_2$ gas bottles supplied with many motorcycle puncture kits can be ideal to re-inflate a rebuilt wheel, if you also keep a spare inner tube in your toolbox.**

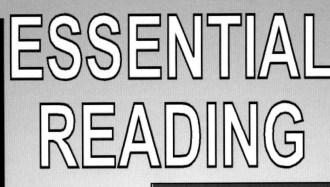
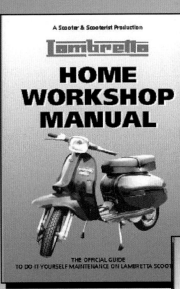

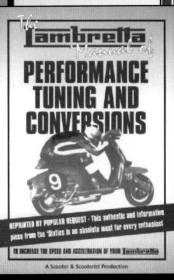
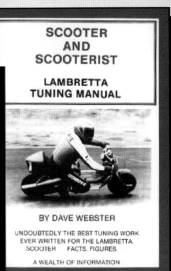

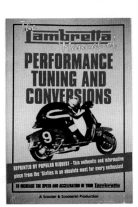

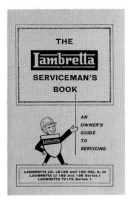

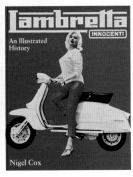

# ENGINE STRIP – THE EASY BIT!

This chapter deals with a full engine strip and rebuild. On a Lambretta almost any job can be done with the engine in the frame – such as work on the clutch, gearbox and ignition system – but it is often far easier to work on an engine that has been removed from the chassis, and particularly to photograph.

## Engine Removal Checklist:

(For more specific engine removal tips, see the Chassis Strip chapter.)

- Drain all crankcase oil.
- Remove bridge piece, running boards and running board support leg (engine side).
- Remove the carburettor from the manifold, but beware of leaking fuel.
- Removal of the exhaust body at this stage can be helpful but is not essential. With standard exhaust systems that haven't been shifted in a while, remove all the nuts holding the exhaust box to the engine (note a bolt under the engine to support the exhaust on later machines), loosen the clamp and from the flywheel side of the machine rest a block of wood on the exhaust and tap the wooden block with a hammer to ease it off. If you are going to replace the old exhaust anyway it may be easier to saw through the downpipe to release the main chamber rather than spending hours trying to separate them.

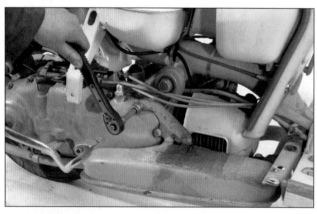

- Disconnect wires from stator plate to junction box or ignition/lighting system (and any retaining straps to the frame).
- Disconnect any earth wire fixed to the flywheel cowling screws.
- Disconnect the rear brake cable. The easiest way is to undo the 17mm nut on the brake pedal clamp. The cable is curved round the adjuster at the wheel end and prone to fraying if you undo it there.

- Use an adjustable spanner over the clutch arm to release tension on the cable so that the trunnion can be unhooked from the arm.
- Remove the rubber cover and circlip/washer that connect the gearchange tie rod to the gear arm protruding from the engine casing.
- Remove the four 10mm-head bolts holding the bracket for the gearchange cable lever and gearchange adjuster block. If you do not want to replace your cables, then doing things this way allows you to keep them in the same position without needing readjustment.

- Remove the rear shock.
- Support the engine or ask someone to help you.
- Loosen the nuts on the main engine bolt, but before fully removing them, tap the bolt each way with a nylon or copper-faced mallet to free it from the frame cones.
- Undo one nut and withdraw the engine bolt.
- With the engine free, it is easiest to lift the scooter off the motor and wheel the chassis away.

With the engine removed, mask off the inlet manifold with tape. Take off the flywheel and head cowlings and scrape off as much dirt as you can. Fully clean the outside of the engine with a brush and Gunk, Jizer or paraffin, being particularly careful of the potential fire hazard.

## Cylinder Head Removal

Undo the four nuts holding the cylinder head. On original machines these M8 nuts are a deep 14mm or 13mm head and have a flat washer underneath. Undo them half a turn at a time in a diagonal pattern to avoid the possibility of warping the cylinder head. The head should come off easily but may not if the wrong washers have been used. If you must prise the head off be very careful not to break any cooling fins or score the gasket face. Remove the head gasket.

# Cylinder Removal

The cylinder should be fairly simple to remove. You may have to tap it gently with a rubber mallet to loosen it. Lift it off carefully.

**Put a piece of rag inside the crankcase mouth as soon as possible to prevent any dirt or components from falling into the crankshaft.**

**If you are having trouble getting the cylinder off, first remove the exhaust studs. If cheap aftermarket exhaust studs have been used, these can often be wound so deep into the threads that they push through and lock on to the cylinder studs.**

# Piston Removal

Remove both piston circlips using quality circlip pliers. A rag heated with boiling water or gentle warming of the piston with a heat gun will help loosen a tight gudgeon pin. The best way to remove the gudgeon pin is with a gudgeon pin removal tool.

**The alternative method is to refit the cylinder so far that it supports the upper part of the piston and then tap out the pin with a suitable drift (such as a 3/8 socket extension). If you try to tap out the pin without supporting the piston there is a danger of bending your con-rod.**

With the piston off, remove the small end bearing and any gudgeon pin shims that may be fitted.

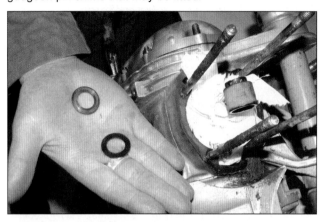

**This is as far as you need to go for a simple 'de-coke' (carbon build-up removal). Scrape off any carbon that has built up on the piston crown, in the cylinder head and in the exhaust port. Clean all components thoroughly and always renew both cylinder base and head gaskets before rebuilding.**

# Side Casing Removal

Undo the 14 10mm-head nuts or bolts around the chaincase.

**If your side casing is held on with bolts it is worth changing these for studs, washers and nuts for several reasons. Firstly, regularly winding bolts into aluminium casings is asking for stripped threads. Secondly, many of the cheaper and smaller clutch compressors only fit onto studs.**

With all the fasteners undone, the easiest way to separate the side casing is to pull on the clutch arm or depress the kickstart. Very rarely should you ever need to tap the casing with a hide mallet to help separate it. Avoid using screwdrivers between the gasket faces.

**As the side casing separates from the gasket more gearbox oil will drip out, so be prepared for it.**

With the casing off, pay attention to several things. Make sure you don't lose the two dowels that are located to the front and rear of the gasket face. Also remove the steel thimble from the centre of the clutch (if you have a pre-GP set-up) or bronze pressure bush (GP) and put it somewhere safe.

 **Check if the kickstart shaft has been rubbing on the top clutch plate. This is a very common problem and can be dealt with.**

## Clutch Removal

Fit a Lambretta clutch compressor (several types are available) over the studs, but not so tightly that it damages the gasket face. Wind down the centre bolt to compress the springs so that the circlip can be removed.

 **The type of compressor shown below can only be used on casings fitted with bolts (rather than studs and nuts) if the legs of the tool itself have first been fitted with studs.**

Unwind the compressor centre bolt. The clutch plates and central pressure plate can then be removed. If you want to re-use the clutch plates, keep them clean and together. The clutch springs can now be removed.

## Clutch Spider ('Inner Bell') and Rear Sprocket ('Crown Wheel') Removal

Tap flat the tab washer around the 22mm-headed centre nut.

You need to hold the clutch spider with a Lambretta clutch holding tool before you can undo the centre nut. Various versions are produced and must rest on the studs to stop the clutch centre turning.

**With this holding tool in place, it is wise to also loosen the front sprocket centre bolt to ease removal later on.**

**We have seen the clutch spider locked with a wide flat screwdriver between the teeth of first gear and the casings in a road-side emergency BUT THIS IS NOT RECOMMENDED as damage can result to the casings or first gear cog if it the screwdriver slips.**

With the centre nut removed, lift out the centre spider by hand. Use a pair of screwdrivers to lever it up if it is stiff.

Lift out the rear sprocket and remove it from the chain. If there is not enough slack in the chain you can either loosen the tab washer and bolts on the chain guides, or wait until the front sprocket is removed to take both sprockets and chain off together. Inside the sprocket is either a pair of needle roller bearings or a single bronze bush (depending on model), with a shim (or sometimes two) underneath.

## Front Sprocket Removal

A con-rod holding tool (of which there are several types) can be used to lock the crankshaft so that the 14mm-headed sprocket bolt can be undone – if you didn't already undo the sprocket bolt when the clutch holding tool was in place.

**If you don't have a con-rod holding tool, you can use two small blocks of hardwood (to prevent damage to gasket surface) between the casings and the gudgeon pin and small end bearing to hold the con-rod.**

**An electric impact socket wrench can be used to shock the bolt undone. I have also seen the front sprocket held to get the bolt undone by sticking a screwdriver between the teeth of the rear sprocket (when still fitted) and chain BUT THIS IS NOT RECOMMENDED since it can damage the chain, sprocket and chain guides.**

With the bolt undone it is possible to remove the cap, spring and cush-drive assembly ('engine shaft shock absorber') before the front sprocket itself and chain.

All these components mount onto a castellated sleeve, which is a splined fit onto the crankshaft. This sleeve should normally pull off by hand if the splines are in good condition. There is a specific Lambretta workshop tool for removing these if they are stiff.

**A stiff sleeve can be removed from the crankshaft splines by gripping it with a pair of vice grips, and resting the grips on one of the M8 exhaust studs or chaincase dowels. Gently tapping the handles of the grips down should be enough to lever the sleeve up.**

# Before Going Any Further!

Two jobs should be done before the gearbox is disassembled.

## Checking Layshaft End Float

Firstly, check the clearance on your gearbox shim ('layshaft end float') by sliding a feeler gauge between it and the bearing outer track in the gearbox endplate. This should only be measured with the rear hub nut done up tight to hold the layshaft into its correct position. The correct float should be between 0.07 - 0.30mm (0.003 - 0.011"). Try successively fatter gauges until the large shim becomes too tight to turn with a finger. If the shim is outside permissible tolerances, then one of a different thickness may be obtained.

## Rear Hub Removal

Next remove the rear hub – if not done already. Undo the Allen bolt that holds the hub nut locking ring, and remove it.

 **A homemade hub holding tool can be very useful for undoing and doing up the rear hub nut. This can take the form of two pieces of metal welded or bolted to an old wheel rim which rests against the casings.**

Various sorts of hub puller have been produced over the years. The Innocenti workshop ones (several types) grip the outside of the hub or wheel studs. Once the puller is tight, give the centre bolt a sharp tap to help shock the hub off.

Most people will only have access to the pattern hub pullers which fit on the centre three threads for the locking ring Allen bolt. For this sort of puller to work, all three of these M7 threads (or M6 on some hubs) must be in perfect condition.

 **To maximise the chances of a pattern puller working, run an M7 tap down each thread to clean them. Also discard the three bolts supplied and replace with longer ones fitted with nuts. Then you can wind the bolts in to their maximum depth before tightening the nuts to hold the puller down evenly.**

## Gearbox Removal

First undo the tab washer and remove the two short 10mm-head chainguide bolts to give better access.

 **On racing engines, or those rebuilt regularly, it may be best to replace the chainguide bolts with studs and nuts to protect the soft aluminium casing threads.**

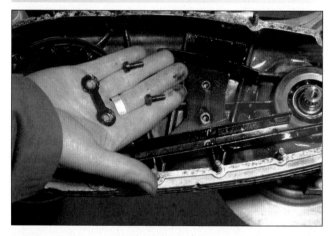

Next, undo the six shallow (M7 x 4mm deep) 11mm-headed nuts and remove the split washers underneath.

There are two threaded M6 holes in the endplate which were designed to be used with M6 T-bar extractors. Fit the extractors into the holes and wind each in until they meet some resistance.

 **The T-bar extractors aren't really needed so long fully-threaded, high-tensile M6 bolts work just as well.**

 **Some Indian endplates were machined without the threaded extractor holes. These endplates must be levered out. Thankfully they are not usually a tight fit. Introduce these to a recycling programme (throw them in the bin) and fit a fully machined replacement to make life easier in the future.**

The endplate starts to lift at one end, but you need to get it to lift evenly. The easiest way is to tap the flat area on the edge of the endplate between the two extractor holes with a soft-faced (copper or hide) hammer. Doing so evens up the endplate and you can wind the extractors in a little further.

You will also need to give the gear cluster shaft (the one poking out) a little tap with a soft-faced hammer to help ease it out of the endplate bearing. Be very careful not to damage the exposed thread. Refitting its nut can help protect the thread.

Take off the large gearbox shim, the small layshaft needle roller bearing and another shim from under that bearing. Now you can remove the four loose gears from the layshaft.

Next withdraw the gear cluster, which is fitted with a shim and a needle roller bearing in a blind hole in the casings.

## Layshaft and Rear Brake Removal

Use a small screwdriver to lift off the rear hub cone and the thin shim from underneath it. If the cone is tight, tap a thin flat-bladed screwdriver into the slot to open it for removal. There are three different angles of these cones and they match certain hubs, so it is important to keep hub and cone together.

Next undo the circlips holding the brake shoes with suitable circlip pliers. Under the circlips should be a metal spring plate then a flat plate, and then the brake shoes. Single piece W-shaped wire circlips are used (without any plates) on later models.

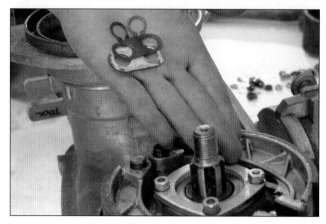

Ease the brake shoes off their pins bit by bit at each end using a screwdriver.

 **TOP TIP** **Mark the positions of the shoes before removal so that they can be refitted in the same position should you chose to reuse them.**

Next use a soft-faced hammer to knock the layshaft through, but be careful not to damage the exposed threads.

 **TOP TIP** **A good way to protect the layshaft thread while tapping it through is to fit one of the rear shock nuts before you hit it.**

As you ease the layshaft through, unhook the two guide pads from the track in the cursor.

# Rear Hub Bearing Removal

Undo the four deep 10mm-headed nuts and wavy washers that hold the rear hub retaining plates (one fat flange, one thin) and remove them. If the studs are bent – as can happen when over tightened – heat around the casings and remove the studs with vice grips. Renew the studs if you do this. You will possibly need a new retaining plate because that may also be bent.

There is a specific Innocenti drift that can be used to knock out the rear hub bearing.

**Most of us don't have Innocenti drifts, so use a large socket on the end of an extension bar as a drift. Make sure whatever you use rests on the outer track of the bearing if you don't want to damage it. An old engine mount fits well.**  **ANOTHER WAY**

**A chromed aluminium 'Sundance' handlebar grip is suitable for many drifting jobs on scooters and pre-heating the casing with a blow torch also works wonders.**  **TOP TIP**

Now you can remove the gear selector fork ('wishbone') which is unusual because it is secured by an M6 bolt and wavy washer with a 9mm head. Withdraw the splined shaft from the outside of the engine. Be aware of the shim between the gear selector fork and the casing which will drop down when the shaft is removed.

## Flywheel Removal

Remove the large wire circlips in the centre of the flywheel and rotate the dust cover in the middle until it can be removed. If it won't turn, clean out any dirt with a small screwdriver. On very early machines, the dust cover may be retained by screws instead of a circlip.

The only good way to hold a Lambretta flywheel while the nut is undone is using a dedicated flywheel holding tool. These are available in various sizes to fit flywheels with different numbers of slots.

Refit the main engine bolt and use this as a point to rest the holding tool against. The flywheel nut has a 17mm head, but there are three different sorts depending on model. **ALL HAVE A LEFT-HAND THREAD.**

**The best alternative to a flywheel holding tool is an electric or air impact socket driver, which can shock the nut undone without the need for a holding tool.**

**If you are stuck at the roadside however, it is possible to lock the crank well enough to undo the flywheel nut by knotting a piece of nylon rope and inserting the knotted end through the plug hole so that the knot is located in the squish area between the piston and cylinder head. Turn the flywheel until you feel the rope lock the piston, then you should be able to undo or do up your flywheel nut.**

With the nut undone, screw in a Lambretta flywheel puller. Spanish Motoplat flywheels use a different extractor thread.

**Double-ended tools are available that work on both Italian and Spanish flywheel threads.**

Tighten the centre bolt of the flywheel extractor (you may still need the holding tool) but if it becomes stiff then tap the centre bolt of the puller with a hammer to help shock the flywheel off.

## Stator Plate Removal

In order to retain your ignition timing settings it is wise to mark the position of your stator plate. One way to do this is to rest the edge of a flat screwdriver on the edge of the stator so that when it is tapped with a hammer it marks both the stator and the mag housing as it jumps down. Be aware though that this is a pointless exercise unless you know that the timing was correctly set in the first place.

 **You can also mark your stator position very accurately by scribing around one of the lugs on the stator back.**

Undo the three 10mm-head bolts that retain the stator, noting that one carries a clip to retain the wiring and the others have wavy washers underneath.

The stator should come out easily. If not then use a screwdriver under the laminates to lever it out. If the woodruff key in the crank is loose, remove it and store it somewhere safe (like stuck to the magnets in your flywheel).

Before removing the stator completely you need to undo the parts that seal the wiring as it leaves the mag housing. Two

screws and washers hold down (in order) a metal plate, a rubber grommet, another metal plate and a gasket. How complicated!

 **It is not necessary to completely remove the stator plate if you only want to remove the mag housing and crankshaft.**

 **For future ease of removal it is a much better idea to change these two small screws for bolts. These are easier to access with the fuel tank in place.**

 **It is good practice to store the stator plate inside the flywheel to prevent loss of flywheel magnetism over long periods of disuse. Don't put a flywheel magnets-side-down onto a dirty bench or it will pick up any loose filings.**

## Magneto (Mag) Housing Removal

Removing a loose mag housing is very little problem. There are two M6-threaded holes to take T-bar extractors (or long fully-threaded M6 bolts), and alternately winding these in half a turn at a time, should pull the mag housing off with ease. If they are stiff do not carry on or you will strip the aluminium extraction threads.

 **If the mag housing of an early Indian GP 150 is difficult to remove it could be one of a batch fitted with Series 1 type caged ball bearings in the mag flange. If you do manage to get the mag housing out then make sure to use the normal NU205 type roller bearing when you rebuild the engine.**

Seized mag housings are more of a problem. Start by applying heat around the outside of the main casing with a blowtorch or electric hot air gun. Try pulling up on the mag housing where the stator wires come through, and tapping on the opposite side. A combination of methods works best.

**On a very badly corroded engine, use a piece of (oak) wood as a drift rested as close as possible to the gasket face and try to tap the mag housing loose, one side and then another. The last resort is to shift the mag housing by hammering the crank through from the sprocket side, but be aware that doing so is likely to wreck the crank.**

# Crankshaft and Drive-side Main Bearing Removal

With the con-rod held at bottom dead centre, gently tap the crankshaft out of the main bearing with a copper-faced hammer to avoid damaging the splines. The crank can be removed at an angle once free of the bearing.

**MB Developments now produce a crankshaft removal tool which will force the crank out without need to hit it and potentially damage the splines.**

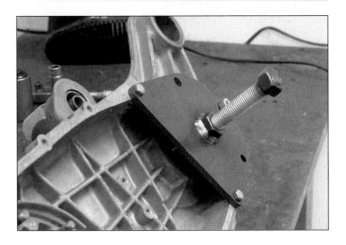

The main bearing is retained by a plate containing an oil seal, and held in by four screws. On original engines these screws are centre-punched, but a small dab of Loctite is sufficient to retain them these days.

By far the best way to undo these screws is with an impact driver. Find a driver bit that fits the screw heads EXACTLY – whether they are slotted, cross or Allen-headed screws – because if you try to undo them and mangle the heads then you are in trouble. Heat applied to the sprocket side of the casing will help loosen the screws.

**Use a socket extension on your impact driver to ensure that the driver does not touch the casing and cause damage when you hit it.**

With the screws removed, you can lever out the plate and the round gasket ('Hallite washer') that sits between it and the bearing.

Gently heat the casing around the main bearing before drifting it out.

Again we used an Innocenti drift, but a Sundance handlebar grip works brilliantly too. Be careful not to let the bearing come out at an angle or it may crack the casing. Innocenti also supplied a puller to remove this bearing but it is not necessary provided you are careful.

## Flywheel Side Main Bearing Removal

 **It is not always possible to remove this bearing without damaging it so if you know it is still OK just renew the large inner oil seal and re-pack the bearing with high melting point grease.**

Inside the mag housing are a bearing, two oil seals, an oil seal retainer and a spacer (not used with the wider GP200 NU2205 flywheel bearings); all lubricated by high melting point grease.

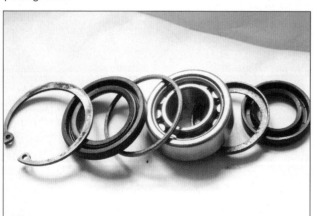

Start by removing the circlip. You will need a large, strong set of circlip pliers to get it out. It is wise to wear some form of eye protection when working with such large circlips.

Next, lever out the large oil seal.

**Note that both oil seals should have the spring-sides facing the crankwebs.**

The GP 200 setup uses a wide NU2205 bearing, but most other engines use a narrower bearing with a spacer ring (shown) under the oil seal to take up the extra space.

There is an Innocenti bearing puller to remove the flywheel bearing and outer oil seal, but since this is not accessible to most people and requires heat anyway, it is normal to do the job another way. The best way to remove the flywheel side bearing is to heat it up over a cooker hob – preferably electric. Do not heat a good bearing with a naked flame if you want to re-use it. If that is the case, heat only the outside of the mag housing with a heat gun.

**Specialist drifts for this job are now available from certain dealers.**

Once hot it should be sufficient to tap the mag housing on a bench and the bearings should drop out. If not, use a large socket and extension as a drift to knock through the seal, seal retainer ring and bearing, but make sure the socket is as large as will fit inside the hole in the mag housing. If the housing is hot enough it should all come out easily.

# CHECKING, SELECTING AND PREPARING ENGINE PARTS

## Crankcase Identification

Do not panic if you are looking at buying a scooter and find that the engine casings are stamped with a different model pre-fix. Confusingly Innocenti did not update the stampings of some casings when the scooter models themselves were updated. Below is a list of the stamped prefixes, which can then be separated into the different scooter models by the first digits of the engine number.

| MODEL | ENGINE PREFIX | FIRST DIGIT OF ENGINE NO. |
|---|---|---|
| LI 125 S.1 | 125LI | 5 – 6 |
| LI 150 S.1 | 150LI or LI150 | 5 – 6 |
| LI 125 S.2 | 125LI | 5 – 6 |
| LI 150 S.2 | 150LI | 8 – 9 |
| LI 125 S.3 | 125LI | 000 – 146 |
| LI 150 S.3 | 150LI | 6 – 74 |
| LI 125 Special | 125LIS | 85 – 88 |
| LI 150 Special | 150LI | 7 |
| TV 175 S.2 | 175TV2 | 1 or 2 |
| TV 175 S.3 | 175TV2 | 5 |
| TV (GT) 200 | TV/2 | 5 |
| SX 150 | SX 150 | 7 |
| SX 200 | SX 200 | 8 |
| GP 125 | 125LIS | 00 |
| GP 150 | SX 150 | 200 |
| GP 200 | SX 200 | 25 |
| JET 200 | SX 200 | 5 |

## Crankcase Check

The Lambretta engine casing is very susceptible to damage from ham-fisted or negligent owners, and with some Italian engines now exceeding 40 years old, there's a good chance that at least one such person has been around your motor. As such, it is very important to give the engine casing a thorough check over before going any further. At the very least give the casing a good clean with Gunk or paraffin and a stiff brush, but it is even better to get the casing vapour blasted or chemically cleaned; particularly if it looks like it will require any welding. On casings that have had a hard life it may be worthwhile testing for cracks using Dye Penetrant Examination (DPE) chemicals available from welding suppliers. A specialist welder should be able to carry out these tests for you if required.

If your casing is in particularly poor condition, it is worth considering a brand new Indian engine casing. At the time of writing (2004) these are often cheaper and the final result better than a heavily repaired Italian or Spanish casing, though some purists may disagree.

 **Some recent batches of Indian casings have been incorrectly machined in respect to the drive side main oil seal retaining plate. This causes the drive side oil seal to leak after only a few miles of use. We have also heard of problems with rear brake shoe pivot hole alignment causing only one brake shoe to contact the drum and incorrect machining of the hub bearing recess which makes it difficult to correctly shim the gearbox. Before purchasing an Indian casing ask your supplier if the one he is selling is likely to be affected by such problems and what he will do about it if you encounter them.**

 If your casings have been sand blasted at some time or another (or even if it is a new Indian casing) then it is worth running a tap down through all the threads to make sure they are clean before fitting any new studs. Spraying brake cleaner into the threads is a good way to clean them. Also if you are going to get anything blasted make sure you leave a bolt in every exposed thread to protect it.

 During the 1980s and on the scooter racing scene it was very fashionable to cut or grind off the engine bump stop from behind the crank casting. This allows the fitment of oversized 4.00-10 tyres and more importantly for racers it meant that the engine could tip further if no rear mudguard was fitted, allowing for faster cylinder strips. The down-side to this modification on a road scooter is that if your rear shock collapses the tyre will immediately come into contact with the mudguard bolts rather than the engine resting on the rubber stop. With 4.00-10 tyres now hard to get (and out of favour) and little need for racing cylinder changes, bump stop removal is inadvisable.

 On ported casings (particularly Spanish ones) check for a hairline crack between the transfer and mag housing where the aluminium can be very thin. Cracks here can cause air leaks, bad carburation and seizure problems. Repairs should only be made by a specialist TIG welder.

## Studs and Threads

Start by checking the condition of all the studs and threads. First try to wobble any of the studs that are still fully seated in their threads. If there is some movement then the best thing to do is to fit a thread insert of some sort. Lambretta casing threads are not supported by a lot of aluminium so it is best to use coiled steel 'Helicoils' or Würth 'Timeserts' because they don't require the holes to be tapped out too far. Timeserts are superior because they are solid and less liable to pull out when a stud is removed. Thicker solid inserts such as Tappex inserts should only be used where there is plenty of meat to support them. If you are not an accomplished engineer then I recommend you take the casings to someone who has experience in fitting inserts. Most bike/scooter/car garages will have the facilities to repair threads (though M7 is not a common size and may have to be ordered in especially) but a local engineering specialist may be even better. It is vital that a quality job is done and the inserts are put in perfectly square. There is nothing worse than not being able to fit your cylinder because one of the studs is pointing off at an odd angle thanks to a misaligned thread insert. Lambretta produced a special tool to help with the alignment of the three chain casing exhaust studs when they are being repaired using Tappex inserts. Weston Scooter Parts have these tools.

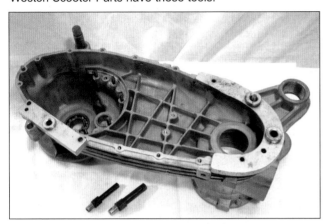

If the aluminium around the thread is cracked or badly damaged, then the best solution is to remove the broken piece and get a proficient TIG welder to build up around the damage so it can be machined back and a new thread cut into it. All this is specialist work and should only be entrusted to someone who comes on recommendation.

Any good studs that need to be removed are best extracted using the double-nut method. Wind two good nuts onto the thread and use a pair of spanners to tighten them together. To remove the stud, use a spanner to turn the bottom nut anti-clockwise (as you look down on it).

To wind a stud in, turn the top nut clockwise. Before fitting studs use thinners and a cotton wool bud to clean the casing threads. A small drop of Loctite Stud and Bearing Fit (or similar) can be used on the stud before fitting. Wipe off any excess. Do not put the Loctite into the casing threads before the stud is fitted.

**Cheap Lambretta chaincase studs may actually screw too far into their threads to be of any use. Specially stepped Lambretta chaincase studs that will only fit to the correct depth are now available to solve this.**

**Studs can also be removed with stud extractors. Various types are available. Those that look like normal sockets are only designed to fit and remove perfect studs so do not attempt to use the type shown on seized, corroded studs.**

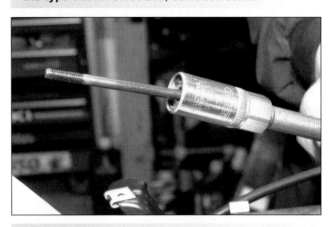

**The type of stud extractor with the knurled wheel that grips the stud shaft (do not use on the threaded section) can remove studs which have threads too damaged to double-nut. Always warm the aluminium before undoing to ease removal.**

One area particularly prone to damage is around the gearbox endplate. It is absolutely vital that every thread is in perfect condition – particularly on tuned motors – because a loose endplate not only means a wrecked gearbox but also that the shaft holding the rear wheel is not given full support – which could be deadly.

You can tell if the endplate has come loose in the past by the condition of the casing around the dowels. If the two dowels are tight, then the casing is fine. If they are very loose then they ideally need a welded repair – which again is a specialist job.

**Some dealers suggest that mildly loose dowels should have the holes cleaned out and Devcon F Aluminium Putty or Araldite used to take up the slack. Smear some putty in the hole, then fit the dowel, then refit a greased endplate to hold the dowels in the correct position while the putty sets. Clean off any excess putty quickly.**

While some dealers suggest you should remove and replace all endplate studs, nuts and split washers, at least the original Innocenti studs were of high quality. After a thorough visual inspection, perfect original studs can be re-used or high-tensile replacements should be sought. Get any damaged threads fitted with a thread insert.

## Gear Control Shaft Bush

Try the splined gear shaft in its casing bush. If the shaft is a very sloppy fit then the bush must be replaced.

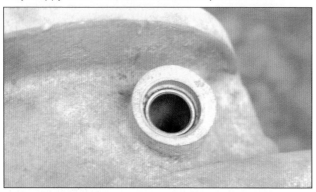

Warm the casings and tap the bush through towards the gearbox with a suitable drift – preferably a shouldered one as shown which can't slip and damage the casings.

**If the gear shaft bush is being replaced then don't throw it away. If it isn't totally worn out then it can be cut in half and makes a good brake pedal bush!**

**Modern replacement bushes are rarely a good fit, and are often too tight. A 12mm reamer can be used to open the bush to the correct size.**

## Engine Mount Silent Block Check

One area Lambrettas really suffer with is their rubber engine mounts: known as silent blocks. The narrow type – used in early LI 125 and 150 engines – gives good support to the motor, keeping the wheel aligned for good handling, but transmits more vibration to the chassis. The wider type used on later 125, 150s, 175s and all 200s has more rubber in it for a smoother ride, but does not hold the engine so well in line. When the rubber becomes worn the engine can sag to one side, the handling deteriorates and vibration increases. Most dealers recommend the fitting of wide engine mounts to early machines for the improved ride they offer. Obviously a longer engine bolt is required.

Damage to silent blocks normally has one of these causes:

- Wear due to aging: Original rubber mounts will almost certainly have given up the ghost by now.
- Poor quality replacements: Getting decent quality replacement bushes has been problematic, with even early batches of some reproduced Italian bushes being improperly manufactured.
- Incorrect fitting: Most wide silent blocks are 'voided', which means that there are holes in the rubber to make the bush softer in a specific direction. If voided silent blocks are not fitted the right way round, they will quickly collapse.
- Design fault: Innocenti realised during production that the engine mount layout was prone to damage; particularly the kickstart side mount. Replacement bushes were subsequently offered with different density rubber on each side to compensate. (*source: Lambretta Works USA).
- Petrol damage: The fashion for using large open-mouthed carburettors on tuned scooters of the 80s and 90s often meant that one engine mount had to spend its life in a fog of fuel and oil, which damages the rubber.

**If you want to protect your engine mounts from the ravages of fuel and even add a splash of customisation, then the chrome covers for car tow-balls fit over the engine mounts, as do the lids from various makes of deodorant can.**

**At the time of writing, three sorts of engine mounts come recommended from dealers: the original SIL Indian ones, recent batches of Casa Lambretta ones (early Casa types were of poor quality) and those from Tutto Lambretta in Italy which are allegedly made in different densities as per the Innocenti technical revisions.**

## Silent Block Replacement

It is possible to replace engine mount silent blocks, and the only advisable way to do this is using heat and the correct tool, because these are an interference fit in the casings. The casings are easily broken or the interference fit damaged if you try to force mounts in or out at anything other than the perfect angle. Pattern versions of Innocenti engine mount pullers are available from several sources.

Here the Innocenti tool is being used to extract the old engine mount.

The same tool can be used to re-fit the new mounts. Voided silent blocks need to be inserted in the correct position. On Italian 3-hole mounts the lowest of the holes should face directly down (6 o'clock), with the remaining holes facing more towards the front of the scooter.

 **SIL in India did their own experimentation with engine mount designs, and they came up with a different fitting style for their two-hole voided mounts. These have the flywheel (left) side mount with the holes located at 8 o'clock and 10 o'clock. The kickstart (right) side mount should have the holes located at 10 o'clock and 1 o'clock.**

A 3-hole flywheel-side engine mount fitted in the correct position with the bottom hole at 6 o'clock, and the other holes facing the front of the scooter.

## Magneto ('Mag') Housing Check

The main thing to check on your mag housing is the condition of the cowling screw threads. These M5 threads are prone to damage, and nothing sounds worse than a Lambretta with rattling, loose cowlings. It is possible to 'helicoil' the threads back to 5mm, or alternatively get the holes fully welded up and re-tap them, but for the modest cost of a new Indian mag housing, it might be cheaper and easier to completely replace yours. Obviously some purists will baulk at the suggestion of using a new Indian component on their scooter, so the damage to their parts will have to be repaired. Also check the condition of the two threaded extractor holes, and if damaged get these 'helicoiled' to M6 again.

 **If you plan to replace your mag housing and are using an original AF ignition system, you may want to have the housing machined to give extra clearance for the ignition pick-up and remove the outer ridge to improve airflow from the flywheel. See: Electrical and Ignition Systems.**

 **Check if your mag housing is actually the correct one for your engine. Early 125/150/175 housings have different transfer port cutaways to 200 housings. It is possible to use a 200 housing in a 150 casing – and Innocenti did so themselves on machines built after 1968 – but it is not ideal and will result in poor gas flow up the left transfer port. It is possible to use 150 housings in 200 engines but these must be machined to suit. If you use an un-machined 150 housing in a 200 motor (as shown) it is possible that the spigot from your cylinder can touch the mag housing at the points indicated, and distort the bore of aluminium cylinders such as the TS1.**

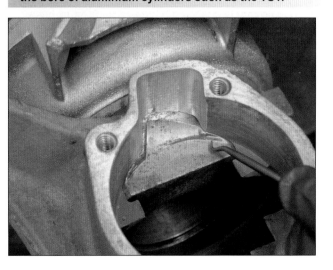

With no crankshaft fitted, try your mag housing in the casing. It should fit quite easily. If it is tight, examine for high spots and rub these down with abrasive paper.

If the high spots are the result of damage to the casing itself, trim with a knife or file away the high spots.

When the mag housing is a perfect fit it should be greased and you should be able to fully seat it without undue force.

## Side Casing ('Chaincase') Check

While there are plenty of variations, side casings that will fit a Series 3 Lambretta come in three basic types:

- **Series 1 & 2:** These are easily identifiable by the extended lug for the kickstart pedal's rubber stop. Early ones only have holes for 6mm rather than 8mm exhaust studs and use a smaller diameter kickstart return spring. These do not have support ribs around the kickstart shaft casting.
- **Series 3 LI/TV/SX:** These have a recess for the kickstart pedal stop, and drillings to fit the ramp that controls the kickstart piston. Early ones do not have support ribs around the kickstart shaft casting.
- **Series 3 GP:** These have a separate casting around the clutch cam to support the bronze clutch thrust bush.

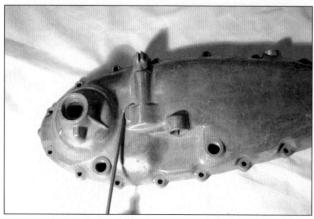

**GP type chaincases (previous pic) are usually easy to identify from the outside because of the semicircular lump in the casting near the clutch rod, which wasn't present on earlier models. Sadly this distinction no longer applies as certainly because the Indians have now started to produce LI/TV/SX-type side casings which also include this lump. Doh!**

The first step is to undo and remove the kickstart bolt. Loosening it is not sufficient as the bolt sits in a slot in the shaft.

**If the kickstart is stiff to remove, put a flat bladed screwdriver in the slot and tap it away from the casing to both open the slot and help shift the kickstart pedal.**

With the pedal removed, next take off the circlip and spacing shim washer. On GP models the shaft is now free to be removed once unhooked from the internal spring.

*LI/SX/TV Models:* Put the teeth of the shaft in a soft-faced vice, and lean your body against the casing to take up the spring pressure.

*LI/SX/TV Models:* You can now use an open-ended or adjustable spanner to unscrew the reference pin from the kickstart piston ('plunger').

**As an alternative to removing the reference pin, you can undo the three 10mm head bolts that hold the ramp ('cam plate') onto the casings. This is both slightly trickier to do, and if your ramp was correctly positioned will require it to be readjusted when reassembled.**

Remove the kickstart piston, piston spring and thrust washer from the shaft. The circlip below can remain in place.

Use a screwdriver to separate the kickstart return spring from the shaft as you withdraw it.

Lever out the kickstart oil seal – these should be changed as a matter of course.

**Very early side casings do not have the extra aluminium support webs around the kickstart shaft (as seen below). Do not use un-supported casings on high compression engines which require a lot of force on the kickstart pedal because they are likely to break.**

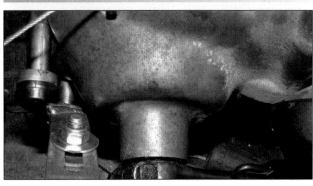

The side casings on all Slimstyle Lambrettas are interchangeable, but if you intend to run a GP-style clutch centre then you will need a GP side casing which has an extra casting to support the bronze thrust bush. On some GP side casings there are no drillings to accept the bolt-on kickstart ramp from earlier models. These can only be used with a GP-style gearbox endplate ('flange') with integral kickstart ramp unless holes are drilled and tapped to accept the early bolt-in ramp.

Damage to side casings is usually confined to wear over the front sprocket bolt if it has been allowed to come undone, and occasionally this will actually break through. Such casings are to be either welded or renewed.

Check the condition of the bronze bush for the kickstart shaft. If this is worn it can be replaced by heating the side casing and tapping it through with a suitable-sized drift. The bronze bush should be flush with the casing looking from the inside. If not, tap it back into place.

**Early kickstart shafts are weak and prone to breaking just where the shaft comes through the bronze bush, as shown below.**

On later models Innocenti thickened the kickstart shaft by 2mm at the weak point and machined the face on the casings further back to suit. The changes were implemented on all engines produced after LI 150/SX 150 engine no. 768530, and SX 200 engine no. 847625. Most early machines were subsequently modified with the tool shown to accept the strengthened kickstart shaft, but if you find that you cannot get the circlip onto your new kickstart shaft – or the shaft rubs heavily on your top clutch plate – then it could be that your side casing still needs to be modified. Specialist Lambretta dealers such as Weston Scooter Parts have the facilities to carry out this modification.

Ensure that the outer kickstart shaft bush is flush with the lip inside the casing so that you have enough room to fit the oil seal. Grease the bronze bushes in the casing. You can either fit a new kickstart seal before reassembly or wait until the shaft is in place to minimise the chances of damaging it.

## Kickstart Check

Wear marks on the kickstart shaft are very common where the shaft has come into contact with the top steel clutch plate. This is usually caused by the kickstart pedal, circlips and shim washer being damaged or worn, allowing the shaft to pull through further into the engine. It is possible to grind away the area that has rubbed to relieve it, but don't go mad because you will weaken the shaft. The main thing to do is ensure that everything fits tightly when it is rebuilt. When rebuilding ensure that the circlips and kickstart shim are all in perfect condition. Different thicknesses of kickstart shim are available if you have slack that needs to be taken up. Original shims are 0.5 or 1mm. MB Developments makes stainless shims in those sizes as well as 1.5mm to suit Indian shafts.

Indian kickstart shafts have been produced with the strong-type shaft, but in the longer early LI-type length. For these to be used successfully in late type casings then a very thick kickstart shim can be required. Note also that some batches of Indian shafts have been incorrectly hardened and may actually bend in use. A bent kickstart shaft does not mean you are a superhero (or a fat b'stard), just that you need to return it to your happy scooter dealer for replacement.

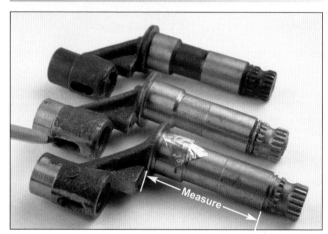

To identify which type of shaft you have, measure from the lower edge of the circlip groove to the thick part of the shaft.

- Early LI (weak type) measures 67.5mm.
- Later LI-SX-GP (thick shaft) measures approx 65mm.
- Indian GP (thick shaft) measures approx 67mm.

The kickstart shaft shown below is the thick post-modification type, and this is essential in high-compression engines. The shiny area is where it has been ground to prevent wear against the top clutch plate. If you do this yourself, do not grind so far as to weaken the shaft.

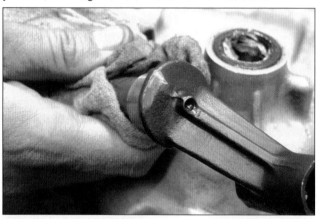

Don't use a good kickstart pedal on a shaft with damaged splines and vice versa. If the splines are damaged then simply replace the offending parts.

Check the condition of the kick-starter piston. It features two teeth that engage with teeth machined onto 1st gear. If either of these teeth are chipped or rounded then the piston will need to be renewed. The same goes for the mating teeth on your gearbox.

 If the circlip and shim on the kickstart shaft have come loose it is possible for the shaft to move in far enough to wear on the 1st gear cog. This often creates burrs that can prevent the kickstart piston from moving out as intended and prevents the kickstart from functioning. File back any burrs so the piston has smooth travel.

The kick-starter piston is retained in the shaft by a circlip, washer, spring and a screw-in reference pin. Due to the design of the engine, this pin can suffer heavy wear. If yours shows any sign of wear it is best to replace it.

There are three sorts of kickstart that look like they will fit this engine, but only two of them fit series 3 casings. The very shortest ones are for the earlier LI series 1 and 2 models and use a slightly different side casing. The very longest ones are for the SX 200 model while the medium length ones are for the remaining machines (LI3, GP etc.)

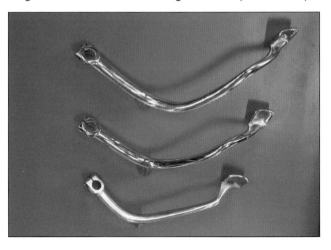

 If the gap in your kickstart pedal pinches closed before the pedal is tight on the shaft then it will eventually cause the splines in both parts to wear and fail. One way round this is to widen the gap by cutting out a thin sliver of kickstart with a hacksaw. To hold the kickstart more securely bore out the bolt hole to 8mm (while the kickstart is fitted to the shaft) and use a high tensile M8 bolt and nyloc nut to fasten it.

## Gearbox Check and Selection

If you are rebuilding a totally standard engine with the original gearbox then all that is required is to check the condition of the gears themselves. However, if your machine has ever been modified then there is a very good chance that it may not contain the original gearbox. If you want to find out which gearbox you have, the information is contained in the Gearbox Appendix at the end of the book.

If your scooter has been tuned in any way then you may want to replace your gearbox with a closer ratio one that is better suited to your needs. Again, all the information is in the Appendix.

Before changing your gearbox, here are some things to take into consideration, particularly in relation to clutch operation.

- Gearboxes with a large ratio jump between 3rd and 4th gears (i.e. SX 150, GP 150 or Spanish LI 150 boxes) are best avoided in anything tuned that has a narrow power spread.
- One of the best types of clutch is the very early ones with the spindle in the middle of the clutch pressure plate. However this type of clutch will only fit with early gear clusters that have a central drilling to accommodate the spindle: e.g. early LI 125/150.
- On highly tuned motors the clutch has an easier life if you use a low ratio gearbox (i.e. LI 125, LI Special, GP 125/200) with a large engine (front) sprocket, compared to using a SX 200/TV 175 or TV 200 gearbox and a small engine sprocket.
- For machines doing lots of town work, pulling heavy loads, or towing a sidecar the early LI 125 gearbox with its low first gear ratio is very handy.
- One favoured original gearbox for racing was the LI Special (Pacemaker) due to a close ratio jump between 3rd and 4th gears, but ONLY USE THE LATE VERSION, because the early Pacemaker boxes were weak and tended to lose teeth from 3rd gear.
- Most dealers' preferred all-round gearboxes are LI 150 Italian, TV 175/SX 200 or GP 125/200 with the correct choice of sprockets to suit your anticipated top speed.

Whatever gearbox you use, you will need to examine its condition. First, check the kickstart teeth on 1st gear for chips. The gear shown is not ideal, but still useable since pristine original SX 200 gearboxes are hard to find. Also check the teeth of each loose gear for chips or wear through the hardening, and check the inner faces of each gear for rounding where it meets the dogs of the selector ('cursor').

Check the condition of the teeth on the gear cluster including the thread and splines at the top. See if a nut runs freely on the thread. Note that the way splines are machined on an Italian gear cluster (left) is different to a Spanish one (right). Despite the different machining the two are interchangeable.

Also examine the bearing surface at the bottom of the cluster for pitting.

If your gear cluster is very badly pitted on the lower bearing face, it is possible to machine it down and fit a replacement bearing track. MB Developments offer this service.

## Endplate Selection

Make sure you use the correct gearbox endplate for your side casing. It is possible (but not always advisable) to use the GP one with integral ramp on all earlier engines, provided you remove any separate ramp from the side casing. It is only possible to use an old-style endplate if your side casing is fitted with a separate bolt-in ramp.

While most of the changes made to the GP were improvements, one problem with the kickstart ramp being built into the endplate is that it has no adjustment. Early systems can be adjusted to get the kickstart to engage as soon as the pedal is depressed, which aids starting. Also operation of the kickstart in the GP system puts added pressure into the already over-stressed endplate studs, so the early system is really preferable in tuned engines.

Check the condition of the layshaft bearing track for pitting. If this is worn the track can be knocked out with a drift and replaced. Also check the endplate face that the large gear shim rests against. If this is very badly scored then the endplate requires renewal.

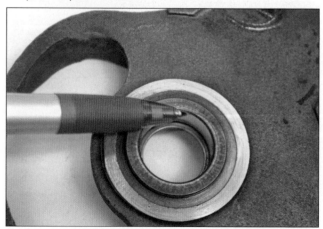

Check the condition of the gear cluster bearing by rocking the inner race. If it needs changing, remove the circlip on the other side and hammer it through. Be aware that since you must knock the bearing out using blows on its centre it is only fit for scrap afterwards.

Special tools are available to knock in new endplate bearings. Tap the bearing in with a drift resting on the outer edge of the bearing so it will not be damaged.

## Gear Selector and Layshaft

Check for wear on the dogs of the gear selector cursor. If the dogs are more rounded than this then the selector should ideally be replaced, but bear in mind that Innocenti or Serveta ones are the best quality so far produced. In this condition the selector would still work fine if used in conjunction with an uprated selector spring such as supplied by Taffspeed or MB Developments. Do not be tempted to use the kickstart piston spring as this is too long and stiff for the job.

Check the layshaft for pitting on the bearing surface. If any damage is bad then the shaft must be discarded, but again less than perfect original Innocenti or Serveta shafts are preferable to non-genuine Indian pattern shafts.

A layshaft is definitely fit for the bin if the hub splines show signs of wear. Also check for thread damage and repair any found using a 1.5mm thread file. A nut must run freely on the thread.

**One of the most important things you can check is to assemble your gearbox on the layshaft to ensure it is taller than the shaft. The gears go on with 4th (smallest) having its flat side facing down, and after that there should be oil slots between each gear. When assembled correctly the difference should be as shown in the following picture.**

If the flat area of the layshaft is taller than the one on first gear (as below) **YOUR GEARBOX WILL NOT SHIM UP PROPERLY** and you must change either the gearbox or the shaft until the gears sit higher. For some reason LI 150 gearboxes tend to be lower as a set and are particularly prone to this problem when used with some types of layshaft.

Change the layshaft o-ring when refitting the shaft.

## Gearbox Shimming and Selection

If your gearbox clearance was too large when you measured it earlier (you did remember didn't you?) then now is the time to select the correct shim to take up the slack. If you have fitted new parts, try a 2.0mm shim to begin with. LI series can use 1.8, 2.0, 2.2, 2.4 or 2.6 or 2.8mm shims to get the correct clearance.

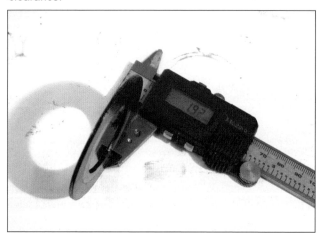

You should check the condition of the 'T'-shaped guide pins that run in the track of the gear selector. If these show wear on their side faces – or are sloppy in the selector fork – then this will be felt as slack at the handlebars. Undo the circlips

and replace the guide pins as required

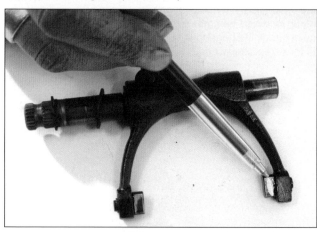

Until recently finding decent quality rear hub bearings had been a real problem. This bearing is not only very important in that it carries the full weight of the rear of your machine, but also because it forms the bottom stop for the layshaft and gearbox, and therefore its position effects gearbox shimming.

As a result it is always worth checking the condition of your old one, since many dealers would still rather use a good original Innocenti bearing than the poor Indian pattern parts available up to now. Lever out the old oil seal then clean and de-grease the bearing. If you spin the clean bearing it will probably sound pretty rattly, but try again after lubrication with a little gearbox oil. If the bearing has spent its life in gearbox oil it may still be fine. Wobble the inner race compared to the outer one. A small amount of rock on the inner race is acceptable, but not any in and out movement.

## Chain Check and Selection

Closely examine your chain for signs that the hardness has started to chip off the rollers or if any of the split rollers on cheap chains are broken. In this case the chain will need replacing.

The other obvious sign of a heavily worn chain is extreme sag when the chain is held horizontally. Compare the sag between a new and a worn chain. A sagging chain does not necessarily need to be renewed – stretched chains are actually required with some sprocket combinations. A chain definitely needs replacing when your top chain guide is at the limit of its adjustment and the chain is still slack.

**Make sure you select the correct chain for the sprockets you intend to use. Standard chains are 80 (15x46 sprockets) or 82 link (18x47 sprockets). Tuners commonly fit bigger front sprockets on more powerful motors, and these can require the use of a slightly stretched chain. Some set-ups however (16x47, 17x46, and 17x47) require a half-link (81-link) chain, which are available off the shelf from various manufacturers. Alternatively you will need to have one made-up especially and preferably riveted. If you ever run a split-link chain, make sure the circlip is on the side visible when you assemble the engine, and the open end of the circlips faces the clockwise direction.**

## Clutch and Sprocket Selection

Check the clutch spider ('inner bell') for wear in its legs caused by the ears of the steel clutch plates. This one is fine, but if the grooves become any deeper clutch operation will suffer. Also check the condition of the circlip grooves in each leg and the tightness of each rivet.

Slightly loose rivets can be tightened by resting the bottom of each rivet on a vice and peening over the rivet tops with a hammer. Alternatively the two parts of the spider can be welded together.

Selection of the rear sprocket ('clutch outer bell' or 'crown wheel') is very important. Firstly, you want one with the correct number of teeth to suit your chosen gearing. Original ones are either 46 or 47 teeth, but 45, 48 and 49 are also available. The next thing to check is which of the three common types it is: cush-drive, riveted or solid.

If your engine contains the cushioned-drive type (identifiable by the visible springs) then it is best to replace it with one of the other types since these often fail.

**Under no circumstances use the type shown below in a powerful engine!**

Examine the condition of the rear sprocket for ridges caused by the ears of the cork clutch plates cutting into the bell. If this damage is bad then the sprocket will need to be replaced.

Early rear sprockets ran on a pair of needle roller bearings, but in later models these bearings were superseded by a phosphor-bronze bush, and this was supplied as the general replacement part. These bushes can be used in any sort of sprocket, however newer solid-type sprockets should never be run with needle roller bearings since the inner surface of the sprocket is not sufficiently hardened to accept them.

Your clutch centre pressure plate ('flange') must be the correct type to suit the gearbox and side casing you intend to use. One of the best sorts is the early one with a central spindle, but these will only fit together with gearboxes that have a drilling in the gear cluster. The next best sort is the GP type, which has a flat disc in the centre of the pressure plate rather than a nipple and a cap ('thimble'). The worst sort was the intermediate one (below), which used the old nipple and thimble centre, but without a central alignment spindle. If your engine uses this type and suffers from clutch drag, then the best solution is to convert to another type.

# Crankshafts

There were a large number of crankshaft modifications through the run of Lambrettas, though by the time the Slimstyle models arrived, most of these had settled on a single part number as the updated spare for many models. These are listed for identification purposes in the Crankshaft Appendix at the rear of the book.

Early crankshafts tended to have very little side float (side to side movement) of the con rod on the big end bearing. This meant that the rod was held central by the webs of the crankshaft, but caused lubrication problems because there was very little room for oil to get to the bearing. The next series of cranks had greatly increased big end float which improved lubrication issues, but required gudgeon pin ('piston') shims either side of the small end bearing in order to keep the con-rod running centrally. Innocenti swapped one problem for another because gudgeon pin shims are a pain to fit and have been known to break-up in use. As a result many people leave them out, which promotes promotes big-end failure and even piston cracking in the long term.

On the very latest 'race' and modified crankshafts using Japanese con-rods available from specialist dealers, both these problems are solved by the use of better big end bearings and rods, and using brass shims either side of the big end bearing as on Vespa crankshafts. These big end bearings last very well, even in tuned applications and the big end shims ensure there is no need for gudgeon pin shims. Sadly, this hasn't meant a complete end to all the problems. Where the crank webs have had to be narrowed around the big end eye in order to accommodate wider con-rods and shims, the crankpins are so poorly gripped by the webs that crankshaft twisting has become a problem in some applications. 'Race cranks' from various UK and European dealers have been prone to twisting, depending on production batch and the performance of the engine to which they are fitted. I know plenty of dealers who are happy to sell them as they are, while others press the pins out of these cranks and rebuild them using Loctite 638 retaining compound, which is normally good enough to keep the cranks straight in engines up to 22hp. Alternatively, MB Developments make marginally oversized crankpins which can be pressed into these cranks to give them a tighter fit and more resistance to twisting. You can even have the crankpin welded to the webs – which is a favoured method of motorcycle tuners – but this needs to be done by someone experienced to prevent the welds pulling the cranks out of alignment as they cool.

When the 'race' cranks are good and run true, they are excellent, but as Italian production varies from batch to batch, it is something of a lucky dip. My only advice can be to ask the retailer if the cranks he is selling are prone to twisting, and what they will do about it if your crank does twist. If you aren't happy with the answer, simply shop around.

**ABOVE: Why Lambretta race cranks are prone to twisting out of line. Compare the width of the crank webs supporting the big end of the Kawasaki crankshaft (right) to the AF Rayspeed GP race crankshaft (left). Also note the brass shims either side of the big end on each crank. These keep the con-rods central, thus doing away with the requirement to fit gudgeon pin shims.**

The other established option is the use of Japanese con-rods in modified Lambretta (or pattern manufactured) cranks. Pioneered by Mark Broadhurst and now offered by several tuning shops, these conversions can be excellent and seem less prone to twisting thanks to tighter tolerances between original style crank webs and the special crankpins used. The only down side to these conversions is that the rod lengths very rarely match those of the original Lambretta cranks, meaning that tuners often have to use aluminium packing plates under the cylinder. The positive thing about Jap rod conversions is that several are now available that allow the use of Japanese pistons with larger gudgeon pins.

The latest Indian GP-type crank uses a 15.7mm-wide big end bearing and rod, and a 22mm crankpin like the 'race' cranks, but does not use any big end shims. These cranks have very little side float on the big end, and are designed to be run without gudgeon pin shims. AF Rayspeed say that these cranks are safe to run in standard engines but that the rods and big end bearings are not suitable for use in tuned engines. It is possible to fit the con-rods and bearings from the Italian 'race' cranks to the later Indian GP webs and the end result is a high quality crank. Indian crankwebs tend to be a tighter fit on the crankpin than many of the 'race' cranks and as such are more resistant to twisting out of line.

By far the most common modification nowadays is the fitment of a GP200-type crankshaft (which has a thicker flywheel taper) to any earlier models so that an unmodified GP electronic ignition can be fitted. This is virtually essential on any highly tuned machine and advisable on all others if only for the convenience of electronic ignition and the superior lighting offered by 12-volt electrics. The pattern GP200 crank below can be used to fit electronic ignition to an earlier machine. Note the wide big end clearance, meaning this crank should be run with gudgeon pin shims.

The early GP 125/150 type crank – identified by the two balancing holes in each web – has the thick taper required for most electronic ignitions, but uses a smaller, stepped big end pin which is inferior to the GP200 type. It also uses the narrow SX-type flywheel bearing. Avoid these cranks in any performance application.

 **TV 175 engines use a longer 116mm con rod – and shorter piston height – than all the other LI-series machines. If you intend to fit electronic ignition to a TV using a GP crank then you must specify a TV 175-length con rod is fitted or use a 'conversion piston'. Many of the 175 kits currently produced by boring out 150 cylinders fit the short LI-SX-GP 107mm-rod crank by using a 175 conversion type piston, which has a longer compression ('crown-to-gudgeon-pin') height.**

## Crankshaft Check

A simple check for a badly worn big end (beyond having a good look at the rollers through the oil slots in the con-rod) is to hold the crank as shown and hit the end of the rod with your palm. Very tired big ends have a loud and noticeable 'ring' to them, which you will soon get an ear for if you try to check a box of cranks at a scooter parts fair.

Before going any further with your examination, first check the condition of the flywheel taper for damage that is often caused if the flywheel nut comes loose and the woodruff key shears. Since it is the face of the taper that is supposed to hold the flywheel (the woodruff key is simply a locator) this face needs to be in good condition. The one shown is only fit for the bin.

Opened keyways should also consign a crank to the scrap, but in an emergency it is possible to glue a key into place with Araldite or a chemical metal such as JB Weld. Light damage to the taper is best solved by filing down any obvious high spots before smearing the taper with grinding paste and twisting it in the flywheel boss until the two mating surfaces have an even matt grey appearance.

The other areas to look for visible damage are the faces on which the oil seals run (two on the flywheel side and one on the other). On a used crank, these points are visible by the polished ring left on the metal by the action of the seal. If any of these rings are intersected by a dent, gouge or deep scratch the seal will not do its job and again the crank should be renewed.

Also look for damage to either thread or the splines on your crank. These can potentially be repaired by filing or re-cutting the thread (though few people will have the correct left hand thread tap for the flywheel nut) but it is much easier to do such repairs with the crank out of the engine.

**If your con-rod has excessive wear then you do not have to renew your crankshaft, it is possible to have the crank rebuilt with a new con rod kit (inc. bearing and big end pin) by a reputable shop. However a worn out LI/SX crank presents a good opportunity to convert to GP 200-style 'race' crank and electronic ignition, thus removing the need for gudgeon pin shims.**

Big end float dimensions are in the Crankshaft Appendix. You can measure this using a number of feeler gauges together and adding their thicknesses up to get your total.

It is highly recommended that you get the alignment ('true') of your crankshaft checked by a specialist motorcycle or scooter engineer using a jig such as the one below. The run-out measured at the furthest point from the centres should ideally be less than 0.05mm (0.002") with some tuners only happy with less than 0.03mm (0.001"). If the run-out is worse than that, then the crank will need to be trued (which generally means whacked – scientifically – with a large copper hammer) to align it.

## Changing the Flywheel Bearing Collar ('Track')

Whenever you want to change your flywheel bearing, you must also change the bearing collar fitted to the crankshaft. This is not an easy job at the best of times. There are several ways of doing it, and none of them is ideal.

Firstly you should apply lots of heat to the collar, no matter which method you chose. I know some dealers who use oxy-acetylene torches to rapidly heat this bearing track until red hot, whereupon it can be flicked off the crank with a screwdriver. This is probably the easiest way if you can generate enough localised heat, but be aware of the

fire/melting hazards of flinging hot bits of metal around your garage.

Innocenti – and other firms subsequently – produced special tools for removing this bearing collar, but they only tend to work on cranks that have had a recent bearing change (i.e. within the last 4 rather than 40 years) and are fitted with older-style metal-caged bearings. The collars of modern plastic-caged GP-style bearings do not have a distinct enough lip for the tool to grip on to. The Innocenti tool tightens around the collar before the centre bolt is done up to pull it off.

**If you try using this tool (or a pattern version) without heat on a stiff collar, you will almost certainly wreck the tool.**

Even after heating it took several goes to get the collar off with the Innocenti tool.

**The common home workshop alternative is to grind the collar off with an angle grinder or bench grinder, but this is highly risky because you can damage the oil-seal faces or your fingers if you slip.**

If you must grind off your collar - use metal hose clips either side of the collar to protect the oil seal face. Only grind on one side of the collar. Usually there is no need to grind right through because when the metal becomes blue it is thin enough that if you tap it with a hammer and chisel, a crack will appear and the collar can usually be prised off.

If you use the cutting disc of an angle grinder you can make a decent slot in the collar. Again it is a good idea to use hose clips to protect the oil seal faces against careless grinding.

With slots ground into the collar you then have the choice of pulling it off using a conventional 3-jaw puller, or using a large chisel to tap the collar off. Hold the crank in a soft-jawed vice and do not do the vice up too tight to avoid bending the crank out of true.

One way to fit a new bearing collar is to rest the crank against your chest, and using a hammer and tubular drift (e.g. Sundance grip!) tap the new collar into place. Resting the crank on your chest means that the hammer blows should be absorbed by your body rather than being able to twist the crank. The sound will become deeper when the collar is fully home.

Alternatively grip the flywheel-side web of the crank – and only the flywheel web – in a large soft-jawed vice to knock the collar on without danger of twisting the crank.

Do not rest the crank on a solid surface to knock the collar on, or there is a good chance that you will knock it out of true. Also do not be tempted to heat the bearing collar in anything other than boiling water to fit it. Overheating the collar will change the properties of the metal and it may either wear badly or spin on the crank.

If you haven't done it already, get the crank true checked once the collar is fitted, just to be sure it is still in line and ready to go back in your engine.

## De-Coking the Piston, Cylinder and Head

Carbon build-up on the piston, head and cylinder needs to be removed for optimum performance.

If a coked piston is left overnight to soak in paint thinners this will greatly ease carbon removal. Others suggest the use of paint stripper or oven cleaner for quicker results.

Use a plastic or tough wood scraper to remove carbon from the piston and head without scratching them. You can use metal scrapers on cast iron cylinders but not aluminium ones.

Do not remove the coating of carbon on the edge of the piston above the top piston ring.

Note the position of the rings so they can be refitted into their original locations if they are to be re-used.

Lift the piston rings out by opening their ends with your thumbs. A thin feeler gauge run around the inside of the ring and a little heat on the crown can help persuade them out if they are firmly stuck into their grooves. Original cast iron rings are very brittle and easy to break. Don't be too hard on yourself if you snap one.

A broken piston ring is good to scrape carbon build-up out of the ring grooves but be careful not to scrape out any aluminium.

Finish cleaning with fine grit wet-and-dry paper, using paraffin as a lubricant. Bring all surfaces to a light polish. Also make sure to remove all remnants of old gasket from the sealing faces of the barrel and then thoroughly clean the cylinder and piston with paraffin.

# Identifying Cylinders

Identifying Lambretta cylinders can be something of a challenge at scooter parts fairs. The first tell-tale is the outside diameter of the cylinder spigot. Cylinders to fit 125/150/175 casings have a spigot measuring 72mm, whereas ones to fit 200cc casings have a measurement of 75mm. The easiest spot check is to try a known cylinder base gasket.

The different 125/150/175 barrels all have different outer cylinder dimensions depending on capacity. You can measure this dimension using a pair of dividers passed between the 3rd and 4th cylinder fins.

- **125cc (nominal 52mm bore):** LI Series 1 125/150 cylinders are now rare, and identifiable by a lump cast into the inlet port and only having three fins below the exhaust port where later models have four. Measuring the cylinder diameter between the 3rd and 4th fins will give a figure of approx 64mm.
- **150cc (nominal 57mm bore):** LI 150 Special Pacemaker barrels are identifiable by two notches in the top fin. The SX/GP 150 cylinder also has two slots in its spigot. Measuring the cylinder diameter between the 3rd and 4th fins will give a figure of approx 69.5mm.
- **175cc (nominal 62mm bore):** TV 175 cylinders should have a visibly larger port sizes. Measuring the cylinder diameter between the 3rd and 4th fins will give a figure of approx 80mm.
- **200cc (nominal 66mm bore):** TV 200 cylinders have a larger inlet port than later 200 cylinders and a plain top fin. Early TV 200 cylinders have a very wide, low exhaust port that is hard on piston rings. Later TV 200 barrels used a narrower, taller exhaust port. SX and GP 200 cylinders have two notches in the top fin.

Further confusion is added at British fairs by the sheer amount of cylinders that have been tuned in the UK, meaning that very often any port height measurements we could supply go straight out of the window. Very often these cylinders will have been ported to accept Japanese pistons, and unless you get the correct piston with the kit (or the tuner has signed and numbered the barrel so you can contact them) you may have trouble setting it up. Bear in mind that over the last few years, the Japanese factories appear to have cottoned on to the unreasonable demand for pistons from defunct Japanese motorcycles, and have been profiteering accordingly. Pistons that used to cost £50 when the tuner first worked on the barrel may now cost £150, making the cylinder financially unviable to bore out and reuse.

Innocenti 200cc cylinders tend to have a lump near the inlet port with a number stamped into it designating which revision it was.

Smaller 125-150-175 cylinders (left) do not tend to have the lump.

Pattern cylinders carrying a symbol of one 'm' outside another near the inlet port are Motoristica Milano pattern cylinders. These cylinders are quite soft and wear rapidly.

# Cylinder and Piston Check

The first thing to do with any cylinder that you remove is to give it a very thorough clean, particularly between the cooling fins and inside the bore. Lambretta's cooling system is marginal in its efficiency at the best of times, so you should give it all the help you can. The exhaust port should be scraped free of carbon and lightly polished to resist further carbon build-up.

Next, check the surface of the bore for scores, smears of aluminium or wear indicating previous piston seizures. If it is in bad condition then a rebore and oversize piston will be required. If you are getting your barrel rebored it should ideally be blasted beforehand to get it totally clean between the fins.

 **Before buying a second-hand cylinder, check first that it isn't already on the maximum oversize!**

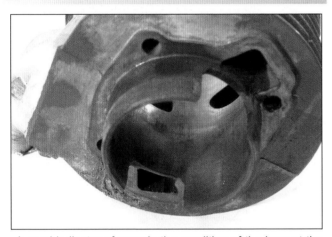

A good indicator of wear is the condition of the bore at the top of the cylinder. If the cylinder has a noticeable lip that you can catch your fingernail in where the top piston ring stops, then there is a good chance a rebore is required. Also any deep scores will require a rebore, or re-plating of a 'Nicasil'-lined aluminium kit cylinder.

The Home Workshop Manual states that the assembly piston to bore clearance of a freshly bored cylinder should be 0.034 – 0.046mm (0.0015" – 0.0018"). This is widely regarded as too tight for an air-cooled cylinder by most tuners. Mark Broadhurst prefers to start with a clearance of 0.051 – 0.064mm (0.002" – 0.0025") for original cylinders using quality pistons and 0.075mm (0.003") with cheaper pistons, or for any tuned original cylinder.

 **If you do ever start with the tight Lambretta specified clearances then you will have to run your engine in very carefully – and for a lot of miles – if you want to avoid piston seizures.**

 **Aluminium cylinders or original barrels running non-Lambretta pistons may well require different piston to bore clearances, so consult a reputable tuner for advice.**

The maximum acceptable clearance for standard pistons/cylinder is 0.15mm (0.006") though larger figures may still be acceptable for non-original cylinders or pistons.
A rough check of piston to bore clearance can be made by inserting the piston (without rings) into the cylinder and pushing it to the top of the barrel. An original Lambretta piston is at its widest 20mm from the bottom of the skirt, so try progressively thicker feeler gauges inserted at least 30mm into the gap. When the feeler gauge is pulled up and the piston starts to lift with it, this can be taken as an approximate figure. Only a specialist re-borer will be able to give you an accurate figure.

 **A 3-legged 'glaze-buster' tool can be used to lightly hone a cylinder after a seizure and to remove polished areas which no longer hold oil. Be careful to evenly hone both the top and bottom of the cylinder or you can end up with a tapered bore. Lubricate the bore as you work it.**

The original Home Workshop manual specifications tell Lambretta owners to check their piston ring gap at the base of the cylinder, below the inlet port. This opposes all modern thought on the matter.

It makes more sense to measure your piston ring gap in the upper end of the bore where the rings actually run. Use the piston to push the ring into the bore squarely and at least a centimetre into the bore so that it is below the wear lip.

 **The Home Workshop Manual suggests all standard 125cc models must have a piston ring gap of at least 0.16mm (0.006") and all engines over 125cc should have a gap of at least 0.2mm (0.008"). Maximum gaps are 0.55mm (0.021") for 125cc and 0.6mm (0.024") for over 125cc engines.**

On tuned engines Mark Broadhurst suggests a wider gap of 0.25 – 0.5mm (0.010" to 0.020") is better on assembly, particularly with Japanese pistons which often have such large gaps straight out of the box. If the gap is marginally too tight it is possible to lightly file the ring ends.

In standard applications the Lambretta piston's ability to cope depends on who manufactured it. Better brands are Asso, Vertex, Borgo, Hepolite or Mahle. Whoever produced it, check for missing or worn-out ring pegs, broken rings and cracks around the cutaways in the piston skirt.

 **If one piston ring is broken or outside tolerances then the full set must be replaced. Avoid the use of pistons with brass ring pegs as these are prone to wear.**

The blackening ('blow-by') so far down the sides of this piston indicates that the piston rings or the bore are badly worn. It is possible to buy new rings if the piston to bore clearance has not exceeded specification, but take care to order the correct type and size. Many different companies have produced pistons for the Lambretta so make sure to tell the part supplier how many rings are fitted, how thick they are and if the piston is an oversize.

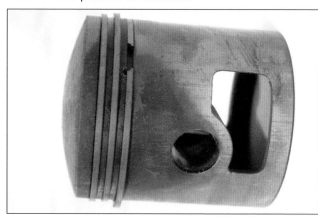

Also check for wear on the gudgeon pin. If there is a lip that you can locate with a finger nail then the pin is worn out and should be replaced.

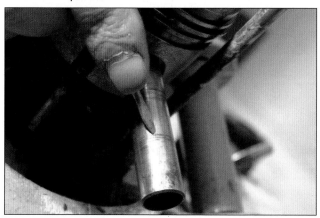

With later types of original crankshaft, gudgeon pin shims are specified to keep the con-rod running centrally on the big end bearing. The crankshaft appendix lists which types require shims. The problem for those seeking to use gudgeon pin shims is that good quality replacements are currently hard to find and poor quality ones can break and wreck your engine. If you do not have access to useable original Innocenti or Serveta piston shims (and quality replacements do not become available in future) then it may be better not to fit any. Wider Japanese type small end bearings can be used to take up the slack at the piston end, but the con-rod is still free to float from side to side, which is not ideal. Converting to a 'race' type crank which uses big end shims is probably your best option.

For good cylinder head sealing, flat off the gasket faces of your cylinder and head by swirling them in a figure-8 pattern on medium-grade abrasive paper taped to a flat surface (e.g. a pane of glass).

Use light oil or water to keep the abrasive 'wet and dry' paper from clogging. When you are finished the gasket face should be totally clean of staining and scratches. The same should be done to the cylinder head to achieve a nice, evenly flat surface.

Most heads have the engine capacity written on them between the fins, but there are other differences worth noting. From the 200cc ones, the centre squish TV 200 and early SX 200 heads are not as good for performance as the later side squish ones. Also note when fitting replacements that many pattern and Indian heads have bigger bowls and lower compression ratios than standard and performance will suffer as a result.

TV 200 models using the centre squish head were specified with a 0.6mm thick head gasket, but the early SX 200 using the same head was supposed to run a thick 2mm head gasket. When the SX was changed to the offset squish head a 1.5mm gasket was specified.

Cylinder compression ratios, gasket thickness and combustion chamber design can all have a large impact on engine performance and reliability. Consult a recognised Lambretta tuner for advice before fitting a non-standard cylinder head.

# ORIGINAL SPECIFICATION ENGINE REBUILD

## Gearbox

When fitting the gear selector cursor to the layshaft be sure to use the correct gear selector spring, not the stronger one for the kickstart plunger.

Uprated selector springs are available from some dealers to reduce the chances of gear jumping, but these do make for a stiffer gearchange which not everyone finds acceptable. Nylon-lined gearchange cables are essential with uprated springs.

Hold the bearings in with your fingers at the same time as forcing the cursor up over them. It is a tricky technique.

You can perform this operation with the shaft inside a clear plastic bag. That way if the balls and spring pop out you won't lose them!

Some new cursors have chamfers machined into them to make fitting easier. These are fitted from the opposite end. Before the layshaft assembly can be fitted, you must first fit a rear hub bearing.

Heat the casing until it will boil your saliva if you spit on it. The rear hub bearing should be cleaned and lubricated with grease or gearbox oil before fitting.

Certain batches of Indian and Japanese rear hub bearings simply don't fit, or have an adverse effect on gearbox shimming. At the time of writing the remade Casa Lambretta ones are most dealers' preference – or original Innocenti bearings in good condition. Certain Indian ones are also ok, but ask a reputable supplier for advice.

It is good practice to degrease the outer edge of the bearing and apply a little Loctite to seal between the bearing and the casing.

If the casings are hot enough the bearing should drop into place. If required, use a drift that rests only on the outer edge to tap it home. Note the change of sound when the bearing becomes fully seated.

Lubricate only the inner seal face of the bearing before fitting the oil seal.

If possible fit the hub oil seal by hand, or tap it in with a hammer. It should sit flush with the edge of the bearing once fitted. Beware of sharp-edged bearings that can damage the seal during fitting.

It is only possible to correctly assemble and shim your gearbox once the layshaft has been pulled in tightly.

 **Several dealers now offer a tubular spacer which can be used to pull the shaft into place using the rear hub nut.**

Refit the thin steel spacer and then the outer flange.

 **If you don't have the layshaft puller tube, you'll have to work the traditional way and use the hub to pull the shaft into place. First fit the thin shim and then the cone that sits on it.**

 **Originally this flange is retained by four M6 deep nuts and wavy washers, but M6 Nyloc nuts without washers are the modern alternative. These nuts should be torqued to 0.48 – 0.53 kg-m. Do not over-tighten these nuts!**

Now fit the hub, washer and hub nut. When done up tightly the layshaft will be pulled into position.

 **A home-made hub holding tool is ideal to allow you to get the hub nut tight.**

 **Put the gear selector in the 2nd gear position (which is the second visible 'ring' from the top) before fitting the layshaft. You'll see why later.**

Two types of gear selector shafts were originally used. The early type was splined at the top and a separate splined arm with a pinchbolt arrangement fits onto it. If you use this early type then there must be no play once the arm is done up.

 **This sort of shaft uses a circlip, below which should fit a steel washer and rubber O-ring.**

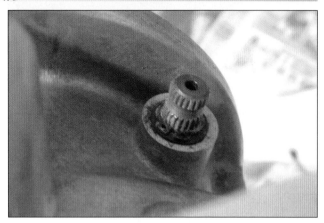

The later type of shaft which features an integral gear arm is to be preferred. These do not use a circlip on the shaft, only the metal shim washer and rubber O-ring.

 **If your gear shaft or bush is worn then the original O-ring might not prevent oil leakage. Slightly oversized O-rings (12 x 3mm instead of the standard 12 x 2.5mm) can be used to ensure a good seal.**

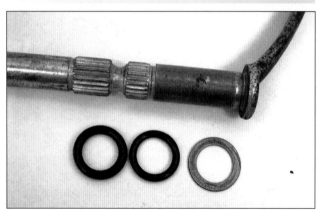

 **Use a blob of grease to hold the inner shim onto the selector fork before fitting.**

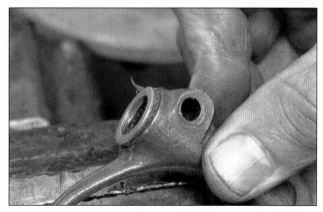

Slot the gear selector fork ('wishbone') into place so that the guide pads locate in the track of the gear selector cursor, and then pass the splined shaft (complete with outer shim and O-ring) down through the casing, through the inner shim and through the gear selector fork.

  **The original M6 pinchbolt has a 9mm head. Do not be tempted to use a normal 10mm-head bolt, because this can foul on some casings and impede gear changing.**

  **A modern alternative to the 9mm headed bolt is a cap-head M6 high-tensile Allen bolt and spring washer. The domed head is important for clearance.**

 **Before tightening the pinchbolt it is essential to check that your selector arm is correctly aligned, particularly with later shafts which can't be adjusted from the outside.**

**With the gear selector in second gear position, a correctly positioned arm should run at 90 degrees to the gasket face and line up with this crankcase stud.**

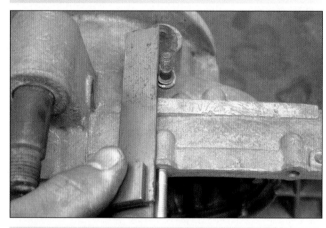

**Another method of checking gear selector shaft alignment is to shift to fourth gear position (selector cursor as deep as it will go, as shown) and ensure you have this sort of gap (approx 5mm) between the arm and the cast rear shock mounting. If the gap is much bigger or smaller than this, then the shaft will need to be shifted by one spline.**

**Some combinations of gear selector shaft and selector fork are incorrectly machined in respect to spline positions. These can be impossible to correctly align. Replacement is the only cure.**

Before fully tightening the pinchbolt it is imperative that the gear selector fork is pushed as high against the shim as possible and the shaft is pushed fully down. Occasionally two shims may be required to eliminate play. If you do not do this then the shaft can float up and down, and gearbox oil leakage can result.

Sometimes the guide pins sit so deep into the gear selector track that they cause unnecessary friction. It is possible to bend the arms out a little so that only the sides of the pins are in contact with the track, as they should be.

Fit the gear cluster needle roller bearing using a little grease to lubricate it from start-up.

Fit the correct shim before fitting the gear cluster. A blob of grease will hold the shim (only one size) in place and lubricate it at start-up.

**An easy way to assemble the gears round the right way is this: 4th gear (smallest) goes first with the flat side facing the hub bearing and thereafter there should be slotted oil grooves (identified below) between each gear.**

Assemble the gearbox so that these oil slots never face one another and everything will be fine.

With the gears correctly assembled you should be able to spin the gear cluster by hand. Next fit the small shim and layshaft needle roller bearing. Run some gear oil down between the gears, over the bearing and around the layshaft to lubricate everything.

The large gearbox shim goes on next. If you haven't changed the layshaft, gearbox, endplate, rear hub bearing or shim, then the end float of the gearbox should remain as it was. If you have replaced any of the listed parts you should recheck your end float.

Ensure that both dowels are in place and fit your endplate. Tap it down with the handle of a hammer.

The endplate was originally secured by thin (4mm) hardened M7 (11mm head) nuts and spring washers. If you have original nuts and they are in good condition then reuse them with new washers. You can use regular full-height M7 nuts in some positions but make sure that the nuts and studs don't protrude beyond the endplate or these may rub on your chain.

There is a correct sequence for doing up endplate nuts – 1,4,6,3,5,2 – with the nuts numbered clockwise from the top as shown. The Indian manual suggests the nuts should be torqued to 1.2 kg-m (8.6 lbs-ft), but most tuners would prefer a higher setting of 1.4 – 1.7 kg-m (10 – 12 lbs-ft).

If everything is assembled correctly, you should be able to fit the clutch centre spider and turn the gearbox by hand. Sometimes it is necessary to fit the nut to pull the gear cluster up into position, or tap the centre of the layshaft to free the gearbox.

If your gearbox will not turn it is possible that the gearbox shim is too large. Try to turn the shim with a finger. If it is tight the endplate will need to be removed and a smaller shim used. If the shim is loose enough to turn, use a feeler gauge to measure the gap between the shim and the endplate. The acceptable range for this gap is 0.07-0.30mm (0.003 - 0.011"). If the clearance is too big even with a 2.8mm shim fitted suspect a worn or faulty hub bearing or endplate.

## The Bottom End

We use the phrase 'bottom end' when referring to the crankshaft, bearings, seals and magneto (mag) housing on a Lambretta.

Start with the mag housing, which should be heated up to around 100ºC using a blowlamp or cooker. Quickly fit a greased outer flywheel side oil seal (25-42-6) with the spring side facing towards the crank. It should fit flush. A fat-bladed screwdriver can help to push it into place, or use one of the specialist drifts that are now available.

Next fit a steel oil seal retainer, with the flat side facing the seal.

If the mag housing is hot enough then a cold bearing (stored in the freezer!) should drop into place. If you are fitting an early LI/SX/TV crankshaft then you should be using the narrow flywheel bearing NU205. GP 200 original and pattern cranks use a wider bearing number NU2205. Note that high load plastic-caged bearings (e.g. FAG or SKF NU2205E) are preferable to the metal caged ones pictured below.

 **If your mag housing cools before the bearing is fully home then the round-type rear hub puller is a good fit to use as a drift.**

 **Never fit a new flywheel bearing without fitting the matching inner bearing track to the crankshaft. Replacing half a bearing is a waste of time.**

If you use the narrow NU205 LI/SX/TV bearing then you will need to fit the metal/plastic spacer ring before the outer oil seal. This spacer is not used with the wider GP 200 NU2205 bearing.

Next fit the inner oil seal (33-52-6) with the spring side facing the crankwebs and a bit of grease on the outside edge. There are various special tools to fit these seals, but anything that rests against the flat of the seal without disturbing the inner lip – such as a small piston – is ideal.

With the seal in place, there should be enough room to fit the circlip. Strong circlips pliers are required. Tap the circlip around with a punch to ensure it is seated properly.

Now pack the bearing with high melting point grease, but leave some space for it to expand. Filling it to the level shown – where the bearing rollers are still visible – is about right. If you overfill the bearing or use low melting point grease then it can be forced out past the oil seals.

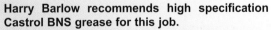 **Harry Barlow recommends high specification Castrol BNS grease for this job.**

Warm the casings to fit the drive side main bearing using a heat gun, blowtorch or electric cooker ring. Move the flame around and take your time to heat the whole casing properly. It should boil spit when hot enough.

The Lambretta Home Workshop manual suggests fitting this bearing using a puller tool (59329 or 70650), but in practice these are rarely if ever used. Innocenti also supplied a special drift to fit this main bearing, but if the casings are hot enough you shouldn't need it.

If you must use a drift, make sure it only rests on the outer edge of the bearing. If you knock a ball bearing in by the inner track you will ruin it. The sound will change when the bearing is fully home.

 **Do not hit this bearing too hard or you will knock it right through and break the casing.**

 Originally Innocenti used a plain 6305 ball bearing for the drive side, but lately many dealers now use a single sealed 6305-1RS (or double sealed 6305-2RS with one seal removed from the sprocket side of the bearing). The remaining single rubber seal (following pic) gives an extra layer of protection in the event of oil seal failure.

Next fit a new gasket ('Hallite washer').

Fit the drive side oil seal (33-50-6) to the seal retaining plate as shown. It only fits in from this side and should locate with the spring side facing the crank webs.

 **Original seal plates are available in steel (early engines) or aluminium (late). The steel ones are preferred, because the aluminium ones are prone to warping when tightened. At the time of writing MB Developments have just had some new steel ones produced in the UK.**

 **Originally the oil seal retaining plate was secured by four crosshead or flat screws which were centre-punched to stop them loosening. Nowadays many dealers prefer to use high tensile countersunk Allen screws to secure the oil seal retaining plate, and a tiny drop of Loctite to retain them.**

 **Do not put too much Loctite onto the screw or you will never get it out. Only use the smallest drip of the weakest strength Screwloc.**

 **Make sure you only use high tensile screws for this job, not just cheap cheesy ones or the heads will shear off or round if you ever try to undo them.**

Do your tightening with an Allen bit on a ratchet in a diagonal pattern. The screws should be torqued to 0.48 – 0.53 kg-m (3.6 lbs-ft). Be careful not to over-tighten particularly when using aluminium seal retainers as these can bend and crack under the pressure. The drop of Loctite means that there is no longer a need to centre punch the screws. If correctly fitted the oil seal retaining plate should sit flat and even.

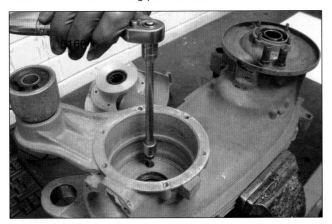

Lubricate the oil seal face of your crank with 2-stroke oil before fitting.

The crank fits in at an angle.

 **While it is tempting to hammer the crank into position NEVER DO IT, because it is too easy to knock the crank out of alignment, particularly on some of the modern race cranks.**

 **The best way to fit a Lambretta crank is to pull it into place using the front sprocket bolt and one of the puller sleeves now available from many dealers.**

 **If you don't have access to a puller sleeve, then you can use the original sprocket sleeve to pull the crank into place. A con-rod holding tool is useful at this point to stop the crank moving while the bolt is done up. Turn the crank occasionally as it is being pulled into position to ease its entry into the oil seal.**

 **For this technique to work it is vital that the crankshaft and bolt threads are in perfect condition. Also beware of forcing the crank in if the splines in the sleeve and the crank are misaligned because they will get damaged. If it feels tight, loosen the bolt, turn the sleeve slightly and try again.**

Once the crank is fitted, check it for free movement. If it seems to rub, suspect the oil seal retaining plate. Rubbing may also be a problem with certain con-rods – especially on long-stroke crankshafts – which require the casing to be machined for extra clearance.

Grease the mag housing gasket and fit it the correct way round with the small tab facing up the transfer port. Also grease the mag housing itself.

Some dealers advise the use of silicone sealant on this gasket for a more secure seal but this makes gasket replacement a messier job.

Slide the mag housing over the crankshaft and onto the studs.

Clean off any excess grease around the crank. On a standard motor use a plain M6 nut and wavy washer on each stud. Torque the nuts to 0.48 – 0.53 kg-m.

## Transmission

The first step is to fit your chain guides.

 Different standard bottom chain guides are available to suit either 15 x 46-tooth (non-GP 200) or 18 x 47-tooth (GP 200) sprockets. Choose the correct one for your sprocket set-up. Good Italian and Spanish bottom chain guides are hard to find at the moment.

 It is possible to use early chain guides together with GP 200 18 x 47-tooth (or larger) sprockets if you saw an inch off each end and ovalise the mounting holes so the bottom guide can sit lower.

 It is advisable to fit an uprated top chain guide in even standard engines. See the following chapter.

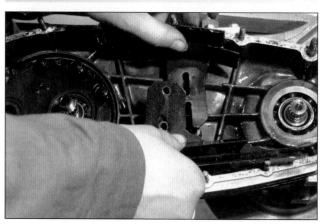

On standard engines, the chain guides are retained by bolts and a tab washer. The standard bottom chain guide overlaps the top one. Position the top chain guide as low as it will go. Do not do the bolts up tight at this point.

The front sprocket and cush-drive ('shock absorber') components are assembled as follows: first the thin dished oil thrower, then the sprocket sleeve, then the front sprocket itself, followed by the sliding dog and then the spring. The spring cap is the last piece to go on. Use a shouldered Innocenti front sprocket bolt or a British remade one in preference to the Indian 'bolt and washer' arrangement.

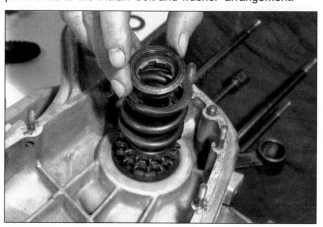

**Aligning the spring cap when doing up the bolt can be tricky. A simple way is to get it roughly lined up, do the bolt up until it almost comes tight, and then give the cap a few light taps with a hammer. The cap will turn and move more freely when it goes into position.**

You can use a con rod holding tool to do the front sprocket bolt up fully at this point. Alternatively if your top end is already fitted, you can use a clutch holding tool to do it up later. The Indian factory torque figure is 3 – 3.5 kg-m (25 lbs-ft), but many dealers prefer to do the front sprocket bolt up tighter than that.

**Many dealers rate German IWIS chains as the best at the time of writing, but original Regina Extra or Reynolds chains are also widely used.**

Fit the rear sprocket shim (sometimes two are fitted) onto the gear cluster shaft before fitting the rear sprocket. It is possible to change the thickness of these shims to set your chain alignment but some dealers don't bother. The technique is shown in the Advanced Engine Building chapter.

Fit the two sets of needle roller bearings (early engines) or phosphor bronze bush (later and GP engines) into the rear sprocket.

**Only use needle rollers in early (riveted) rear sprockets. Recently produced (solid) sprockets for the GP must be used with bushes because their centres are not hardened enough to cope with bearings.**

Fit the clutch centre spider, tab washer (over the longer rivet) and nut. Use a clutch holding tool while doing the centre nut up to the recommended torque figure of 6.7 – 7.5 kg-m (48.5 – 54.3 lbs-ft).

**If you haven't already done so, the front sprocket bolt can now be tightened with this clutch holding tool left in place and used to lock the chain. This is the preferred method because there is no chance of twisting the crank out of line.**

Bend up one side of the tab washer to secure the centre nut using a drift or punch.

**Adjustable pipe pliers can also be used to bend up this tab washer.**

Now it is time to adjust the chain guides. Note that they are called chain guides not chain tensioners! Turn the chain by the rear sprocket so that any slack is in the top chain run. Slide up the top chain guide until there is around 6mm of up and down play in the chain between the top guide and the front sprocket. The Home Workshop Manual suggests 12mm but this is widely regarded as too much.

Now tighten the bolts to 0.48 – 0.53 kg-m and bend up the tab washer to secure them.

 **Examine your clutch springs for height before fitting, if they aren't all level then replace the entire set. Originally TV 200 used the strongest standard springs, followed by SX 200/TV 175, and the other models used the weakest available. Modern replacements do not make this differentiation, but strengthened ones are available and advisable in most applications. Clutch springs do lose their strength over time when left in an engine so it is best to replace them occasionally.**

Sit the clutch springs into the clutch spider. A blob of grease will help hold them in position.

**Note that it is normally only possible to change your clutch with the engine (or scooter) laid horizontally, otherwise the springs tend to fall out of position. A tool was developed in the racing fraternity which has five fingers on it that poke through the holes in the clutch pressure plate. The fingers support the springs so that the clutch may be rebuilt with the scooter standing on its tyres. These tools have been produced commercially and are available from specialist dealers such as Taffspeed.**

Now fit the clutch pressure plate ('inner flange'), not forgetting the thimble on pre-GP set-ups, which can be retained with grease while the engine is being completed.

**Some manufacturers produce cork plates that**  **may be as much as 15.5mm thick across a set of four, which can be too thick for use with GP 3mm top steel plates and GP clutch bells. The correct specification for GP clutch plates is 14mm thick across a set of four corks (3.5mm each) which can be checked by sliding them between the jaws of a 14mm spanner.**

The clutch plates should ideally have been soaked for 24-hours in gear oil before fitting. Start with a cork first . . .

. . . then a steel and so on.

**There are two different thicknesses of top steel clutch plate. The thin one is used in early set-ups. It may not work with later sprockets because the ears of the top cork plate do not always sit deep enough into the bell.**

Compress the clutch and fit the clutch circlip. Ensure that the ends of the circlip are both supported by the spider as shown, rather than being exposed. Indian genuine SIL clutch circlips are actually stronger than the Italian versions and work well.

**If when assembled the ears of your cork clutch plates are very near to the top of the slots in the sprocket it is permissible to bend the ears of the cork plates down a little so that they can't pop out.**

Finally use a screwdriver to locate the springs into their correct positions.

**With the clutch compressed you must be able to move the ears of the cork clutch plates up and down a little with your fingers. If the plates have less than 1mm free space in which to separate then the clutch is sure to drag. Solutions to this problem are covered in the next chapter.**

## Side Casing

Start by greasing the bushes through which the kickstart shaft runs, and replace the oil seal as a matter of course. These often leak.

**It is possible to fit this seal after the shaft to prevent the seal lip being damaged by the splines during assembly.**

Fit the kickstart spring with the kinked end connected to the kickstart shaft. The shaft is retained by a circlip and shim, both of which must be in good condition. These shims are available in different thicknesses. Use the fattest shim that still allows you to fit the circlip snugly in its groove. This should prevent the kickstart shaft from rubbing on the top clutch plate, which is a common problem.

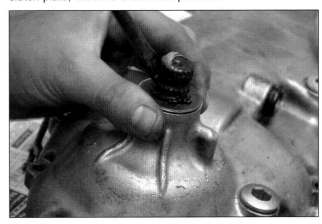

Ensure that the kickstart shaft already contains the circlip and small spring pressure plate. You can now fit the piston and spring, which can be held into place with a blob of grease.

Turn the casing in the vice so that the kickstart shaft moves to this position. You can now screw the reference pin into the depressed piston. Fit a new reference pin, if there is any visible wear use a small drop of Loctite on the thread to ensure that it doesn't come loose.

**ONE TO WATCH** Be very sparing with any Loctite used on the reference pin. Put too much in and you will glue the piston into the shaft so the kickstart won't work.

On side casings with a bolt-in ramp, the shaft is now held in place and the spring remains pre-tensioned so it is easy to fit your kickstart.

## Kickstart Positioning & Adjustment

Due to the splined fit, the kickstart can be located in several positions. This one is clearly too low since the stop on the pedal is far below the rubber buffer in the casing.

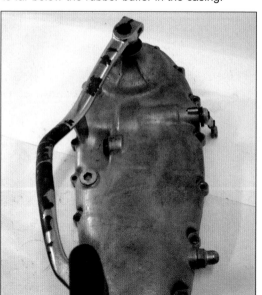

This position is slightly too high since the stop is touching the casings. Do not be tempted to pull the pedal down and fit it in this position because you will find that your kickstart piston is permanently engaging with 1st gear and clicks when you start up.

**ONE TO WATCH** Some pattern kickstart shafts have the splines machined in the wrong position so that it is almost impossible to get correct positioning and adjustment.

Try to get the kickstart pedal on the correct spline so that it rests against the rubber casing buffer. On pre-GP motors you can then adjust the bolt-on kickstart ramp for perfect operation by loosening the three 10mm-head bolts and moving it.

Shown below is the ideal position for the shaft and ramp. The kickstart rests on the rubber buffer and the reference pin holds the kickstart piston only just at the bottom of the ramp. In this position the kickstart piston should engage with the first gear almost immediately as the pedal is depressed, giving you a longer 'kick' before the pedal touches the floor.

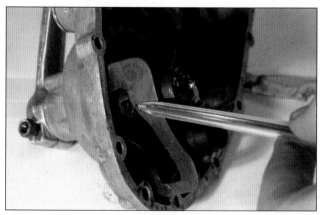

The main chaincase gasket should be lightly greased. Silicone sealant can be used where the gasket face is damaged. Now refit the side casing.

**If you are using a pre-GP clutch, check that the pressure thimble is still in place before you fit the casing. For GPs use a blob of grease to ensure that the phosphor bronze pressure bush stays put while the casing is fitted. Also make sure you refit the two location dowels before the casing goes on.**

**For a proper restoration, where nuts are used, the original chaincase nuts are 6mm deep (slightly deeper than standard M6 nuts), and each should have a wavy washer underneath.**

**Put a strip of masking tape on the side casing marked 'NO OIL', to serve a reminder not to start the engine until it has been oiled.**

## Top End Preparation

The gap for the small end bearing on many pistons is wide enough to accommodate a standard Lambretta small end bearing AND two gudgeon pin shims, but wider Japanese-type small end bearings are available instead for use with cranks that do not require the fitting of gudgeon pin shims. There should be no more than 1mm space either side of the bearing/shim combination that you intend to fit.

Only use gudgeon pin ('piston') shims if you can get quality ones, and if your crank requires their use. Don't use poor quality Indian shims or gear cluster shims by mistake because these can break up and destroy your engine. Presently there are still some stocks of genuine Spanish Serveta shims still available but these will eventually dry up. In every other case – particularly with 'race' or 'Jap-rod' cranks – no gudgeon pin shims should be fitted and a wider small end bearing used to take up the gap.

The cylinder makes a good stand to hold the piston while fitting the rings. Oil the grooves before fitting the rings.

**Be sure to check you have sufficient ring gap before fitting a new set of rings. See previous chapter.**

Lightly lubricate the cylinder bore with two-stroke oil. Smear it over the entire surface with a clean finger.

Fit one of the piston circlips, making sure that it is the right type for your piston. It is good practice to have the gap in the circlips facing the top or the bottom of the piston so that the massive G-forces exerted at the change of stroke don't make them compress over time.

Fit your cylinder base gasket. On restored engines many rebuilders only use grease as a sealant because it makes gasket removal much easier in the future. Others prefer gasket cement or silicone sealant. Fit your small end bearing to the crankshaft and lubricate both small and big end bearings with 2-stroke oil.

If your engine requires the use of gudgeon pin shims, hold these either side of the bearing with a blob of grease.

**The normal way to build an engine is to fit the piston to the crankshaft using the remaining gudgeon pin and circlip, prior to fitting the cylinder. With Lambretta 3-ring pistons and barely-chamfered barrels it sometimes proves easier to fit the piston to the cylinder first, to the depth of the last ring.**

**Always make sure that the arrow or 'S' stamped onto the piston crown faces the exhaust port.**

Slide the piston and barrel onto the studs together, and then push in the gudgeon pin, which should also be lubricated with 2-stroke oil.

**A 5/8" or 16mm diameter wooden dowel chamfered almost to a point can be of great use in aligning the piston shims and small end bearing with the gudgeon pin. Push the dowel through with the gudgeon pin and everything should stay in line. Note that you can only do this if you haven't previously fitted one of the piston circlips.**

Fit the remaining piston circlip(s) and slide the cylinder down. If everything is right the barrel should seat on the gasket without being forced. If it does need forcing then do not ignore it, find out why.

**Rogue circlips can be prevented from dropping into the crank by stuffing a rag into the crankcase mouth, but remember to remove it before lowering the cylinder!**

The SX 200 models originally used a fat 2mm aluminium head gasket with a concentric squish head. When the offset squish head was introduced the gasket was changed to 1.5mm. The SX 150 was originally supplied with two thin head gaskets. While better performance may be available from fitting a thinner gasket than specified to your engine this may make the compression ratio dangerously high for modern petrol and may also reduce the piston to head clearance to an unsafe amount. For details of how to check piston to head clearance see the following chapter.

**While it may be tempting to fit a thinner head gasket than intended to an original SX 200 to boost power a little it is probably safer to use the thick type gasket considering the poor quality of modern fuel.**

Other engines require the use of a thin gasket. The TV 200 used a thin gasket of 0.6mm (modern 'thin' pattern gaskets are normally 0.5mm). This should be pushed down over the studs with a long socket. Some builders fit these gaskets dry if the cylinder and head have been lapped, while others prefer the use of Loctite, or silicone sealant.

**A proprietary compound called Wellseal is good for sealing head gaskets.**

Fit the cylinder head using flat or wavy washers and plain nuts. Remember to put the long cylinder cowling nut in the correct place (lower kickstart side). These nuts should be torqued in a diagonal pattern to 1.9 – 2.2 kg-m (17 lbs/ft).

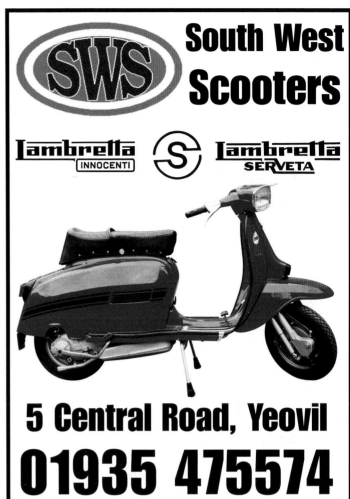

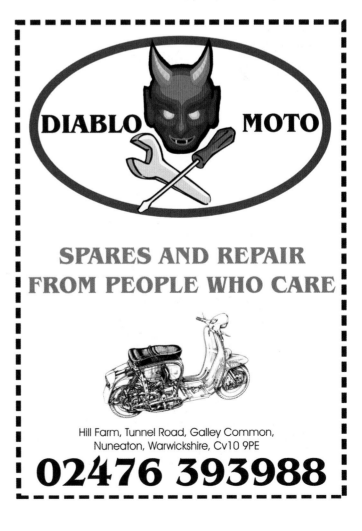

# ADVANCED ENGINE BUILDING

Plenty of ways to improve on Innocenti's method of mass-producing engines have emerged over 40 years of use. Mark Broadhurst of MB Developments assisted with the production of this chapter which includes plenty of useful tips not only for building tuned engines, but also hints that can improve the assembly and reliability of standard motors.

## Gear Cluster Bearing Track Removal

If your engine has been run without oil or stood for a long period of time then there is a fair chance that the gear cluster bearing has worn out. The needle roller bearing itself is easy enough to replace, but the track it runs in is harder to get out because it sits in a blind hole, so it can't be removed from the far side. Innocenti did manufacture a tool to remove these, but even when new they didn't always work too well. Instead you can use hydraulic pressure to remove the track. To do this you need to have a piece of solid steel bar machined so that the last 5cm has a diameter of 22mm exactly. Please note that this is an advanced job, and should not be attempted without a 22mm bar or there is a good chance that you will wreck your casings.

After heating the casing with a blowtorch until it will boil spit, pack the bearing with grease.

Insert the steel bar – which must be a snug fit. Hit the end of the bar with a decent-sized hammer and the hydraulic pressure generated in the grease will begin to lift the track out of the casings.

You will need to repack the bearing regularly with grease after each couple of blows – or at least when you hear a change in tone – but eventually the track will lift out.

Underneath the track is a steel shim. Don't forget it when the track is being replaced. Replacement is done by tapping a cold track into a hot casing.

## Crankcase Porting

If you are going to fit a tuned cylinder, you will get best results by matching the transfer port cutaways to the cylinder. There is nothing to be gained by over-porting the casing though. If you don't want to do it yourself, there are plenty of tuning shops who will carry out this work for you.

# Engine Bottom End Assembly

If you are going to leave mag housing studs in place make sure that they are all high-tensile and sit 14mm clear of the casing. Again, stepped studs have been produced which only fit in by the prescribed amount.

Drive-side oil seal plates can be a problem. Modern aluminium Indian ones (left) tend to warp. Steel Spanish ones (centre) are good, as are steel Italian ones (right) though these have a groove machine into them which racers used to fill with epoxy resin to try and raise crankcase pressure. Check second-hand retaining plates for warping or cracks around the screw holes. MB Developments had such trouble finding decent drive seal plates that they have since started to produce their own.

This is a typical problem with Indian oil seal retaining plates. As the outer edge has warped down, the inner edge has come up and rubbed against the crank web. Note the use of high tensile Allen screws to hold the retaining plate. These are first degreased and Loctited (sparingly!) into place.

The rubbing problem was cured by linishing the face of the drive plate to allow extra clearance. The inner lip of the seal is greased to ease fitting over the crank.

Many of the aftermarket race cranks of recent years have been prone to twisting. Some dealers strip and rebuild even new cranks in order to Loctite the crank pin, which is normally enough to keep them in line. MB Developments go one better and use slightly oversized crankpins as well as Loctite retaining compound. The MB-produced crankpins are 1mm longer than standard and require 0.5mm to be skimmed off the inside of the magneto housing where it faces the crank web. The remaining 0.5mm gives extra clearance between the flywheel and the stator plate which was particularly needed with AF Electronic ignitions.

Mark prefers to use clear silicone instant gasket as a sealant on the magneto housing and cylinder base gasket faces. Only a fine smear is required.

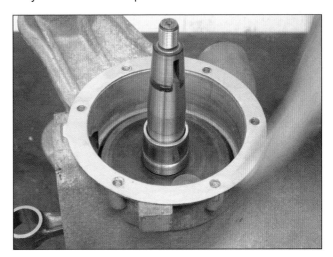

**With the mag housing only locating onto studs, there is room for it to sit at a slightly different angle each time it is fitted. In order to locate it in the same position each time – so the ignition timing marks stay relevant – first centralise it with a countersunk M6 Allen screw.**

Mark fits mag housing studs and nuts in one go by first winding a new Nyloc nut onto the stud until it is flush and then winding it into the casing as if it was a bolt. He fits a washer underneath the nut and uses a dab of Loctite on the stud. The casing threads have to be in very good condition for this to work.

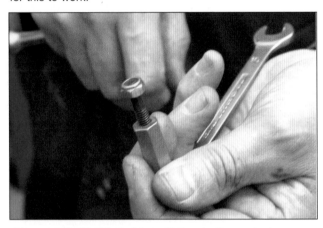

The new studs will wind in until they bottom out whereupon the nut will tighten up to finish the job.

With the mag housing fitted, check that there is some clearance between it and the crankweb – particularly when using cranks built with aftermarket crankpins (e.g. MB Developments' 41mm long pins). If you do not have enough clearance you can either machine the mag housing face or add an extra mag housing gasket.

## Engine Top End Assembly

Mark uses a 'long' cylinder head nut with a short bolt in it to act as a stud fitting tool. The stud bottoms out on the bolt and can be wound in using the nut. Once at the required depth the bolt can be backed off a little which frees the long nut to be wound off by hand. Mark only uses specially-made high tensile studs.

**Genuine Vespa PX200 cylinder studs are very good quality and have a longer thread at the nut end which makes them suitable for use even with non-standard length cylinders. They also have slightly fatter threads which take up play in loose casing threads. Avoid the use of Indian or remade Italian cylinder studs.**

**Mark fits the cylinder studs with just a light smear of grease on the sides of the stud thread to help if they ever need to come out again. Never put any grease on the end of the stud or into the casing thread as the hydraulic pressure caused when the stud is wound in can crack the casing. If the threads are not in the best condition then Loctite would be preferable.**

The small end bearing is lubricated with two stroke oil before fitting the piston. Also lubricate the big end bearing.

Lambretta gudgeon pins tend to be a tight fit (Japanese ones usually slide in by hand) so lubricate the gudgeon pin holes too.

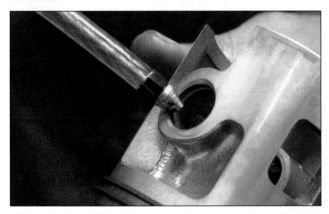

The standard TS1 piston uses fine wire circlips with tails. Always ensure you use the correct circlips for the sort of piston you are fitting.

This engine is being assembled with a Yamaha-rod crank which is 3mm longer than standard. In theory the use of a 3mm thick packing plate should get all the barrel and piston heights correct. MB also produce 2.5mm ones which are useful on Spanish and Indian casings which tend to be taller at the gasket face than Italian ones, by anything up to 1mm.

The transfer openings in the packing plate need to be opened out to match the porting of the casings. Mark uses an angled scribe to accurately mark where to cut.

The cylinder is assembled onto the piston without sealant in order to check port timings.

Mark checks all his port timings using a large diameter degree disc which requires the transmission side engine mount to be removed. The larger disc makes it possible to measure port timings to fractions of a degree.

**Other tuners such as Taffspeed and Harry Barlow use a computer programme to calculate port timings from measurements of the relative piston and port heights inside the barrel.**

A length of welding wire mounted to the casings is bent for use as a pointer. The end is cut to a point for greater accuracy.

Mark usually determines port opening by eye – looking as close as possible along the dome of the piston – but you can check with a feeler gauge too.

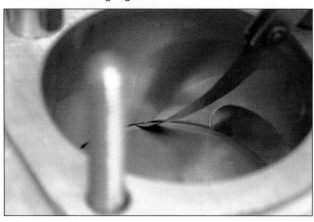

Once the correct packing plate for the required timing has been ascertained, the packing plate is coated lightly with silicone and the cylinder is fitted for real.

MB have returned to using aluminium head gaskets for TS1 and other kit engines now that they have found a source of heat treated aluminium gaskets. Most head gaskets available in the UK are of a soft, shiny material which does not last in large bore, high performance motors. Other firms like Taffspeed get around the problem by recessing the cylinder head – so it has enough piston clearance to be run without a head gasket – and dowelling it so it always sits centrally on the cylinder. The advantage of using head gaskets is that Mark has different thicknesses which make it easier for him to set the correct squish clearance. Always measure the thicknesses of the gaskets because they do tend to vary. When the right gasket has been selected, he prefers to use Loctite retainer as a sealant, but only a very fine amount so none ends up in the bore.

Mark uses 'long' 13mm-head M8 nuts on all four studs with plain washers underneath. He prefers to torque these to 2.4 – 2.8 kg-m (18 – 20 lbs-ft) before the clearance is checked.

Mark uses a twist of 1.5mm thick solder (2mm thick is better if you can find it) to check piston to head clearance. Insert through the spark plug hole and turn the engine over by hand.

The piston will come up and squash the solder against the head. Test the clearance at four points around the head as shown below.

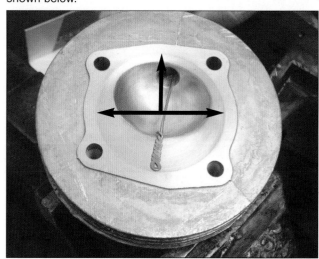

This method of clearance checking through the plug hole is handy if you do not want to disturb the cylinder head, but some tuners argue that the readings at the top and bottom of the piston may seem larger than the true gap due to the piston rocking in the bore when pressed on only one edge. For greater accuracy two 'V'-shaped pieces of solder may be held into position on the top of the piston with blobs of grease, the head refitted and the crank turned past TDC. The head is then removed. A more accurate picture of the clearance is obtained because the piston did not have a chance to rock due to being pressed simultaneously on all sides, but without being dowelled the head may not go back in the same position when it is fitted, thus affecting the relative clearances around the piston.

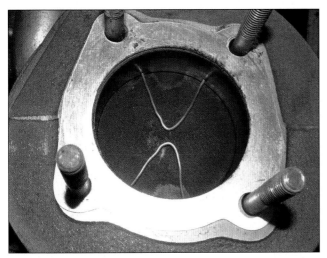

Measuring the thickness of the compressed solder with Vernier calipers gives you a reading of the available clearance. This reading of 1.96mm is larger than Mark would use in a TS1, so a thinner gasket was needed. Normally he would prefer a 1.0-1.5mm squish clearance (lower the better) on a 150-250cc engine, but no less than that or you risk the piston touching the head at high rpm, particularly with Lambretta con rods.

Test the squish at four points around the piston: to the left, the right and also the narrow squish band near the plug hole.

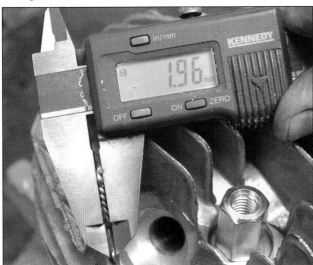

If you get a much higher reading on one side than its opposite number then the head is off-centre. Loosen the cylinder head nuts a little and tap the head with a rubber mallet on the side with the high reading. This should centralise the head a little better. Retighten the nuts and check the squish clearances again. This is not an issue if the cylinder has been doweled in the manner favoured by Taffspeed.

MB have had specially shouldered high tensile stainless exhaust studs made.

Use a deep socket to push the exhaust gasket into place.

Mark fits his exhausts using a flat washer, then a spring washer and finally a brass nut.

Silicone is used on the inlet gaskets too. This TS1 engine has one extra gasket (three in total) because an inlet packing plate is being used to space the reedvalve away from the piston. Mark fits a stud to TS1-type inlet manifolds and matches it to the inlet port shape so airflow is not disrupted. You may need to D-shape a washer to fit under the nut.

It is good practice to tape up the opening of any inlet port until the engine is fitted, to prevent stray objects falling into the motor.

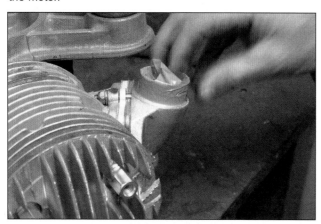

## Transmission Preparation

**One popular racer adaptation is to modify the gear arm to get rid of the tie-rod circlip/washer assembly and replace it with a simple nyloc nut. The best way to do this is to cut off the old pin and drill and tap the arm to accept a short M6 stud. Loctite the stud into place. With this set-up it is much quicker and less fiddly to remove an engine. Also if the tie rod and stud wear so that the gearchange becomes sloppy it is no bother to change both of them without stripping the engine.**

**Racers or those with very powerful engines may consider the use of an uprated gear selector spring (top) to prevent jumping out of gear under power. The gearchange action will be a little stiffer but it is better than possibly wrecking your gearbox. Note that some people find the gearchange too stiff with uprated springs fitted.**

Racers or anyone who may regularly need to change their gearbox may like to modify their engine casings so that the gearbox endplate may be removed without the need for extractors. Mark cuts a slot into the casings so that he can get a screwdriver under the front of the endplate. Together with a 'crow's foot' tool at the rear, the endplate can now be removed very rapidly.

On powerful engines the rivets holding the clutch spider to its centre are prone to coming lose, so it does no harm to weld them up.

Indian phosphor bronze rear sprocket bushes can suffer with a lack of lubrication. Filing a small groove down the full length of the inside and outside surfaces will improve lubrication.

One tip for improved clutch action is the fitment of a rear sprocket (outer clutch bell) that has been machined to allow the bottom clutch plate to sit deeper into it when the lever is pulled in. This modification drastically reduces clutch drag with the machine in gear and prolongs clutch life. Several shops supply sprockets that have been modified in this way.

 **An easy alternative to machining the clutch bell is simply to bend up the ears of the bottom cork clutch plate to allow more clearance between the plates when the clutch lever is pulled in. Beware of distorting the cork plate while doing this though.**

Assemble your clutch sprocket (clutch bell), bush (or bearings) and centre spider. Lay a ruler across them as shown. For correct operation the centre spider MUST be the tallest part, but only by a small amount (ideally no more than 0.1mm). Even with brand new Indian sprockets and clutch centres this isn't always possible as the clearance is much larger. The only alternative is to take your clutch centre spider to an engineering shop and have it machined to reduce the clearance. MB Developments offer this service.

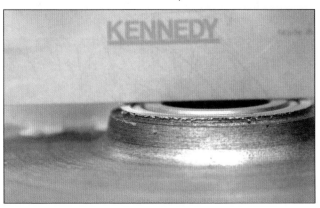

## Chain Alignment

While most people never bother, it is possible to fit different shims under your rear sprocket to adjust your chain alignment. A properly aligned chain and sprockets will not only last longer, but also waste less power. Start by fitting a 1mm shim. It is a waste of time even bothering with this if your sprocket has lots of up and down movement and rock because the clearance listed previously is too large.

There is an original dealer tool that can be used with a dial gauge to check chain alignment. Alternatively rest a ground flat metal bar on the gasket face and use a magnetically-mounted dial gauge to measure the height of the front sprocket teeth. Move the bar so that the dial gauge rests on the teeth of the rear sprocket and calculate the height difference. The rear sprocket is allowed to be up to 0.25mm lower than the front sprocket, but no more than 0.05mm higher. This difference can be adjusted out using fatter or thinner shims or even a combination of two shims under the clutch sprocket. Five different shims are available: 0.8, 1, 1.2, 1.4 and 1.6mm thick.

**It is actually possible to adjust the height of the front sprocket by your choice of dished oil thrower. Italian ones are 0.5mm thick whereas certain Spanish ones are 1mm thick.**

A less-accurate method will be to use the depth gauge of a set of Vernier calipers to measure the difference. In this case we used the flat side of an aftermarket clutch compressor as a surface to measure from.

Be very careful that you measure at the correct point on the teeth of the rear sprocket. Measure the teeth below the turrets of the clutch bell because those below the slots for the cork plates are often machined down and will give an incorrect reading.

One common mechanical problem in the racing world – and even on standard Lambrettas – used to be failure of the top chain guide, which would bend or even snap off and jam the transmission. Mark pioneered the use of plastic/nylon-faced aluminium top chain guides which last almost indefinitely and are widely copied. The use of these is advisable even on standard engines.

With the advent of nylon-faced guides many racers abandoned the use of bottom chain guides all together, but Mark still prefers to fit these to road-going engines. Due to poor quality control on Indian spares these lower guides sometimes need to be manually adjusted to ensure the correct chain clearance along their entire length.

*(Following photo)* Note the use of studs and nyloc nuts to hold the chain guides rather than bolts and a tab washer. This is an old racing trick to avoid damaging the aluminium casing threads by regularly fitting bolts.

Even with a plastic-faced top chain guide you should still allow for 6mm up-and-down chain slack at this point. Note that the Home Workshop Manual suggests a 12mm clearance, but most dealers now think 6mm is better.

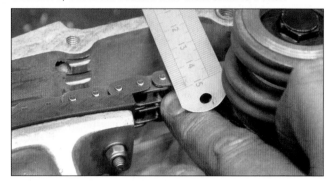

Stronger, uprated clutch springs should be fitted as a matter of course in tuned engines. Consult the supplier of your tuning kit about the strength of springs they recommend.

An alternative route to uprating your clutch to cope with extra engine power is a 10-spring conversion. This is carried out by fitting five Vespa PX clutch springs around the outside of five Lambretta springs. By varying which of the five springs are standard and which are 'uprated' it is possible to balance clutch bite against your ability to pull the lever in. Other popular alternatives are a centre-spring fitted over the 22mm clutch nut or a 5-plate clutch conversion. Thinner steel plates are usually required with a 5-plate conversion to prevent clutch drag.

**TOP TIP** If your engine makes much over 20hp then it may well be worthwhile investing in a 6-plate conversion which requires lengthened inner and outer clutch bells as well as an extended kickstart shaft and a side casing packing plate. These are available from various sources.

Surflex '1062-B' clutch plates have traditionally been the preferred ones to use in any application. Never use Surflex '1062-C'. Allegedly the C stands for crap. If possible soak new clutch plates in oil for 24 hours, but at the very least pour fresh oil over them before installation.

**ONE TO WATCH** Some batches of Surflex clutch plates have been manufactured too thick for use with certain combinations of clutch spiders, rear sprockets and top steel plates. The original Innocenti GP specification was for clutch plates to be no more than 3.5mm thick – or 14mm for a set of four plates. Sets of plates measuring over 15mm are likely to cause clutch drag in some engines. One solution to this is to run 'thick' Surflex corks with thinner steel plates such as those produced by Taffspeed. Alternatively it might be necessary to switch to using a brand that produces plates of less than 14mm as a set.

Mark prefers to use the early LI-type 2.5mm top clutch plate in preference to the 'thick' 3mm GP type. The thin type allows more room for the plates to separate with the clutch pulled in, thus reducing clutch drag at a standstill.

The downside of using the thin top plate is that with certain combinations of clutch centre spider and rear sprockets ('outer clutch bells') the ears of the top cork plate can sit so high that the plate escapes the slots in the bell and spins freely. This is solved by bending down the ears of the top plate so they sit deeper into the bell.

**TOP TIP** If you also bend up the ears of the bottom cork plate, this gives more room for the plates to free off with the clutch in. It is easier to do this with the clutch disassembled and the ears of the plates held in a vice.

**TOP TIP** Another cure for clutch drag is to use 'Yamaha-type' long clutch levers, which actually pull the clutch a little further at full travel.

**TOP TIP** If you have tried all the recommended solutions to allow your clutch plates to free off when compressed (machined clutch bell, using a 'thin' 2.5mm LI top clutch plate, bending up the ears of the bottom cork plate etc) then your final option is to use thinner steel plates for extra clearance. Taffspeed produce 1.2mm-thick steel plates for their 5-plate clutches - rather than the original 1.5mm.

**ONE TO WATCH** With the clutch compressed you must have at least 1mm of free up and down movement on the ears of the cork clutch plates to avoid clutch drag.

This is how close the kickstart shaft runs to the top clutch plate. Mark has cut down a casing to test the clearance between a correctly assembled kickstart mechanism and the clutch of any freshly assembled motor. If things were really bad you could theoretically fit a second chaincase gasket to increase clearance, but this is inadvisable.

# TAFFSPEED RACING
## The Performance Scooter Tuning Center
**128 Corporation Road, Newport, South Wales, NP19 0BH**

Since the beginning of the 1980's, **TAFFSPEED** have been at the forefront of Lambretta tuning & race engine development!  It was the knowledge we gained from our racing that enabled the Frankland brothers; Ian & Terry aka "The Terrible Taffs" to become the one of the worlds leading tuners of LAMBRETTA's!

In the mid '90's we were the first "Scooter Tuning Shop" to invest in a Dynojet Rolling Road & the exhaust gas diagnostic equipment that went with it! This in turn enabled us to  speed up the development of our present range of BSAU.193(1990)T3 LAMBRETTA  Exhaust Systems!
Regarded by many of our customers as still the best all round systems available!
Many of which are still giving good service ~ some 10years on!

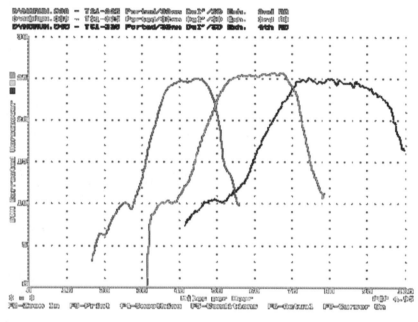

The graph shows what can be expected from a typical **TAFFSPEED** ported 225cc TS1 engine unit using a Dell'orto 32mm Flat~slide carburettor with our **TAFFSPEED** designed Road Race Replica exhaust system producing 25bhp through the gears!

**TAFFSPEED** can supply various specialist tuning parts & services eg; crankshafts of various strokes (54, 58, 60, 61, 62) & conrod configurations, 14t to 24t drive sprockets & quality duplex drive chains & tensioner kits, 5 or 6 plate clutch basket conversion kits, BSAU exhaust systems, Hydraulic conversion to discbrake backplate, uprated front fork suspension springs, pistons, rebores, porting & honing or re-Nicasil plating of alloy cylinders. gas & alloy welding, specialist machining work,

Our latest **TAFFSPEED** Lambretta rear damper units are now available with a choice of a steel or billet aluminium body & in 2 lengths to suit the Series I & II or Series 3 Li models onwards!

**Email: sales@taffspeed.co.uk     www.taffspeed.co.uk**
## WORLD WIDE MAIL ORDER SPARES SERVICE
## Tel: 01633 840450 or Fax: 01633 246175
**INTERNATIONAL Tel: +44 1633 840450 or Fax: +44 1633 246175**

# EXHAUST SYSTEMS

Lambretta exhausts have a very hard life. They are located close to the ground where they suffer corrosion due to water splashed up from the wheels. They are directly attached to a fairly vibratory engine and they even have to follow every bump hit by the rear wheel. To be honest it's a surprise that they last as long as they do.

## Original Fitments

As a general rule, original type Slimstyle silencers are interchangeable, but quality, performance and accessibility all improved as production went on. As such, it is worthwhile fitting a later GP-type Series 3 exhaust to any standard model when a replacement is sought.

- Series 3 type – as used right up to the late SX. There were various sorts, denoted by the four-leaf Clover end to the tailpipe.
- GP type (Italian) – slot-ended tailpipe.
- Spanish type – visibly similar to series 3 but with a different chamber-to-pipe angle.
- Most pattern exhausts have a round-ended tailpipe.

In addition to those above, the Indian factory for a time fitted a version of a '60s performance pipe which has since gained the title Indian 42mm 'big bore'. Other versions of a similar system (Clubman) are also still available. These pipes are modifications to the standard system to improve power output. The Clubman-type is widely regarded as one of the best performing exhausts for standard or moderately tuned road Lambrettas. They have the advantages of simple fitment, standard looks, good ground clearance and extreme value for money to their credit. The main defect is that they are noisier than genuine silencers, but so are most other performance exhausts. Due to the fixed brackets they are not adjustable to take account of modified cylinder lengths or pack plates.

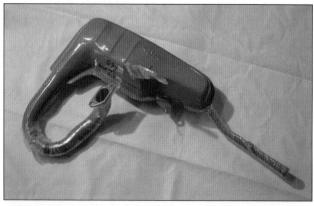

**Above: the AF 42mm Clubman, in 'Ancillotti Orange'.**

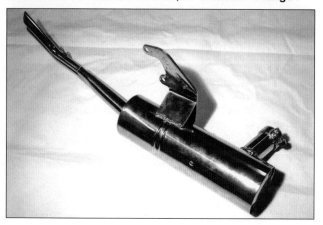

**Above: A twin outlet teapot, yesterday. Made for going slower.**

## Performance 'Expansion Chamber' Exhausts

There are massive performance gains to be had from simply changing the exhaust on a Lambretta. The best results of tuning will only be realised when matched with a suitable performance pipe. Even a totally standard machine will benefit from the fitment of a 42mm big-bore or a Fresco. For TS1 or Imola cylinders you have no option but to change the standard exhaust since these cylinders use a different exhaust flange and gasket.

Your choice of performance exhaust should reflect your intended use for the machine. High-revving exhausts will usually give the best top speeds if your machine is capable of sustaining high speeds without seizing (e.g. if it runs an aluminium cylinder) and isn't over-geared. Those who often run with 2-people on board, do a lot of town work or want to pull tall gearing for lower rpm cruising on the motorway should choose an exhaust that has more low-mid rpm performance.

## Understanding Dyno Graphs

The graph below compares the power output of a Clubman exhaust and that of a Kegra-type JL KRP2 expansion chamber when fitted to a tuned Lambretta 200. The following graph was produced by Worb 5 in Germany and differs from those Dynojet ones commonly shown in Scootering magazine in several ways:

- Power is shown both Kilowatts (KW) and PS; which is the German equivalent of Horsepower (HP). Despite a 3% difference in the way HP and PS are calculated they may be considered as the same.
- The vertical power scale is compared to engine rpm rather than road speed as the horizontal axis.
- Curves are also shown comparing torque output (expressed in Newton Metres) to engine rpm.

As you can see the peak power increase available with an expansion chamber is quite large: up from 19hp at 7,500 rpm with the Clubman to 23hp at almost 8,000 rpm with the KRP2. This doesn't necessarily make the KRP2 a better pipe, because it depends on how you expect to ride (fast or slow, alone or with a passenger), and what gearing you plan to use. The Clubman may not have such a high peak power output, but it actually makes more power than the KRP2 from 3,000 rpm right up to 6,500 rpm which gives an easier ride around town. The trick to understanding dyno graphs is not to pick the exhaust with the biggest power output or the highest rpm, but to find one that makes power at the correct revs to suit your engine and riding style.

HONDA 205cc CONVERSION

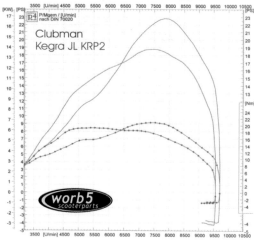

Clubman
Kegra JL KRP2

## Lambretta Performance Pipes

There are currently too many different sorts of Lambretta exhaust available to list them all, and new models are still being designed even now. As such, the best we can do in this book is offer a few hints and tips.

- Taffspeed, Kegra, JL, and MB pipes have all been designed with interchangeable stub manifolds so that the same chamber can be fitted to original or TS1/Imola cylinders.
- If you have a drastically shortened or raised cylinder you will need an exhaust with adjustable mountings to accommodate this. Most British-designed systems are adjustable, but original type exhausts are not.
- If your TS1 type cylinder has suffered a stripped thread and had the exhaust studs taken from M7 (which fits 11mm-head nuts) to M8 (which takes 13mm-head nuts) this can cause clearance problems when trying to fit an exhaust with a tight U-bend such as a PM Tuning. Original Vespa 90 wheel rim nuts – if you can get them - solve this problem since they are M8 thread but only 11mm spanner size.
- When fitting an exhaust, slightly loosen all the bracket mountings and shake it around or run the engine for a minute to settle it in position before tightening it up. Most exhaust failures come from systems being under strain when they are bolted up. Where rubber mounts are fitted there must be a tiny amount of flex to allow the system to absorb vibrations without fracture.

## AF Rayspeed NK Exhausts

**Pros:** Interchangeable stub manifold to suit original or TS1-type cylinders. Fair mid to high rpm performance.
**Cons:** Peaky power delivery doesn't suit all engines. No rear silencer mounting. Rear running board requires trimming.

## Fresco Exhausts

**Pros:** Simple and effective pipe for low-mid rpm power. Modified 'over the kickstart' version of the original Italian design is currently being remade in India/UK. Interchangeable muffler now fitted.
**Cons:** Solid mounting of remade batches un-adjustable for different cylinder heights. Rear running board requires trimming.

## Gianelli TS1/Imola Exhaust

**Pros:** Lightweight under-the-floorboards fitment for that standard look. Stub manifold for TS1 and Imola fitment. Good high rpm performance.
**Cons:** Peaky power delivery doesn't suit all engines.

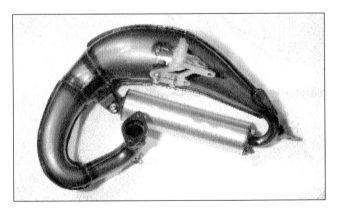

## Jahspeed Exhausts

**Pros:** Shapely fully-blown design. Various performance levels available.
**Cons:** Not a stub manifold type so cast iron OR TS1 fitting.

## JL Exhausts

**Pros:** Past manufacturer of Taffspeed and Kegra pipes and now selling 'his own' pipes to dealers everywhere. Layout based on Kegra (KRP1 and KRP2) and Taffspeed designs so performance is comparable. The pipe sold as JL KRP3 is based on the Taffspeed 'Road' pipe, and JL KRP4 is based on the Taffspeed 'Race' pipe.
**Cons:** As Taffspeed/Kegra.

## Kegra (JL) Exhausts

**Pros:** Regularly improved, fits with original bodywork, KRP1 suits low rpm use and standard engines. KRP2 suits mid to high rpm use and is good for top speed. Interchangeable stub manifolds. Now only produced by JL.
**Cons:** High revving KRP2 not so good for 2-up use due to lack of low rpm power. Rear mounting onto chaincase studs requires perfect casing threads.

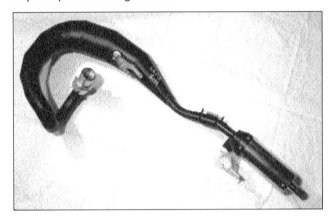

## MB Developments Exhausts

**Pros:** Regularly improved, most versions fit with original bodywork, several performance versions available suiting general mid to high rpm use, interchangeable stub manifold. New versions are currently being produced in stainless steel for MB Developments by Scorpion.
**Cons:** Low slung manifold of early ones vulnerable to speed humps. Rear mounting onto chaincase studs requires perfect casing threads.

## PM Tuning Exhausts

**Pros:** Lightweight, tidy construction, nice sound, adjustable fit, regularly improved, interchangeable muffler options. Good mid to high rpm performance.
**Cons:** Supplied unpainted. Requires a slight cutaway to the back of the right hand running board. Separate versions for TS1/Imola (PM 28) or original-type (PM 25) cylinders. Lower performance stainless steel ones also now available.

## Taffspeed Exhausts

**Pros:** Regularly improved designs, fits with original bodywork, several performance versions, interchangeable stub manifold. The Taffspeed 'road' pipe has excellent low to mid rpm performance which is good for engine reliability and 2-up use.
**Cons:** Lack of high rpm performance requires up-gearing or revised cylinder porting to reach high speeds. Rear mounting onto chaincase studs requires perfect casing threads.

## Scorpion Exhausts

**Pros:** Rust-free stainless steel construction. Performance better suited to iron cylinders than TS1.
**Cons:** Requires trimming of the rear running board and sidepanel.

# ELECTRICAL SYSTEM – THE SPAGHETTI NIGHTMARE

Lambretta electrical systems are perhaps the most difficult area of these machines, not because they were especially complex – which they weren't – but because they had so many variations. There were no less than four manufacturers of 4-pole flywheel and stators and three different ones for Italian 6-pole systems. With each of these having AC and DC versions and being altered from model to model you can see that it is almost impossible to catalogue every part and every variation accurately. Instead we have offered tips on each of the specific electrical components found on a scooter.

If you are hunting for spares (such as points, condenser or HT coil) for a specific machine then you are best to consult a knowledgeable shop quoting the model, year and component manufacturer. A Lambretta parts book can come in especially handy here for quoting the specific part number. The wiring system for most Italian Lambrettas came in two flavours: battery or non-battery. Many UK-supplied machines tended to have batteries as standard to power parking lights, whereas many of the more recent Italian imports were never fitted with batteries to begin with.

Subsequent Spanish and Indian production used more complicated and different wiring to include electronic ignitions and indicator systems, and these were changed regularly throughout production. Colour wiring diagrams for several systems are supplied in the appendix at the rear of the book, but these may not cover all the variations produced in Spain and India. For help on Spanish electrics consult Serveta specialists Bedlam Scooters or Totally Scooters. For assistance with Indian parts try AF Rayspeed or Scooter Restorations. Also see www.scooterhelp.com

## Various Tips

- Swapping known good parts for suspect ones is the best way of tracing intermittent problems.
- A length of wire fitted with a crocodile clip at each end is useful for tracing broken wires or connecting substitute components.
- If you have to repair broken wires, solder and seal all connections with heat-shrink sleeving which is available from good electrical suppliers such as Maplins or RS Components.
- **IMPORTANT:** Note that on all 6-volt systems, the speedo light bulb should be 12-volt 2.5-4Watt. A 12-volt bulb helps to absorb excess electrical power.
- Early 4-pole models earth the ignition through the brake light switch, so if the stop light bulb blows the engine cuts out.
- The change-over from 4-pole to 6-pole ignitions happened from machines of the following engine numbers: LI 125 – 36626, LI 150 – 631475, and TV 175 – 507945. Variations of the 6-pole design were fitted to all subsequent models.
- Never run a battery type stator plate (Italian wiring: green, brown and two yellow wires) without the battery connected because the coils can burn out. To test for a damaged coil try sparking each of the yellow wires against bare metal with the engine running. If one of them doesn't spark then the coil is probably faulty.
- Machines wired with a second 6v battery in the toolbox, or Indian pre-'86 machines carrying a 12v battery which is wired POSITIVE EARTH have been given a UK 12v conversion using a Lucas rectifier and Zener diode. Full details of this system are available in Mark Haines' Unofficial Lambretta Manual Update.
- Indian non-battery GPs after engine number 73000 (but pre-electronic ignition) have a different stator and wiring so that the headlight bulb circuit is supplied at 12v, but the other circuits run at 6v.

- Do not trust the colour coding of Indian components!
- Always make sure there is a good earth wire between chassis and frame. Many Lambretta electrical problems are caused by this simple omission.
- Ensure that your bulb holder junctions are in perfect condition. Both ignition and lighting systems rely on good connections here.
- Indian points ignition components (flywheel, stator and HT coil) should be kept together and not mixed with Italian parts.

## Headlight 'Bulb Holder' Junction

- The headset wiring does look complex but in reality it couldn't be much simpler because all the terminals are colour coded, and all the terminals of the same colour are connected together.

- Polish all wiring bullet connectors with wire brush to ensure good connections.
- Lambretta bulb holders are prone to having the terminals come slightly loose over the years, thus making bad connections. It is possible to re-punch the rivets that hold them, but it is often more reliable to solder across the back of them or place a small piece of wire to bridge connecting terminals before the bullets are pushed in.
- On all 6-volt models the speedo bulb acts as buffer to absorb any surplus power in the event of an electrical surge, and to prevent all the other bulbs blowing. The problem with this system is that the bulb only earths through the speedo cable, which both runs in grease and also can be known to snap. In order to provide a better earth for the speedo light bulb, some dealers make a small alteration to the wiring in the headset. This is explained in the Headset section of the Chassis Check chapter.

## Headlights

- Headlamp adjustment on LI 3 models is by slackening the three fixing screws and moving the whole rim and headlight unit. On Special/SX/TV/GP type (below) there is a lens adjustment screw to alter the beam angle – anti-clockwise lowers the beam and vice versa.

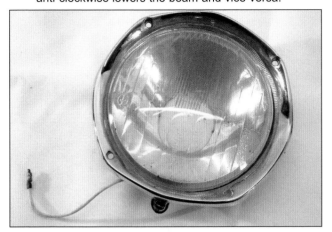

- 'Halogen' conversion bulbs are available in Bosch-bayonet fitting and provide a worthwhile increase in light output. These are suitable for all glass headlights but beware fitting them to plastic lens headlights due to the increased heat produced.

## Handlebar Switches

- Original LI-type trapezoidal headlight switches are hard to get, though some specialist dealers may still have small stocks. At the time of writing remade Indian switches are available but not always effective. Different wiring was used for 4-pole, 6-pole and AC or DC versions of these switches.

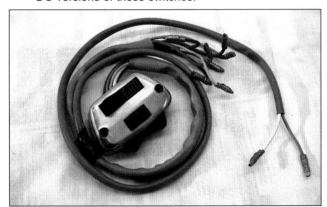

- TV/SX/GP-type horn/dip switch. Recently reproduced in Vietnam, Italy and India, but not all to a high standard (at the time of writing). Only some types actually work. The original switches had different lines and colouration for different models though typically there were cross-over periods.

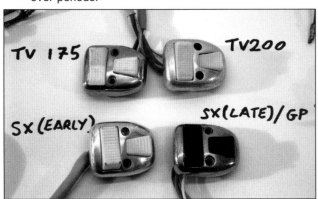

- Later Spanish and Indian indicator models used various types and fittings of indicator switches mounted on modified lever housings.

## Ignition Switches

The forked tag on the pink wire below is intended to fit under the forward most of the three bolts that secure the headset to the fork clamp. Because the securing nut is masked by the headset it makes changing an ignition switch very difficult without removing the headset from the fork. One alternative is to cut off the forked terminal and replace it with a small ring terminal which may be secured under one of the screws for the throttle rod arch-bracket.

- Early LI-models had no ignition switches at all and made do with an ignition cut-out button on the back of the headset.
- Different key ignition switches were originally fitted depending on whether the machine was wired for a 4-pole, 6-pole AC or 6-pole DC stator plate.
- Do not throw away an old lock just because you have no key for it. New keys are available from Weston Scooter Parts simply by quoting the number stamped on the lock barrel.
- Indian battery-type GP key ignition switches work fine on a non-battery Italian scooter, but if you use a non-battery Indian switch (i.e. without the anti-clockwise key position) on an Italian machine then the rear light will not come on in the third key position due to different wiring of Indian machines. Consult a specialist dealer for parts or information for these models.

| MODEL | ELECTRICAL SYSTEM | PART NUMBER |
|---|---|---|
| Early TV 175 S3 | 6v DC 4-pole | 19701040 |
| Special, TV, SX, GP | 6v DC 6-pole | 19781070 |
| GP 125, early Jet 200 | 6v AC 6-pole | 19781050 |
| Early Indian GP | 6v DC 6-pole | 22981070 |
| Indian 6/12v mid-series GP | 6/12v AC 6-pole | 22981050 |
| Indian GP 200 | 12v DC 6-pole | 22981070 |
| Indian GP 200 Electronic | 12v AC Electronic | 22081050 |

# Horns

- These are supplied in 12v or 6v, AC or DC versions so it is important to state which sort of system the horn is intended to work with when ordering a replacement. A 6v or 12v AC horn works with the common AF or Indian AC electronic ignition kits. DC horns are noticeably larger.

# Brake Light Switches

- These often need replacing due to corrosion caused by their exposed position.
- Very early switches with a single wire leading to them are of a type that earths the ignition system through the switch, and will stop the ignition when the bulb is blown or if the switch fails.
- Late Indian/Spanish machines will have a second brake light switch fitted in-line on the front-brake cable similar to that used on the Vespa T5. These use two separate sections of outer brake cable, which not only means that the horncasting has to come off to change a cable, but it also makes the front brake action feel spongy. Given that few MoT testers will know if your Lambretta should have a front brake light switch it may be preferable to dispense with the in-line switch, tape up the wires and fit a normal cable. Alternatively if your scooter is to be converted to hydraulic front brake it may be possible to extend the wiring back to the headset and use a switch mounted in the handlebar master cylinder.

# Batteries

Original fitment Lambretta batteries are all lead-acid type.
- 6v machines use 6N11-A4
- 12v machines use 12N5-3B

If a new battery is being fitted then it is important that the breather bung is removed and replaced with the supplied breather pipe which should route out below the floorboards. New batteries are normally supplied 'dry' and should be filled with acid by a dealer and allowed to settle or trickle-charged for 24-hours before use.

 **Ensure battery connections are tight. Poor connections may be signalled by the rectifier fuse blowing.**

 **Don't run DC system scooters without the battery attached since this can damage the rectifier or stator plate.**

# Junction Boxes, Regulators and Rectifiers

Many types of regulator (early AC models), rectifier (early DC models) and junction box were used on Italian models through the years. They can be identified by matching up the colours marked for each wire and looking at the internals of the box with the cover removed. AC regulators are identifiable by the fact they usually have no fuse, whereas DC rectifiers are more complex inside and are fitted with a fuse.

- Italian 4-pole AC (early non-battery LI 125/150) machines use a rectangular regulator with a metal cover on the floorboard strut.

- Italian 4-pole DC (early TV 175) uses a fused rectifier on the floorboard strut

- Italian 6v DC (battery) 6-pole machines have a square plastic box on the rear of the footboard strut which is a Ducati rectifier. The colour codes are: VIOLA = purple, MARR = brown, VERDE = green, GIALLO = yellow, ROSSO = red, GRIGIO = grey.

- Some LI 125 Special and 150 Specials for the Italian market came with a rectangular type wiring junction box (left) which often fails. These can be changed for the later round type. The first round type junction box (in centre - AC Italian/Indian/early Spanish) has groups of paired bullet connectors. It is important not to get this confused with the AC 12volt version (as supplied with many electronic ignition conversions) which has all the sockets except the green (ignition) pair connected together.

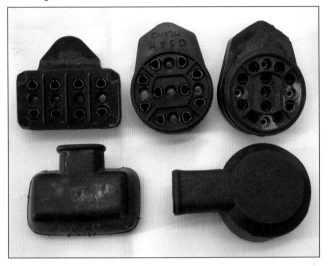

- Later AF Electronic and Indian non-battery systems use a 3-terminal AC regulator that is interchangeable with that used on non-battery Vespa PX models. AF Electronic DC versions use a rectifier interchangeable with the PX electric start Vespas.
- Several firms (such as Scooter Loopy in the UK) are now making specific mounting brackets for AF/Vespa-style CDI units and rectifier/regulators so that they can be fitted to the rear frame support tube around the original HT coil position.

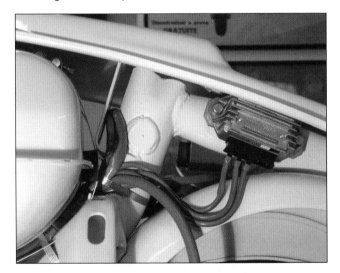

## Rear Lights

Complete rear light units are interchangeable between different manufacturers, but the lenses themselves are often unique and specific to one brand. A single model of Lambretta may have used several different rear lights during its production run, so it is not always possible to predict which type of rear light was fitted originally.

Pre-GP models were fitted with one of three rear light housings. The Carello one (top left) is identifiable by a cast-in reflector. The other pre-GP housing (top right) has drillings to accept lenses and reflectors from CEV or Aprilia. A plastic light housing (bottom left) was introduced for the GP model, originally made by CEV. The pressed Serveta housing (bottom right) takes an ugly light unit, but is popular with customisers since the steel is more easily chromed.

The lenses on the top row (Carello and GP) are unique to their respective housings. The CEV and Aprilia ones have different screw hole positions but will both fit onto the same housing which carries both sets of holes. Each uses a special bulb housing/reflector. The original Aprilia one is chromed steel and prone to rust. The CEV uses a more deeply dished aluminium one.

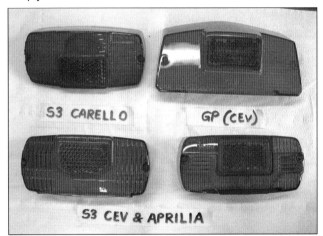

Remade gaskets and polished aluminium reflectors have been produced by Casa Lambretta that fit both CEV and Aprilia rear lights.

## Points System HT Coil

- For reliability the best coil to use on an Italian Lambretta is the plastic-bodied Ducati PX type (right), which was also fitted to Ciao mopeds. Some stocks of these are still available but on most versions the holes are slightly too far apart to fit without re-drilling one of the mounting holes in either the coil or the frame. A similar Ducati coil was used on certain Malaguti mopeds and this one actually has the correct hole spacing to fit on a Lambretta frame. The metal-bodied Ducati coil (left) is often unreliable so most dealers prefer to replace them with the plastic type.

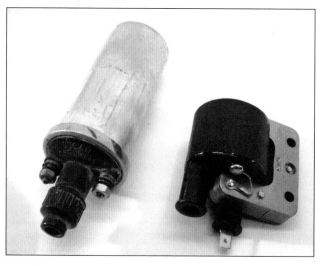

- If you must use a metal-bodied Ducati coil then the correct connections are: No 15 = (+) positive terminal goes to green wire from stator. No 1 = (–) negative to earth via exposed earth wire to the cowling. These coils will still work if the connections are reversed but the spark will be significantly weaker.
- Only use the correct coil with Filso ignitions (No. 00811384) because these stators are sensitive to HT coil characteristics. Filso stators will work with a plastic-type Ducati coil.
- A healthy coil should produce a spark that can jump a 5mm gap from the end of the HT lead.

Note the thick vibration insulator used between this old-style HT coil and the frame on our early LI.

## Stator Plates

- A major source of stator plate problems are coils that come loose on the laminates of the stator backing and break their earth wires. Loose earth tags are also prevalent so all these parts should be checked for tightness.
- Early Italian production (LI-TV) was fitted with 4-pole 6v points stators by four different manufacturers: Ducati, Dansi, Filso or Marelli. Keep flywheel and stator manufacturers matched. A 4-pole stator has only two visible coil windings and four magnets in the flywheel.

- Later Italian production (LI-SX-TV-GP) was fitted with 6-pole, 6v stators wired for either battery or non-battery systems. Three manufacturers (Ducati and Dansi for UK market, also Filso in Italy) made these systems but all use the same points and condensers.
- Italian 'Electronic' GPs were fitted with a Ducati 6V electronic ignition stator plate of a unique type.
- Most Spanish machines were fitted with 6-pole Motoplat 6v or 12v stators utilising unique points and condenser. Some models were wired for battery use.
- Later Spanish machines were fitted with a unique Motoplat 12v electronic ignition stator.
- Most Indian machines came fitted with 6-pole 6v or 12v points systems though some used 12v for the headlight and 6v for all other circuits. Some were wired for battery use.
- The last Indian GPs came fitted with 12v electronic ignition wired for AC non-battery use.

## Points-Type Stator Plate Overhaul

One of the most common forms of damage to a stator plate is split sleeving around the wiring. Six-pole stators like the one below come in two forms with different wiring. Battery ones – as most often found on British market machines – are wired with two yellow wires, a green and a brown.

**Pre-prepared sections of wiring with all the correct bullet terminals and sleeving already fitted are now available and considerably simplify the stator repair process.**

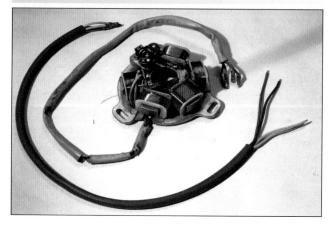

Non-battery stators – as are more commonly found on Italian imports – are wired with green, purple, pink and brown wires. Stators were produced by Ducati (most common), Dansi (fairly common) and Filso (fairly rare). It is possible to use one brand of stator with a different brand flywheel though this is best avoided where possible.

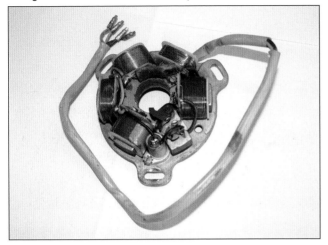

There are several different sorts of points. Early ones (right) were single spring type, but these were superseded by a preferable double spring type (left) which is less prone to 'points bounce' at high rpm.

 Good quality remade Lambretta points brands are FA and CTE (CTE part no. 013558-2). Some of the Lambretta points supplied in the UK are actually Vespa PX points, and while they appear to be the same, the cam heel length is slightly different, which makes correct timing much harder to achieve.

 Some points – most notably New Old Stock (NOS) ones – come with a coating to protect the contacts until they are used. This can be removed with electrical cleaner and a rag, or lightly sanding with a piece of folded 400-grit wet and dry paper gripped between the contacts. Do not do this while the points are fitted to the stator because any grit that falls onto the felt pad will quickly cause wear to the cam and points heel.

 Test the points with a multimeter to make sure they make and break contact before fitting them.

If you intend to repair the wires and sleeving without a piece of readymade 'kit' wiring, then first note the lengths of the wires and sleeving by marking them on a bench.

Remove the old points and condenser. These are both cheap enough that you may as well replace them as a matter of course. Cut the black wire from the condenser to the coil and then unscrew both components.

 It is a good idea to make a drawing of the stator and the wiring connections before you remove them so that it can be rewired correctly. Taking a picture of both sides of the stator with a digital camera is even better.

Heat up the solder joints so that the wires can be withdrawn.

 Only hold the soldering iron on the joint just long enough to melt the solder – any longer than necessary and you risk melting the plastic coil housings. In this respect a powerful soldering iron of 50W or more can actually be more effective since the heating duration is reduced.

Apply a thin coating of solder to the end of new wires by dipping them in electrical flux and then applying solder to the tip. Electrical flux-cored solder will do if you have no separate flux. This process is called 'tinning'.

Heat the joint and pass the tinned end of the new wire into place through the melted solder.

 **Hold the wire very still while the solder cools. A good joint should have a shiny silver finish. A matt grey finish indicates a 'dry joint' which does not have such good conductivity and can prove unreliable.**

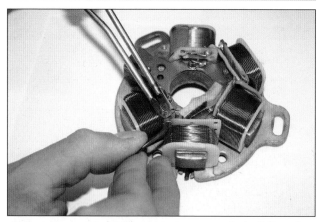

Use a piece of insulation tape to ensure that all the wires stay at the correct length relative to one another. Make sure that they are more than long enough before cutting the ends.

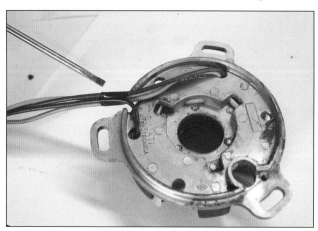

Getting sleeving over new wires is an acquired technique. Slide the wires into the sleeving as much as you can at first. Next grip the ends of the wires inside the sleeving with one hand (top) while stretching the sleeving a little with the other. Swap your firm grip to the other hand (bottom) and release with the first. The sleeving will pull itself down the wires. Repeating in this way it is possible to slowly 'worm' the sleeving into position.

 **A piece of cable attached to a solid object can be used to pull wires into position through sleeving. First slide the sleeving over the cable, attach the wires and then slide the sleeving over the wires using silicone spray as a lubricant.**

 **One significant cause of electrical unreliability comes from the use of cheap red and blue connectors and crimping pliers from the market. These are inadvisable in most scooter applications but especially unsuitable for Lambretta stators because they are so fat that it makes them tricky to get through the mag housing sealing plate. Professional (original) type bullets or spades should be used, but note that these require specialist crimping pliers.**

New points should be treated with electrician's flux to help the solder run before the wire is soldered to them.

Solder a wire into place on one tag and when it is cool bend the other tag over to hold the outer sleeving of the wire.

 **The original points screws have a small head and can be hard to get to. If possible fit one with a slightly larger head for improved access.**

 **If you take apart your points, ensure that all the parts go back together properly. If assembled incorrectly the spring can permanently earth the contacts and you get no spark!**

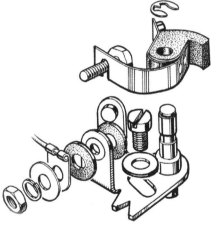

Rather than solder two wires to the condenser it is easier to continue the same wire from the points. Fit the points to the stator plate, route the wire past the condenser and then mark it so that a small amount of sleeving can be trimmed away.

**The condensers fitted to all 6-pole stators are the same. The condenser from early Vespa PX points models will also fit but these do not have the securing plate.**

First 'tin' the bare section of wire, and then solder it to the condenser using the minimum amount of heat and solder needed to do the job. Condensers are easily destroyed by prolonged heating.

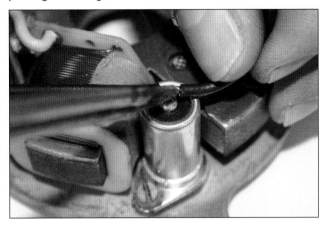

Finally trim off the remaining end of the wire and solder it into its correct position on the low tension (LT) coil.

**Ensure that the bolt holding the points together is tight. Original bolts had a 6mm head whereas aftermarket ones tend to use 5.5mm or smaller. It is best to fit the 6mm bolt for ease of use. Also bend the terminal down towards the head of the bolt to minimise the chances of it coming into contact with the flywheel.**

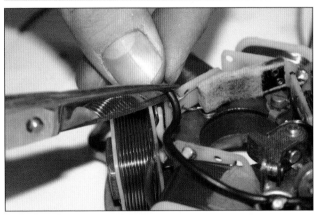

Put a light smear of gearbox oil or High Melting Point grease on the felt pad which lubricates the flywheel cam. This stops the heel of your points wearing and constantly going out of adjustment.

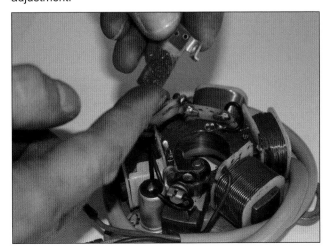

# AF Electronic Ignition Systems

Ray Kemp first had these excellent electronic ignition systems built (by Ducati) in the 1980s. The lightweight aluminium flywheels are based on that of the Lambretta Luna-range design and are ideally suited to high-revving engines.

**AF flywheels use a 4-tongue dust cover. Both the AF-supplied plastic and aluminium ones tend to break. If you can find a genuine Innocenti J-range aluminium dust cover, these will last much longer. Alternatively, Vespa PX flywheel bungs can be glued into the inspection holes.**

AF Flywheels can break after many years in high performance engines – usually from cracks forming around the boss and between the apertures. At the time of writing they are the still the lightest electronic ones available, and thus quite sought after – even with broken fins.

*STOP PRESS – At the time of writing AF Rayspeed are in the process of having these flywheels remade in India.*

Two sorts of AF electronic stator plate were supplied: AC, and a DC battery version. Partly due to the popularity of the TS1 kit – which required removal of the battery tray – the AC non-battery ones were more in demand. They were also more reliable.

The AF ignitions are very similar in function – if not exactly the same in wiring – to the Vespa PXE stator. They use basically the same CDI boxes and lighting regulators as the Vespa, and these are normally extremely reliable.

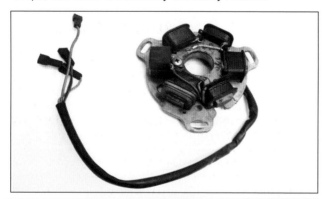

**AF ignitions had a tendency for the black trigger coil (pick-up) on the stator to rub on the inside of the flywheel due to insufficient clearance in the design. The standard answer was to put the mag housing in a lathe and machine back the inner face that the stator sits against by 1mm. The closely fitting flywheel means you also need to shave the heads of the bolts down and possibly lower the tops of the mag housing studs to ensure that they don't rub on the flywheel.**

**Rather than machine the mag housing Taffspeed machine the flywheels back by 1mm on the face indicated below to give extra clearance for the pick-up. This does not weaken the flywheel but does allow it to be fitted to any unmodified engine.**

# Indian Electronic Ignitions

Scooters India Limited introduced electronic ignition to their GP models around 1993. The stators are laid out essentially the same way as the AF Rayspeed Ducati ones (apart from wiring colours), but the flywheels are totally different. Compared to an AF flywheel they are heavy, which makes them better suited to standard machines since the weight means the engines tick-over more evenly. The Indian flywheels are produced with taller fins supposed to aid cooling, along with taller cowlings to match. Most British dealers machine down the fins so that they can be used with standard cowlings and running boards.

The problem with the Indian ignitions is that several companies are now making them. Some of them are fine from the box but some don't even have the keyway in the right place and won't time up properly. Others have had weak bosses that split along the keyway.

All the original electronic ignition flywheels are designed to fit onto the fat-tapered GP crank because thin-tapered early cranks are prone to shearing woodruff keys or even snapping when used with heavy flywheels on powerful engines. More recently some electronic flywheels have been modified with the fitment of an SX-LI-TV-type boss so that older engines can be converted to electronic ignition. If you are building a powerful engine it is far better to convert to a GP200-type crank for the improved big-end lubrication, wider flywheel side main bearing and fatter taper. The SX-LI-TV-type flywheel can be used successfully on lower performance engines provided that a quality conversion has been made. Scooter Restorations use a special UK-made boss which is oversized slightly to prevent splitting at the keyway. The central hole of the stator plate has to be bored out by 1mm to suit this conversion.

Note the positioning of the woodruff key slot in these two flywheels relative to the nearest rivet. The points flywheel (left) has the keyway positioned anti-clockwise of the rivet. The electronic flywheel (right) has the keyway positioned clockwise of the rivet. Some Indian manufacturers have been producing electronic flywheels with the keyway in the wrong (i.e. the points) position. Avoid these conversions because it will be impossible to correctly set your timing without massively extending the bolt slots on your stator plate.

Modern Indian electronic ignition flywheels are not without their problems. MB Developments now weld around the boss to support it, and weld the boss to the flywheel to prevent the rivets coming loose when used with powerful motors. This isn't always necessary but with variable Indian quality it is better to be safe than sorry, particularly if destined for a powerful engine. Also check that the screws holding the magnets in place have been tightened up properly. Oh, and make sure that all the coils are held tightly onto the stator too.

## Original Ducati Electronic Ignitions

These ignitions fitted to only very few of the last Innocenti GP200s are now extremely rare. The ignition circuits are very similar to the AF and Indian ones though colour coded differently. The lighting system was still 6-volt. The flywheel is cast aluminium and looks similar to the Ducati points flywheel except for the obvious difference that two of the magnets have overlapping extensions to trigger the pick-up coil.

Reports are that the original GP Electronic systems weren't particularly reliable due to failures of the red CDI/HT unit (below) and problems with loose earth tags and broken LT wires on the stator plates.

## Vespa PXE Conversion Electronic Ignition

This was a conversion pioneered in the 1980s by Mark Broadhurst while working for Beedspeed Scooters. The stators are constructed either by moving all the coils from a Vespa PX Electronic stator plate onto a 6-pole Lambretta stator (this is the inferior way since the coils are prone to coming loose), or by drilling out the rivets that hold the Vespa backing plate onto the stator and mounting on a Ducati Lambretta backing plate in its place. It says something for Italian production that the rivet holes still line up after all those years. The finished stator should have all the coils mounted in the same position as the Indian/AF systems.

The flywheel was constructed by machining down a Vespa PXE flywheel enough to fit inside the Lambretta mag housing and removing the rivets for the centre boss which should then be replaced (in the correct position) by a bolted-in Lambretta one from a Ducati flywheel. Again all the holes mysteriously line up perfectly. A lightweight plastic fan was usually screwed to the flywheel for cooling.

This system then used the original Vespa CDI box and regulator. Apart from disintegration of the occasional plastic fan and the aluminium cracking around the centre boss and ripping out of the odd flywheel, this was a fairly reliable conversion.

## AF/Indian/Vespa/GP Ducati Ignition Fault Finding

This text assumes that if you have an Indian stator it has been wired up as per the AF/Vespa colour coding which is:

- WHITE = Earth to stator
- RED = black Pick-up coil
- GREEN = Low Tension (LT) power coil

These colours match up with the colour coding on commonly supplied PX-type black or blue CDI units.

Original GP Electronic stators are wired up this way:

- GREEN = Earth to stator
- RED = black Pick-up coil
- WHITE = LT power coil

 **A Vespa-type CDI box may be used with an original GP Electronic flywheel and stator if you swap the positions of the white and green wires.**

To carry out the following tests you need to be able to use an electronic multi-meter set to measure resistance (ohms Ω). Check these figures in sequence.

**1.** Measure between the terminal of the White earth wire (Green on original GP) and the mag housing or stator plate backing. The resistance should be a short circuit (i.e. less than 0.1 ohm).

**2.** Measure between the terminal of the White earth wire (Green on original GP) and the terminal of the Red pick-up wire. On all stators you should expect a reading of 95 – 120 ohms.

**3.** Measure between the terminal of the White earth wire (Green on original GP) and the terminal of the Green LT power wire (White on original GP). The reading should be in the region of 450 – 540 ohms.

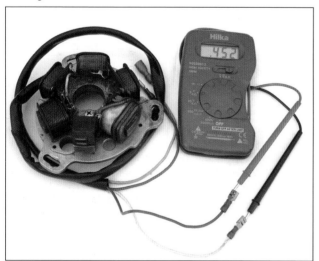

If your measurements from tests 2 or 3 show a much lower measurement this normally indicates a short circuit, possibly from a trapped wire or broken insulation, but occasionally from a faulty coil. If either of the tests show infinity (∞ or a flashing 'I' on digital meters) then it means a broken circuit, either due to a faulty coil itself or more commonly a loose earth tag or broken earth wire particularly coming from the LT coil. Both pattern LT coils and Pick-ups are available as spares and can be fitted to fix a dead stator plate.

It is possible to test the function of the CDI boxes, but substitution for a known good one is a far more simple way of testing. One of the good things about electronic ignitions is that they suffer far less from intermittent problems than contact breaker systems. Normally one works or it doesn't work. With that established it is a simple matter of isolating the faulty component and replacing it to get it working again.

 **The white lead and tag coming out of Vespa-style CDI units is a secondary Earth connection. While it should be connected to a chassis earth the CDI should still function if this short earth lead is broken, as long as the white wire from your stator is in good condition and well earthed (and vice versa).**

## Flywheels

 **If the crank taper shows any signs of prior damage file off any high points and 'lap' a flywheel onto it by putting a smear of grinding paste onto the taper and turning the flywheel backwards and forwards to improve the way they mate. When they match, both surfaces will have a slate grey colour. Thoroughly clean off all grinding paste.**

 **Brass 6-pole flywheels with a riveted-on aluminium fan – part no. 31.46 – are often found on early (post-4-pole) machines (LI-TV). These flywheels were prone to having the fans come loose and also loss of magnetism, so were superseded by the fully cast aluminium types. Magnets can be recharged at specialist dealers who still have the Innocenti flywheel re-magnetising tool.**

Generally the later cast LI-TV-SX flywheels (part no 31.56.4) are better than the brass ones, but not always. Try to use Ducati ones if available.

 **The later 31.56.4 flywheels have a 1mm thicker (28mm) boss than the early 31.56 version and will not fit into early stator plates unless the centre hole through the laminates is bored to 29mm to suit. The best type is the Ducati one with the riveted centre boss.**

 **Filso flywheels with the cast-in boss (below) are only useful as a door-stop. Do not fit them to a scooter because the centre boss will eventually come loose.**

 **Equally the Dansi flywheel with the cast-in boss is unreliable and only fit to throw at people you don't like.**

When the GP range was introduced the flywheel was modified to suit the fatter crankshaft taper. GP flywheels also have part no 31.56 but the hole for the crankshaft is visibly larger.

# Serveta Motoplat Electronic Ignition

The Serveta electronic ignition has an odd flywheel with triangular cut-outs for the holding tool. The system is reliable and has an extremely high electrical output, but with a heavy 3.2kg flywheel fitted to the thin SX crankshaft taper it isn't really suitable for powerful engines. There are two types. The AC version has only one yellow power wire, while DC type (shown) has two.

# Variable Timing Electronic Ignition Systems

At the time of writing three new Lambretta ignition systems are due to be released. All of these offer variable ignition timing which has the potential to boost power across the rev range when compared to normal 'fixed' ignition timing. Generally a two-stroke engine will gain power with more ignition advance at low rpm, but this needs to be retarded to a safe level at peak power to prevent detonation. Ideally the ignition advance should be tailored to a particular engine configuration but even a broadly set pre-programmed unit can still offer advantages over fixed timing.

- Tino Sacchi's Italian-made Varitronic system uses a light 1.85kg steel flywheel fitted with a nylon fan. It is pre-programmed to vary the timing between 10 and 30 degrees according to engine rpm. The stator plate has a 12volt 90Watt output.
- MB Developments are due to release a similar European-made system, also using a steel flywheel with aluminium fins and a 100Watt 12volt stator. The MB Euro system can be run with a pre-programmed variable advance box which is switchable between four different ignition maps, or it can be used without the advance box using fixed timing.
- Finally PM Tuning are developing a fully programmable advance/retard box to work with Indian or AF flywheels and stator plates. This system can store ten different maps to tailor the ignition timing: two of which are changeable on the move via a handlebar switch. Users can design their own ignition maps on a laptop and download these into the ignition box. This race-spec system is really only for serious speed junkies.

# IGNITION TIMING

Being petrol-powered the Lambretta engine relies on a spark to ignite the fuel/air mixture in the cylinder. For optimum efficiency this spark should fire while the piston is still on its upward stroke, just before it reaches the top of its travel. Thus timing is quoted as degrees of crankshaft travel Before Top Dead Centre (BTDC). For any meaningful attempt to be made to time an engine, you must first accurately locate Top Dead Centre (TDC).

There are two popular methods of establishing TDC and timing your engine – each with their own supporters and detractors. For convenience we will show you both and leave it up to you to decide which path you choose.

The Positive Stop method has advantages in that it can be carried out with little more than a broken spark plug, a bolt and a cheap dial gauge, and also that you can time an engine without taking the cylinder head off.

Those in favour of the Dial Gauge method say that it removes any errors that may occur in doing things 'by eye', and yet the other camp claim a dial gauge can never truly locate TDC because of the 'dwell period' where the needle shows the piston is at the top of the bore and yet the flywheel can still be rocked backwards and forwards by a couple of degrees. Personally I think that the Positive Stop method is sufficiently accurate, and will appeal to the majority of readers simply for the fact that it requires less in the way of engine stripping and tools.

## Timing Settings

For totally standard machines, the traditional timing figures are as follows (± 1°):
- LI-SX-TV (all capacities): 23 degrees BTDC
- GP (all capacities): 21 degrees BTDC

 **The above figures were established when leaded petrol was in regular use, which had higher resistance to detonation than modern unleaded fuel. As such many tuners suggest it is probably better to set all untuned machines closer to 19 degrees, and certainly no more advanced than 21 degrees for totally standard LI-SX-TV models.**

The required ignition timing for tuned engines depends on numerous factors (state of tune, fuel used, cooling efficiency, carburation etc.) so it is not really practical to suggest specific timings. Those commonly used for TS1 type engines range from 19 degrees BTDC (Before Top Dead Centre) – which is more risky depending on set-up – to 16 degrees BTDC; which should be safer but perhaps with marginally less punch at lower rpm. You should select your timing on the basis of advice from your tuner.

 **If you are trying to select a suitable timing figure yourself by seat of the pants testing, then always start with a low figure (e.g. 16 degrees) and advance your timing a degree at a time.**

 **Never work from timing marks on a mag housing unless you know them to be correct. They will be different if the flywheel or crank has been changed and particularly if you have converted from points to electronic ignition. It is far better to check and remake them as necessary.**

## Ignition Timing – Positive stop Method

This method of timing relies on the fact that if you turn a crankshaft in one direction until the piston meets an obstruction and mark the housing, then turn it back the other way to meet the same obstruction and mark the housing again, your TDC point will be exactly half way between the two marks. The key to this method is producing a reliable piston stop.

A piston stop can be produced by hollowing out an old spark plug and putting a bolt and washers through it. The bolt should protrude from the tip of the plug thread by around 15mm, but may need to be longer with certain types of cylinder head.

 **If you make a piston stop this way, then the bolt must be totally tight. Any movement when the piston touches it will produce inaccuracies in your result. Araldite all the pieces together, but make sure that the spark plug threads are still clean.**

After a thorough clean (removing any filings) fit your flywheel onto the crank using the woodruff key for alignment and with the nut tightened. Always use a perfect woodruff key and ensure that the keyway in the crank and flywheel are in good condition.

 **Lambretta flywheel woodruff keys are the same as Vespa PX clutch ones.**

 **To refit a points-type flywheel more easily, turn the crankshaft so that the woodruff key is in the 5 o'clock position.**

 **Some 4-pole flywheels fitted to early machines have no timing mark arrow. As such you should scribe an arbitrary arrow somewhere into the flywheel and use that when following the instructions below. Any point you choose will be fine as a basis for marking the mag housing even if the marks themselves are not in the usual positions.**

 **For greater accuracy, continue the arrow right to the edge of your flywheel with a scribe or hacksaw mark.**

With the piston at the bottom of the bore, screw your piston stop into the plug hole. First turn the flywheel anticlockwise. It will stop when the piston touches the bolt. There is no need to force it, so just rest it gently on the stop. Mark the mag housing opposite the arrow on the flywheel.

FIRST STOP MARK

Now turn the flywheel in the opposite direction until it stops. Again mark a point opposite the arrow. Doing this by eye can introduce errors if your eye is not in line when making the marks.

When you have marked the stop positions, then TDC will be directly between the two marks. There are many ways to find the mid-point but the most sensible and accurate will be with the correct size of degree disc. It just so happens that Cambridge Lambretta Works have produced one that is almost the same diameter as a Lambretta flywheel and with the correct hole bored in it to fit on the crankshaft it is ideal for the job.

Remove the flywheel and fit the degree disc onto the crank with a flywheel nut to retain it. Adjust the disc so that the two marks are an even number of degrees either side of the TOP mark. In this instance the two stop marks are 23.5 degrees either side of the TOP mark – which is where you should put your mark for TDC.

 **Since you now have several marks on your mag housing it will be wise to mark your TDC point a different colour so you don't get confused.**

 **On most common systems the TDC mark should be at approximately 1 o'clock on the mag housing, with the firing mark closer to 12 o'clock.**

 **Finding TDC by measuring around the mag housing with a steel rule is possible but not too accurate. Wrapping a strip of paper around the marked area of the casting, marking the two points and then folding it in half between them will give a mid-point which can be marked if you put the paper back in position. You could even use a set of dividers to find the mid-point. These methods will all work but only the degree disc will also help you calculate your firing point.**

Once you have established your TDC point, then finding the firing point is simply a question of counting ANTI-CLOCKWISE from TDC by the number of degrees that you require. In this instance the engine was to be set at 19 degrees, hence the second coloured mark at that position.

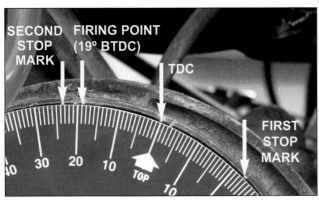

## Ignition Timing – Dial Gauge Method

Fit your flywheel as described previously. Remove your cylinder head and mount a dial gauge onto the studs as shown.

MB Developments produce this dial gauge bracket which fits diagonally across two of the cylinder studs on all types of casings. When set up and spaced correctly from the cylinder, turn the engine over to find Top Dead Centre and zero the gauge at that point.

**There is a 'dwell period' of a few degrees of flywheel movement where the needle still shows TDC. Turn it one way then the other until the needle starts to move and try to make sure that your TDC mark is halfway between the two points.**

Mark the mag housing with a pen in line with the arrow on the flywheel. This mark is your Top Dead Centre (TDC) point.

This TDC point will never change as long as you use that crankshaft, flywheel and mag housing. As such it is worth marking the TDC point in a more permanent way – i.e. with a punch.

Refit the flywheel and line it up with the TDC mark. Then turn it ANTI-CLOCKWISE until the dial gauge has moved the distance (in millimetres) that corresponds with the required ignition timing. For instance if you want a timing of 19-degrees (with a standard LI-SX-GP 58mm stroke crank and 107mm con rod) then turn the dial gauge back by 2.0mm. For the figures to be relevant your dial gauge readings have to be accurate to ±0.02mm. When you are happy with the dial gauge reading, mark the mag housing again with what will be your firing point.

**Note that if you use a crank with different stroke or even a different length con-rod then the dial gauge measurements will change. The dial gauge measurements for most common crankshafts are listed in a table in the Ignition Timing Appendix.**

The punch mark (left) on this mag housing is at 23 degrees, which is not too safe for modern unleaded fuel. The point to the right (indicated with black-tipped screwdriver) is 19 degrees, which Taffspeed suggest setting even standard engines to nowadays.

19° Mark (-2.0 mm on DIAL GAUGE)     TDC

## Stator Plate Fitting

The original fitment uses bolts and wavy washers but MB use high tensile Allen screws (with a tiny dab of Loctite) fitted with wavy and flat washers. To optimise your chances of being close to the correct timing position, start by putting the stator in the central position on the slots, or if the stator has washer marks from a previous position, try it there first.

A cable clip should be used to hold the wiring away from the flywheel. The original one is straight and intended to fit on one of the stator plate screws. MB Developments have had curved ones produced which fit better onto the mag housing studs.

## Points Setting

Before you can properly set the timing on a points ignition, you must first set the points gap within the working range, which is 0.35mm – 0.45mm. First of all, loosen the points screw a little so that the contacts can be adjusted without closing back up. Use a screwdriver in the V-shaped notch (or cam-screw on some early stators) to open the gap.

Turn the flywheel until the points look fully open through the slot in the flywheel. Insert a 0.4mm feeler gauge between the contacts of the points and loosen the screw so that the points close onto the gauge. Retighten the screw and your points gap should now be set. Check everything is okay by turning the flywheel clockwise a couple of times to see the points open and close, and then use the feeler gauge to check the gap again.

**In theory having a smaller points gap will produce a stronger spark since the coils are being charged for longer between firings. As such tuners like Harry Barlow prefer to set points ignitions closer to 0.35mm, but you may need to adjust your stator position to ensure that the ignition still fires at the correct point.**

## Points Ignitions – Finding The Firing Point

There are a couple of suitable methods to determine the exact point at which the contacts open. One method uses a battery and a bulb. Connect up a 6 or 12-volt battery and 12-volt bulb so that the negative terminal of the battery is connected to the engine casings. Connect the positive terminal to one side of a bulb and the other bulb connection to the green wire coming from your stator plate.

Rotate the flywheel CLOCKWISE towards the firing point. The bulb should glow brightly.

At the exact spot where the points open the bulb will glow slightly dimmer. The point where the brightness changes is the actual firing point. If the flywheel arrow is positioned ANTI-CLOCKWISE of your firing mark then your timing is too ADVANCED. Take the flywheel off and rotate the stator slightly clockwise. Refit the stator and flywheel and check again. When the bulb dims at the exact point that the arrow on your flywheel lines up with the firing point you marked on your mag housing, then your timing is correctly set.

 **A simpler method to establish the opening point uses a cigarette rolling paper (or other thin piece of paper). Turn the flywheel until you can see the points opening through the viewing slot. When they are open insert the cigarette paper and turn the flywheel back slightly until the points grip the paper. Now pull very gently on the paper as you are turning the flywheel clockwise. The paper will be released at the exact moment the points open. Check if this is when the arrow on your flywheel aligns with your firing mark on the housing. If not then adjust the position of your stator plate as described previously.**

 **Be aware that adjusting your points gap will have an effect on your ignition timing. It is best to first set the desired gap as described above, and then move the stator to select the desired firing point. Once the stator is in roughly the right position, the timing may be fine-tuned by setting a different points gap but never exceed the 0.35-0.45mm range. A slightly smaller gap retards the timing (fewer degrees before TDC) and vice versa.**

## Electronic Ignition – Finding The Firing Point

Once you have established the TDC and firing marks for an electronic ignition, there is (supposedly!) a simple visual check that can be made to see if the timing is in the right ball park.

If the timing is correct then the pair of parallel marks on the black ignition pick-up should line up with a matching pair on the flywheel when it is positioned at the firing point. If not then you will have to take the flywheel off and move the stator until the lines match up. *Note: the poor condition of the red pick-up wire was spotted and repaired later!*

 **If the flywheel is an early Ducati AF Rayspeed one, then you can be reasonably sure that the two timing marks on the flywheel are actually in the right position and your timing should be as desired. The same can not be said of Indian flywheels which seem to be made in several different factories each with very different concepts of 'accurate'. Some may have marks in the correct place, but we have seen flywheels with the centre boss positioned in totally the wrong place, and this makes it virtually impossible to time them correctly. With the inconsistency of Indian electronic ignition manufacture it has become essential to check your timing is correct with a strobe.**

## Final Flywheel Fitting

Make sure to use the correct nut and washer for your flywheel. The shallow one (left) is for very early LI. The deeper one (centre) was used from 1964-on. It has a 21mm-wide boss and uses a washer with an outside diameter of 21.5mm. Finally one that is both deeper and wider was introduced for thick-taper GP flywheels (right) and this has an outside diameter of 23mm.

You may need to take the flywheel on and off several times to move the stator. Once you are happy with its alignment torque the flywheel nut up to 6.9 kg-m (50 lbs-ft).

 **No matter what sort of ignition system you use, always make sure there is a good earth wire between chassis and frame. If you don't make a good physical connection then the engine earths to the chassis through the cables. Since these run in grease, this can not be regarded as a reliable electrical contact.**

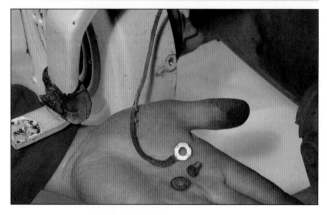

## Strobe Timing Check

 **A strobe timing check is essential when using Indian electronic ignitions since the accuracy of the timing marks on the flywheel can not be relied upon.**

To check the ignition with a strobe you will need to connect the stator to a coil or CDI ignition box. Cheap AC strobe guns that fit in line between the HT cap and the spark plug (which must be earthed to the engine) are the ones to use. More expensive battery-powered DC strobes can give false readings unless a 'distributor-less ignition adapter' is used. If your motor is in the frame and ready to run then you can simply fit a cheap AC strobe in line and start the engine to check the timing. It is highly unlikely that you will cause any damage to your engine by running it for a short period even if the timing is way out. It is possible (but not as good) to strobe test ignition timing with the engine out of the scooter using a powerful electric drill fitted with a socket attachment to spin the engine up for the test. Obviously the drill would not be able to turn the engine with the spark plug in place, so the plug is merely earthed against the engine casings to still be able to spark.

Paint both your firing mark on the mag housing and the arrow on the flywheel with bright paint – Tippex works fine – and turn the engine over, either with a drill or by starting it. You may need to be in a darkened environment to see it. With the engine running as fast as the drill will turn (it needs to be at least 2,000 rpm) the strobe should flash and make the arrow of the flywheel appear stationary. If the flywheel arrow lines up with your timing mark on the mag housing then your timing is set. If the arrow shows up clockwise of the mark then the stator needs to be moved anti-clockwise and vice versa. Moving a Lambretta stator Anti-clockwise Advances the timing, so clockwise retards it.

 **Depending on the gap between the magnetic pick-up on your stator and the flywheel, the timing can swing around a few degrees as the engine is revved. If possible, do the strobe test with the engine running at around 6-7,000 rpm. If the arrow on the flywheel appears anti-clockwise of your timing mark, then turn the stator clockwise and repeat the test until they line up. Strobe testing at the actual rpm you expect your engine to cruise at is the best way to set your timing.**

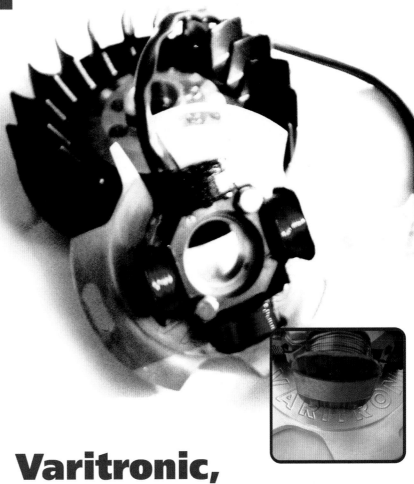

# CARBURATION AND FUEL SYSTEM

## Standard Carburettors

Original Lambretta carbs are small and primitive devices, but they do a good job on standard machines; particularly when you consider the economy figures that can be achieved if you take it easy. For most British scooterists however, 'taking it easy' has proved only marginally more popular than crucifixion. As such, many UK Lambrettas found themselves fitted with significantly larger carbs in the eternal quest for more speed and power. Through the 1980s the 'bigger is better' attitude ruled, but in recent times many people have been converting their scooters back to standard or running more sensible-sized carb conversions.

The original Italian carb fitments were as follows.

**18mm**   (Dell'Orto SH 18) – LI 125/150, LI 150 Special
**20mm**   (Dell'Orto SH1/20) – TV 175/200, LI 125 Special, SX 150/200, GP 125
**22mm**   (Dell'Orto SH2/22) – GP 150/200
(Component details are listed in the Carburation Appendix)

- Carb manifolds are available in two different stud spacings: 125/150/175 or 200. While 18 or 20mm carbs can both fit each other's manifolds be aware that these were changed from model to model to match revised inlet port shapes on the various cylinders used. You should make an effort to obtain the correct one for your cylinder or at least match the manifold to the inlet port for optimum performance.
- Indian machines have been fitted with Spaco (Indian copy Dell'Orto), Jetex (GP 200) and Mikcarb (GP 150) carbs during their production. The Mikcarb layout is based on a Japanese Mikuni design and is totally different to that of the Dell'Orto.
- Very early GP 200 carbs came fitted with 123 main jets as opposed to 118 listed in most books. The 123 jet was also used on later Indian machines running the 42mm 'big bore' exhaust and this size jet is an advisable starting point on any standard GP 200 fitted with a performance pipe. If you can't get a 123 main jet then a 122 'INC'-stamped Dell'Orto jet is perfectly adequate.

 Jetex 22mm carbs are now commonly available as a replacement carb for the GP 200, or as an upgrade for various models. When these work as intended they are excellent, but improperly machined ones are fairly common. Don't go crazy trying to set one up without first trying another carb to prove that yours isn't faulty.

 On 18, 20 and 22mm carbs there are a choice of slides to fit. Those with a part number ending – 2 – are weaker, while those with – 1 – are richer.

 If you buy a Dell'Orto 22mm carb assembly, watch out for Lambro (3-wheeler) ones which are sometimes supplied as spare parts. These are essentially the same – and will work – but have no outer lip on the carb mouth to retain the carb hose. These are then prone to leaking fuel at the hose joint even when clamped tightly.

## Carb Removal

To remove the carb first undo the clamp bolt using an 8mm socket.

 Getting a carb off a manifold can be very tricky if it hasn't moved in years. You can try heating it with a rag drenched in boiling water, but for heavens sake don't heat it any other way; particularly with a naked flame. If you can't grip the carb in a gloved hand and twist it to get it off, then it may be tapped off from the other side of the scooter with the words "a carburettor is a sensitive instrument" ringing in your head. One way is to rest a piece of wood (gaffer-taped to prevent splintering) against the back of the carb and tap it to encourage the carb to start moving. Once loose you should be able to twist and pull it off the manifold. It is easier to do this if the rear shock is removed, thus lowering the carb.

 The Scooter Surgery method of getting standard Lambretta carbs off the manifold is to loosen the clamp bolt and then insert a close-fitting bar of some sort wrapped in rag into the mouth of the carb. By levering the bar from side to side at the same time as you pull on the back of the carb the clamp is forced open a little and the carb comes off. Only use a side-to side movement of the bar (in this case a ratchet handle) to avoid damaging the carb slide.

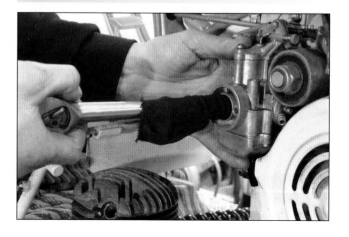

Detach the throttle cable inner from the hook in the arm.

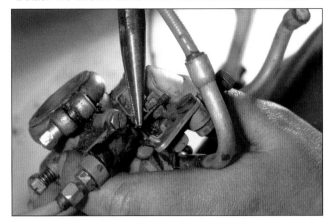

Unscrew the choke fixing and remove the plunger from the cable. If the rubber tip inside the plunger is damaged it should be renewed.

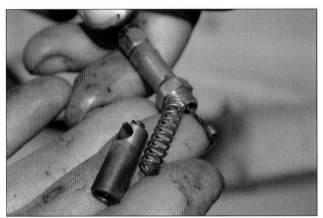

## Repairing Stripped Choke Fixing Threads

Standard Lambretta carbs are made of a very soft alloy and it is very common for the choke fitment thread to strip.

By gently tapping the choke housing with a ball pein hammer while it is resting on a vice it is possible to slightly bend in the alloy enough that it will grip the thread of the fitting once more. In future do not over-tighten the choke fitment since the threads will never be very strong. Use Loctite to ensure it doesn't come loose with vibration.

## Carb Strip and Clean

If your carb is filthy then it is very easy to make things worse by opening the body and allowing dirt to get in, so clean the body as best you can before going any further.

**Petrol, paraffin or spray Carb Cleaner and a toothbrush will do the trick, but all are highly flammable so be careful.**

Remove the screws that retain the float bowl. This area should be scrupulously clean, but with old scooters very often rust particles from inside the fuel tank clog up the fuel filter and float bowl.

Withdraw the pivot pin and remove the carb float and float needle together. Examine the float for damage. If you shake the float and can hear anything sloshing inside then it will need to be replaced.

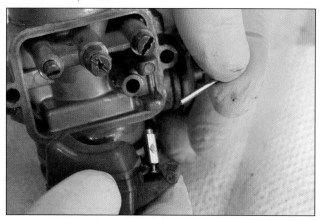

The long jet on the left is the choke ('starter') jet, which richens the mixture for starting when the choke lever is opened. The short jet (centre) is the idle or slow running jet which takes care of fuelling when the engine is on tick-over. The long jet with the hexagonal head (right) is the atomiser, which mixes air with fuel coming from the loose main jet (bottom) when the throttle is open. Jets should be cleaned by blowing through with a high pressure air line. Generally their sizes are stamped on the sides.

 **Another way to clean jets is to twist together two strands of copper wire and insert through the drillings. Rotate the jet on the wire to clean it.**

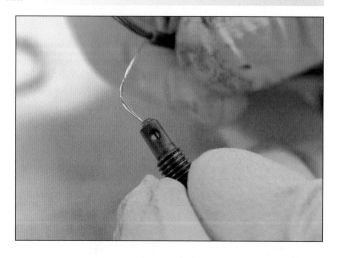

Remove the union for the fuel pipe, which is known as a fuel banjo because of its shape. Remove any accumulated crud. Also lever out the fuel filter with a small screwdriver and give that a thorough clean.

Remove the carb mixture screw and spring. The longer one (left) fits 22mm carbs, while the short one (right) is for 18 and 20mm carbs.

Undo the carb-top screws and withdraw the slide assembly. If the slide looks particularly worn – signified by polished metal 'high spots' – then it should be renewed. A very badly worn slide probably indicates that the carb body is past its sell-by date and may also need to be renewed.

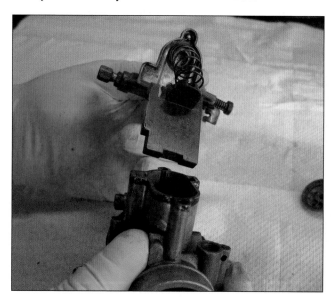

If you plan to chemically clean the carb then continue stripping it down. Unhook the slide and spring, withdraw the slide rod, and remove the rubber sealing washer.

Two types of carburettor clamp were originally used. The older cast ones (left) are probably better than the modern folded steel ones (right).

Various types of float needle are available. The modern ones are red-tipped and are produced to survive the ravages of unleaded fuel, so it is important to fit one if your carb has the old black-tipped type. If the needle shows any sign of wear – or your scooter is prone to flooding if left stood with the fuel on – then renew it.

Once stripped, clean as thoroughly as possible with lint-free cloth and proprietary spray-on 'carb cleaner' and blow through with compressed air. Normally a good manual clean to this standard will set straight any fuelling problems.

**If your carb has been stood without running for a long period (i.e. several years) then the fuel can evaporate away leaving a filthy emulsion of two-stroke oil which can clog up all the internal drillings of the carb. Immersing the main carb components in an ultrasonic bath is the modern way of carb cleaning, and various companies now offer this service in scooter and classic motorcycle magazines.**

**Dean Orton was shown another quick – if more dangerous – way of cleaning old carbs by an Italian classic bike enthusiast. The carb should be stripped of all plastic parts – ideally including the plastic bush that fits onto the manifold. It is impossible to remove these bushes without damaging them, so do not attempt this without a replacement to use. Use a piece of wire to attach the four bare alloy components together and immerse them in a bucket of neat battery acid for 15 seconds. It will bubble like hell. Using a pair of pliers carefully withdraw the parts – being careful not to splash or drip acid on anything important like your skin – and immerse in another bucket of fresh, clean water for a minute or two. Shake the parts in the water to ensure all the acid has been washed out. Blow-dry the parts with compressed air or allow them to dry naturally before rebuilding with new gaskets, O-rings and a new plastic bush. This process will not remove thick, encrusted dirt which should be scraped off first, but it will clean out all but the most clogged internal drillings.**

After acid-cleaning the carb will have a new matt-grey appearance.

These are the only real service parts required for a Lambretta carb strip.

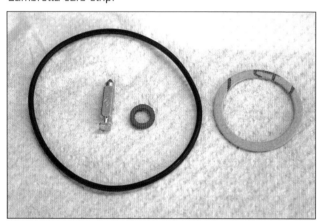

Refitting the float bowl O-ring can be a bit of a game. In most cases the original is safe to re-use unless showing visible signs of damage.

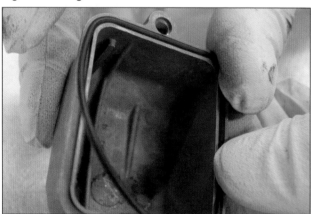

Replace the jets and float/needle assembly.

Reuse the fuel filter unless damaged, but replace the fuel banjo gaskets wherever possible.

**On 18mm carbs which don't have a lug to locate the banjo, hold the carb upright and looking from the banjo bolt position, locate the fuel inlet at the 8 o'clock position.**

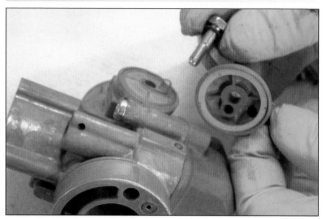

Don't forget the rubber washer when reassembling the carb top.

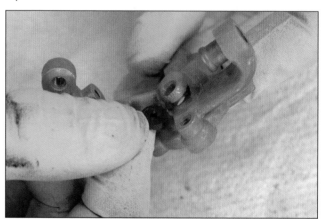

If your engine barely runs with the tick-over screw wound fully in, it is possible to bend down the tab that it rests against slightly to put the screw back into a useful range.

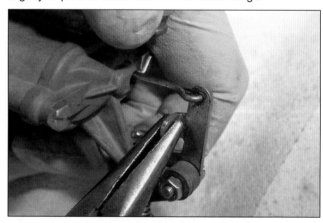

## Setting the Mixture Screw

The mixture screw (indicated below) should be wound in until fully seated (do not force it) and then wound back out the prescribed amount. The Lambretta Workshop Manual suggests half a turn out as a base setting for most carbs, but many dealers prefer starting one and a half turns out. From there the screw can be fine-tuned to obtain the most even tick over. Hesitation to pick-up when the throttle is opened and a slow settling-down to tick-over are possible indicators that the mixture screw is in too far. Spluttery pick-up and a very smoky tick-over are possible indicators that the mixture screw is out too far.

Remember that this screw only controls the fuelling at tick over and makes no appreciable difference to jetting once the slide is past 1/4 open. On all Dell'Orto-based Slimstyle standard carbs, wind the screw OUT (Anti-Clockwise) to RICHEN (higher proportion of petrol), and IN to WEAKEN.

 **Tick-over setting should only be done with a warmed engine.**

 **If your engine suddenly needs a significant adjustment to this screw to regain tick-over this is normally the indication of a more serious problem**.

## Fuel Flow

Never underestimate the damage that can be done to an engine by receiving insufficient fuel. Old fuel taps often become clogged with paint or grit, particularly after restoration. If this is a recurring problem then you should coat the inside of your fuel tank with a solution such as Petseal or fit a new tank. Many fuel taps simply don't flow enough fuel in the first place for the thirst of a tuned engine, which can consume as much as a pint of fuel in a minute.

**Even on a standard machine you should look for a tap to flow at least half a pint in a minute. If your tap doesn't meet this criteria then you would do well to fit a fast-flow fuel tap (right). These are essential on any tuned motor and advisable in any case whenever a replacement tap is required.**

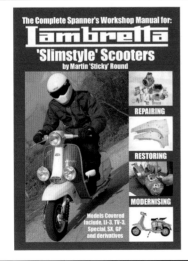

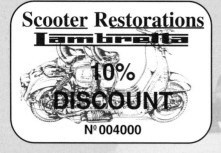

# CHASSIS STRIP

## Good Practice

● Keep fasteners (nuts, screws etc.) together with the bits that you take off. Bag them up and tape the bag to the relevant part.
● Take digital photos as you dismantle to remind you how things go back together.
● Be aware of the fire and fume risk of working with machines containing petrol.
● Obtain a Lambretta Parts Manual for your particular scooter model.

## Running Board Removal

Remove the sidepanels. Almost every engine or ignition job requires you to also take off the running boards. These are fixed with 8mm-head nuts.

It takes a long, thin socket to reach some of the nuts.

 **If you are one of the many who are undertaking the restoration of a recently discovered wreck – and you intend to replace many of the old parts with new, then in many cases it is easier to simply cut off the rusty nuts or screw heads with bolt croppers rather than trying to undo them.**

Since we were also taking off the legshields, the bolt croppers proved to be essential.

You need to remove the central bridge-piece before you can get the running boards off. Access is not too bad with a standard Lambretta exhaust but becomes murderously difficult with some of the aftermarket sports exhausts.

**To improve access to the bridge piece nuts, remove the rear shock.**

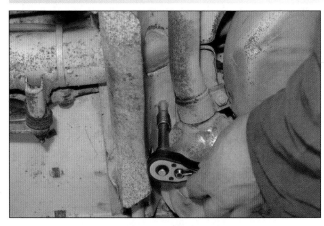

The bridge-piece has four rubbers: two edge gaskets and a round one (or rectangular on later models) under each screw hole.

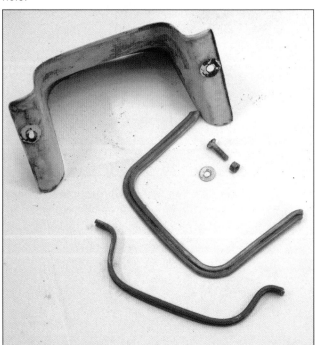

The outside edges of the running board are connected by studs cast into the plastic runner strips. These need to be partially lifted to free the running boards.

Note the rubber spacers under each screw hole.

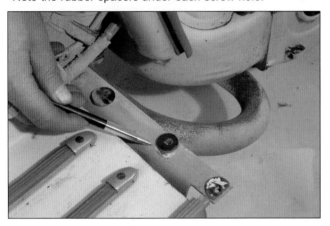

This early Series 3 is unusual because the rear of the runner is secured by two nuts whereas later models only use one. Again there is a rubber gasket between the running board and its support strut. Also note the push-over panel buffer on this early scooter (flattened from use!), where later ones use a clip-on type.

## Exhaust Removal

Remove the exhaust. This is held on by a clamp on the downpipe, two nuts on the main bracket and a third on the tailpipe bracket. Later models featured another bracket that bolted the exhaust to the underside of the engine. Removal usually requires a lot of wiggling.

 **It you can't get the exhaust to come off the downpipe, rest a block of wood against the body of the silencer from the far side and hit this with a hammer to encourage movement.**

 **If the exhaust is seized onto the downpipe and you plan to bin it anyway then the easiest way to get it off is to saw through the downpipe.**

## Seat Removal

The seat fixes to the seat arch with four M8 bolts (13 or 14mm head). The nuts and black wavy washers underneath are accessed through the toolbox door. Metal washers are used between the seat bracket and the frame.

Our LI was fitted with saddle seats. Most Slimstyles for the UK came with a dual ('bench') seat. The pillion saddle is a later LI-type – identical to the front and fitted using wedge shaped metal adapters.

On later machines fitted with a dual seat, the four rear holes are occupied by the seat catch bracket. It is easier to take off the pillion seat or seat catch after the fuel tank has been removed.

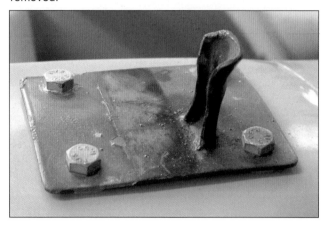

## Air Filter Box Removal

To take off the airbox, first unscrew the air scoop from under the seat. Note the rubber gasket fitted.

Remove the air hose and filter. The airbox is retained by a nut and peculiar square-headed bolt which fits into the frame bracket shown.

Between the airbox and the frame is another rubber gasket.

## Toolbox Removal

Next to come off is the toolbox, which fastens using special kinked screws. These are retained by 8mm head nuts held in place by tab washers. The two lower screws hook into the frame near the toolbox door. On some machines there are plastic plugs to hold these in position.

## Fuel Tank Removal

Empty the fuel tank, remove the fuel pipe and unscrew the fuel tap nut. This has a strange double thread design, so hold the tap still as you are undoing the nut. Next undo the tank strap bolts to release the fuel tank. Swing the bottom of the tank forward to remove it. Note the position of the many tank rubbers

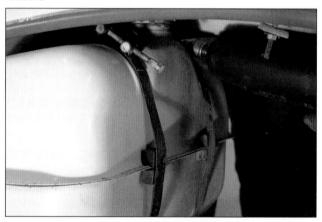

## Rear Brake Pedal Removal

If you need to take the engine out of the chassis, it is normally easier to undo the 17mm nut on the rear brake pedal cable clamp than undo the cable at the rear of the engine.

This early LI uses a grease nipple on the brake pedal pivot point. These were abandoned on later models. The brake pedal must be removed if you want to get the legshields off. Start with the circlip which in this case broke during removal.

 **Unhook the return spring from the pedal with care because if you let the spring go suddenly it will damage the brake light switch.**

With the pedal rubber taken off, the pedal can be removed from the pivot point and withdrawn through the hole in the legshields.

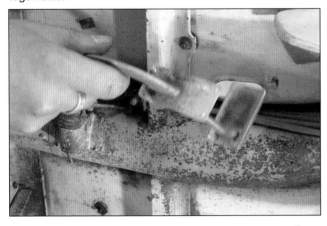

## Horncasting and Front Mudguard Removal

It is easiest to remove the mudguard and horncasting as a single unit. Start by locating the six screws which secure the mudguard to the legshields. Some of these are hidden under the floor runner channels. If these screws are hard to undo it may be better to cut them off. Our LI was fitted with unusual alloy end caps featuring brass spacers. The spacers were integrated into the alloy casting of later models.

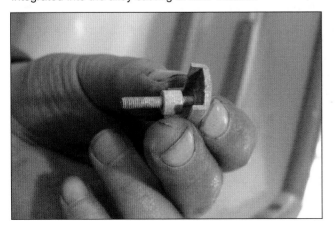

Next undo the top horncasting screws – which in the case of our LI also supported an accessory bag hook – followed by the two lower horncasting screws. Warming the aluminium horncasting with a heat gun will ease removal of tight screws.

Next carefully prise the horncasting badge out of its clip.

**When rebuilding you should put a dab of grease on this clip to ease badge removal in the future.**

The main horncasting screws are Allen bolts hidden behind the badge. With these undone the mudguard and horncasting can be removed as a single unit.

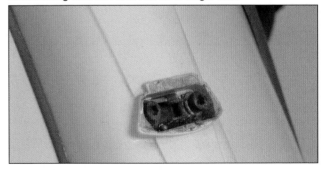

## Legshield Removal

Once all of the floor runner screws have been undone, only these two bolts hold the legshields in place. Remove these and the legshields can then be carefully withdrawn.

# Working with the Engine in the Frame

It is possible to do many tasks on a Lambretta engine without removing the engine from the chassis. Once the running boards are off you have enough access to do any carb, ignition or transmission work you require. It is also possible to remove the head, barrel and piston with the engine in the frame, but this is a much harder squeeze depending on the cylinder setup of your scooter.

The first step is to remove the rear wheel, prise out the rubber engine bump stop and remove the rear shock. The back of the engine will now swing further up offering improved access to the cylinder.

Next, withdraw the cylinder cowling after first undoing the single large bolt (two bolts on later Indian cowlings) and two slotted hex-head screws into the mag housing. This job is much easier with later exhaust systems, but with early ones you may need to lift the cowling a little until you have room to access the nuts to remove the down pipe.

With the cowling off you have access to the four cylinder head nuts, and if you remove the inlet manifold it will also be possible to get the whole top end off. If you are going to carry on and drop the engine out, be sure to undo the earth wire that fastens to one of the flywheel cowling screws before you attempt it. Also make sure the stator wires are no longer clipped to the main frame tube.

# Engine Removal

For the purposes of our work we wanted the engine completely out of the chassis. The control cables should be undone next. Cleverly, this can be done on Lambrettas without losing adjustment of the cables.

First put an open-ended spanner over the clutch arm and turn it forward so that the clutch ferrule can be unhooked from the arm.

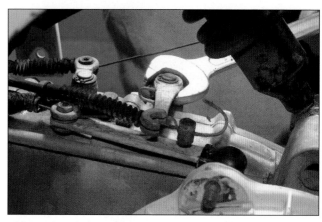

Slide the rubber cover off the gear arm/tie rod joint and remove the circlip and shim that hold them together.

Remove the two 10mm-head bolts that hold the cable adjuster block (and rear brake cable guide) to the top of the engine.

Remove the two gear lever arm support bracket bolts and the whole control cable assembly can be withdrawn as one. Note the gaskets employed under these brackets which may be saved for re-use. These are not essential and never supplied in gasket sets (but are available separately).

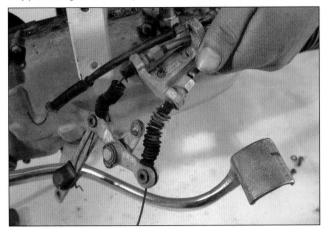

Ensure that the rear brake cable is undone at the brake pedal end, if you haven't already done so.

The rear shock is best removed by alternately tapping it top and bottom using a piece of wood as a drift. If the steel bushes are seized then the rubber around them can give way and the shock must be renewed. Spraying lubricant such as WD40 or Plusgas into the bush in advance can help avoid this.

Check that the stator plate wires and carb have been entirely disconnected from chassis before proceeding.

Undo one of the 24mm-head main engine pin ('bar', 'spindle') nuts and use a copper hammer to get the pin moving. These are often stiff so spray lubricant should be employed to ease movement. Tap the pin back and forth a few times to loosen it from the cones before trying to knock it right through. If you do need to hit it hard, wind one of the nuts back on to protect the thread.

Undo both nuts then put several washers on one end of the pin. Tighten one of the nuts over the washers to pull the engine pin through and start it moving.

It is always best to extract the engine pin towards the kickstart side of the scooter (as shown) because the flywheel side engine mount is weaker and can break if forced in other direction.

Once the pin is moving, knock it as far as you can into the engine mount and then use a drift to knock it right out. A 1/2-inch drive extension bar makes a good drift for this job but not a screwdriver! With the engine pin out (note that we forgot to undo the clips holding the stator wiring – doh!) the engine should now be entirely free. It is easier to lift the scooter off the engine rather than vice versa.

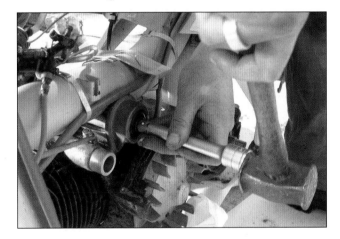

## Headset Removal

Undo the headlight rim and disconnect the white earth wire from the bulb holder. Pull the bullet connector, not the wire itself. Undo the bulb holder clip and remove the headlight unit.

Unscrew the headset top screws from below the main headset. This screw has a curved shake-proof washer.

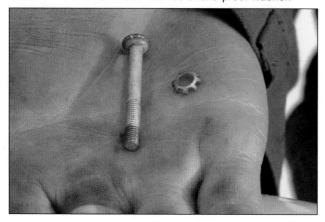

Push the speedo outer cable as far up through the forks as you can. This should release enough slack to lift the headset top. Unscrew the cable from the speedo and unplug the speedo bulb holder.

 **TOP TIP** **To prevent the speedo cable nut from falling down inside the forks attach an elastic band to hold it in place, or stuff paper into the top of the fork tube.**

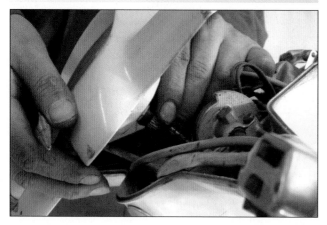

Detach the front brake cable by undoing the knurled adjuster nut. You may need to lever out the 'top hat' outer cable stop to free the cable completely. The speedo cable is detached from the hub by unscrewing the knurled aluminium nut.

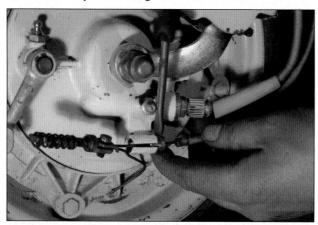

Undo the handlebar lever pivot bolt. As standard these use strange round-headed nuts underneath which can be loosened with pliers or vice grips before unscrewing the pivot bolt from above.

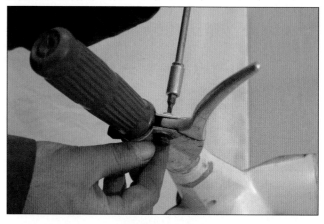

The lever pivot bolt, nut and star washer arrangement.

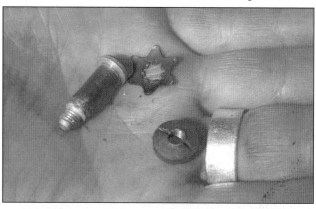

Be careful when withdrawing the levers since they should contain anti-rattle springs and caps which may fly out if you aren't prepared to catch them.

The end of any decent cable should be finished with a removable ferrule fitted over the end of the fixed nipple.

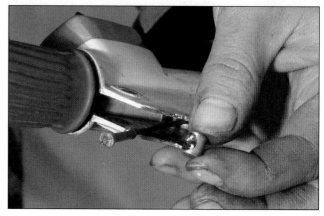

Depending on the type of cable used, you may now be able to withdraw it from inside the headset, but if the nipple is too large then the inner cable must be pulled out entirely. Since it will be badly kinked at the adjuster end it is better to cut the inner cable if withdrawal is required.

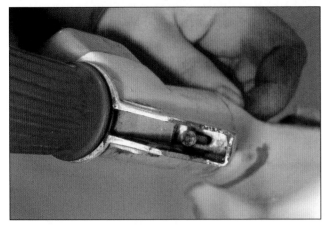

To remove the headset you will also need to detach the clutch, throttle and both gear cables before undoing the main clamp bolt with an 8mm Allen key.

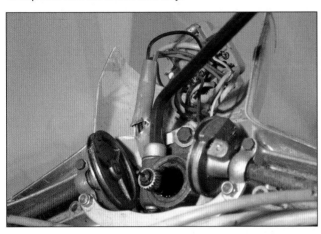

If you only need to get the forks out, it may be possible to undo the clamp bolt and lift the headset off the forks with many of the cables still attached. You may need to undo a couple of the cable ties to do so. The best technique is to hold the forks steady between your legs while lifting and twisting the headset from side to side.

# Front Wheel and Fork Removal

Start by undoing the two wheel spindle nuts. These have 21mm heads; which is the same as spark plug socket size. The wheel will not drop out until you pull out the special locating washers which sit in recesses in the fork links. Disc brake machines will also have the back-plate attached to the right hand link by a stud and nut arrangement which will also need to be loosened.

**Occasionally if the spindle is in poor condition you will find that the spindle nut on one side does not undo because both nut and spindle turn together. In that instance you need to find a thin spanner that will fit the other spindle nut behind the link. If you tighten that nut it should hold the spindle tightly enough to remove the outer nut. Some cycle spanners are thin enough for this job.**

A special C-spanner is used to loosen the fork locking ring.

**If you don't have the right C-spanner then it is possible – but not recommended – to loosen the locking ring by putting a chisel into the cutaways of the ring and tapping the ring loose with a hammer.**

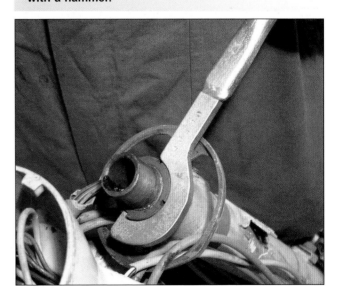

Next, lift off the spacer ring. Its internal tongue should be a good fit in the slot through the fork thread. If the tongue is damaged then review this spacer ring.

Another special tool is used to undo the top bearing race ('cone'). This tool is genuine Innocenti (and should be used the other way up!), but cheaper pattern ones are available.

**If you don't have the right spanner then it is possible – but not recommended – to loosen the locking ring by gripping the nut with a very large pair of vice or pipe grips.**

The forks should now drop through the frame and can be withdrawn.

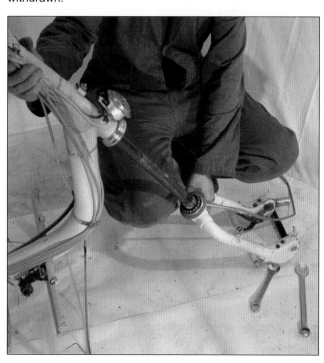

# WESTON SCOOTER PARTS
## Lambretta Specialist & Museum

Come and see the Largest Collection of Lambretta Scooters & Memorabilia in the World

# MANY ORIGINAL PARTS & ACCESSORIES IN STOCK
## Tel: 01934 614614 - Fax: 01934 620120
## Mobile: 07768 491663
### E-mail: enquiry@westonscooterparts.co.uk
### Website: www.westonscooterparts.co.uk
## Address: Weston Scooter Parts, 77 Alfred Street, Weston-super-Mare, Somerset, BS23 1PP

Opening Times: 10am-5.30pm Wednesday to Saturday & Some Sunday Mornings.
Closed All Day Monday & Tuesday

**Main Agents for**

### Casa Lambretta

# CHASSIS – CHECKING AND SELECTING COMPONENTS

## Frame

Before going to the trouble of painting and restoring a frame, first make sure it is straight. Most problems – even bent or twisted frame tubes – can be rectified if you are willing to spend the time and money to do it. In the UK there are companies with hydraulic jigs for straightening motorcycle frames and with ingenuity these could reasonably be employed to straighten a Lambretta frame. Italian restoration specialists Rimini Lambretta Centre instead commissioned this unique jig which they use to re-align damaged Lambretta frames.

 **A good way to check for frame and body alignment it to do a 'dry run' of all the major body components (sidepanels, legshields, running boards, horncasting, mudguard and headset) before painting. This way you can see if the floor struts or running board support arms are straight and carry out any 'adjustments' without damaging your paint. See the Chassis Rebuild chapter for assembly instructions.**

**Frame Alignment Check 1:** Measure from the bottom of the toolbox door opening to just above the weld on the headstock tube. This measurement should be 50cm for all series 3 machines.

 **If your measurements are out it doesn't necessarily mean that your frame has been in an accident. Particularly with Spanish or Indian frames it is not unusual to find that the seat arches or other brackets have been welded in the wrong position at the factory. In that instance it is possible to cut them off and weld them back in the correct position.**

**Frame Alignment Check 2:** On an early LI-TV machine the measurement from the top of the toolbox door opening to the chrome-ring should be 43cm. On later LI-SX-GP machines with no chrome ring the measurement to the steering cone should be 45cm. Variations of a few mm in production are normally nothing to worry about but if the measurements are a over a centimetre out it's a good pointer that the frame has been in an accident and may need straightening or scrapping.

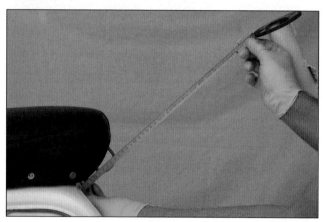

**Frame Alignment Check 3:** with the bottom bearing cone still in place look straight down through the headstock tube. When you are in line with the frame, the bottom bearing cone will be visible as a black ring. If the frame has had a hard front end knock the black ring will appear fatter at the front of the machine than it will at the back.

Stand bolts often pull through the frame strut ('cross-member'). If the holes have just been distorted then it is sufficient to hammer them flat with a ball pein hammer. If the holes have split then they could do with welding and repairing properly.

**Rather than hammering back distorted frames you can actually pull the cross-member back into shape by tightening thick metal support brackets either side of the hole.**

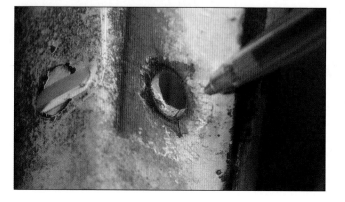

Early frames are fitted with this type of horn bracket mounting.

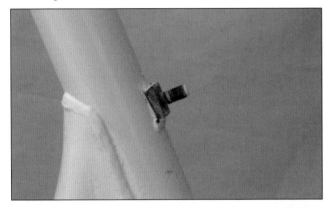

Later frames use this type of mounting.

Fit the small 'L' shaped rear footboard hanger bracket with its M7 bolts on the kickstart side. Use a straight edge to check the alignment of the cross-members ('floor struts') and floorboard support brackets on each side and adjust as necessary. Also check the security of the cross-members and re-weld if required.

If you have had the struts or seat arch welded back on you need to check that there is a visible gap between the tops of the struts and the bottom of the seat arch (approx 5mm) otherwise your floorboards won't fit back on without bending them.

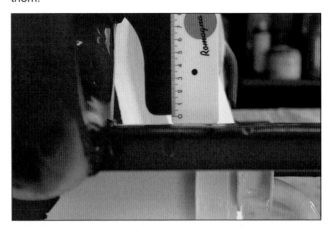

## Centre Stand

The easiest way to change stand feet is to cut or saw them opposite the locating pin.

Then prise the rubber off the pin.

These steel roll-pins very often seize into the stand. Knock them in a bit further to get them moving, then use a pin-punch from the other side to knock them right out.

Replacement stand feet should be supplied with new roll-pins. Nip up the leading edge in a vice to make them easier to fit.

 **Instead of using a roll-pin, screw an M6x40 stainless steel bolt into the rubber. It will fit straight into the stand without tapping a thread and makes stand foot replacement much easier when the feet wear out.**

Align the stand rubber with the hole in the stand and tap the roll-pin into place.

 **Several firms are now making polished metal stand feet for Lambrettas. These secure using grub screws so are much easier to fit. Make sure your stand cross-member is securely welded if these are used because they will put extra strain on the frame.**

 **If you do fit metal stand feet these will bash your running boards every time the stand comes up. Recent remade series 3 stands come with a built-in rebound buffer on the stand spring side and these may be employed to prevent damage.**

# Running Boards

LI-TV-SX running boards have a curved profile over which the sidepanel fits, whereas GP ones have a noticeable corner in the pressing.

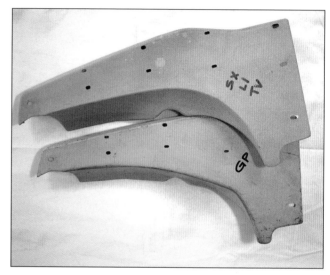

Late Italian GP and all Indian running boards have a steel support rib spot welded on the inside.

 **Welding such a support into the kickstart side of earlier running boards is a good idea to prevent damage from kickstart use.**

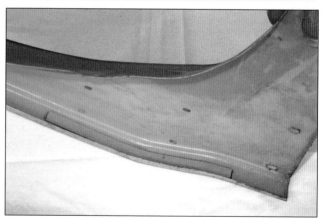

Running boards for most Spanish machines use rubber floor mats instead of plastic runners so do not have running strip fixing holes.

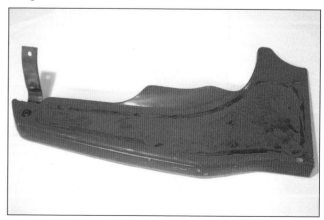

## Bridge Pieces

Two different bridge pieces were used during Italian production, with different rear rubbers to match. Early ones (top) are noticeably narrower.

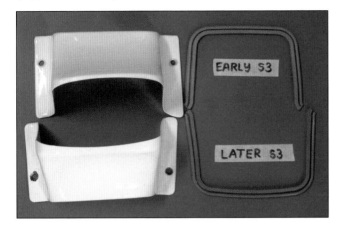

## Horncastings

The top horncast with the narrow grille and mounting for a shield badge is LI 125/150 (later 'series 4' LI was the same but takes a rectangular-type badge). The SX/TV-type horncast (centre) is the same length as LI, but uses a wider grille with a central rib. The GP horncast (bottom) is visibly shorter and uses a grille with no rib. The SX/TV and GP grilles are interchangeable for fit.

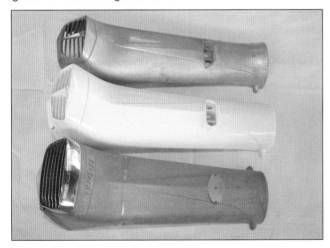

Early TV/Special-type machines using the chrome ring under the headset take a horncasting with these small cut-aways in. Later TV/Special and SX models (without the chrome ring) have a plain horncasting. You can't tell the difference by the part number – they are both the same.

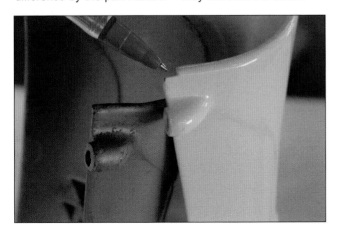

Late SX-type machines (and LI 4) have a horncasting to take the square badge (left), whereas that of the early SX (right) takes the shield type badge.

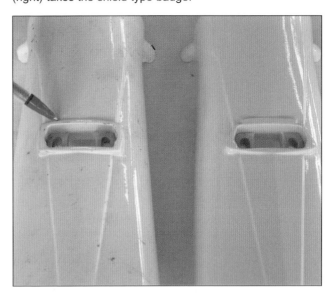

## Headset Identification

Headsets for early LI-TV-Special machines with the chrome steering lock ring are identifiable by the small gap of around 3mm between the bottom of the headset and the steering lock.

Later headsets have a much deeper casting to take up the space where the chrome ring would have been.

The headset tops of TV/Special models were also changed when the later 'non-chrome ring' headsets were introduced. This is the correct gap you should have with an early chrome ring TV/Special headset and headset top cast A1972.

The top for later Special/SX headsets (cast P1241) is narrower and leaves this nasty gap if fitted to an early 'chrome-ring' type handlebar.

SX-type headsets with this sort of cutaway are for Servetas which have headlight alignment screws protruding here.

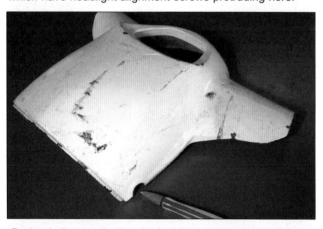

During Indian production the headset casting for the GP was revised to include lugs for mirror mounts and a thicker flared end with matching gearchange and switch housings.

The conditions of the headset clamp and chrome ring are important in order to get the correct clearance between your headset and bodywork. The clamps are easily distorted so it is often better to wire brush and paint them rather than re-plating them. A new replacement (right) is an alternative but Italian pattern ones are often poorly machined so that standard outer cables won't even fit into the positions provided until drilled to the correct diameter.

**If the outer cable holes are so big that the cables drop out it is possible to bend the clamp slightly to grip the outer cables more firmly.**

Early type gearchange castings (top) have thinner castings with a noticeable lump in the metal where the lever pivot bolt goes through. Holes that have been worn oval by seized pivot bolts are a common problem, cured only by replacement or welding and careful re-finishing. Mildly ovalised housings can be repaired by drilling both the lever and housing to accept an MB Developments oversized pivot bolt, which has an 8mm (rather than 7mm) shank.

As with the castings themselves being thin (early) or thick (late) there are also thick and thin levers to match. Either sort will function correctly, but if you are restoring a scooter properly you could do with the right type. Most remade Series 3 levers tend to be of the later, thick type. Series 2-type levers are different again and parallel along their length.

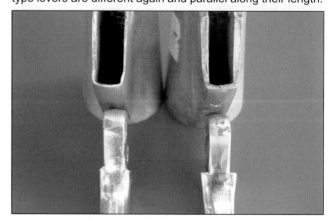

This is what it looks like if you fit late 'thick type' aftermarket levers onto an early headset. Classy . . .

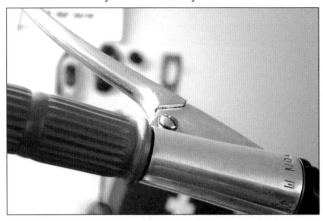

Original late-type GP levers (top) are a strange shape and have a very small ball-end. Earlier ball-ends (centre) had a larger ball, while remade levers (bottom) are often different again.

 **Later Serveta models were fitted with kinked 'dog-leg' levers as standard, and these can be an advantage to riders with small hands.**

Use a Dremel with a sanding attachment to remove any rust from inside the gearchange section so it will turn smoothly on the handlebar.

 **Lambretta gearchange castings are prone to wear where the outer cable sits, particularly if non-standard cables have been used. One solution is to bore the casting enough that a steel Vespa 'top hat' cable end can be fitted. These may need to be shortened slightly otherwise it can be impossible to select 4th gear on some types of headset.**

On early headsets a flat plate on the gearchange rod locates into the gearchange casting via a slot in the tube. This metal-to-metal join is prone to wear giving a sloppy gearchange action. Later types locate the rod using a plastic component which can also wear, but is more easily replaced.

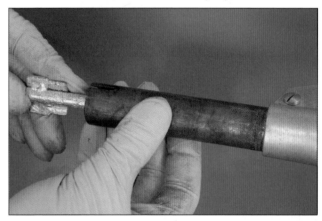

Some dealers suggest that welding these parts together – ensuring that the rod is straight and central – is probably the best way to cure unwanted slop. File the weld flat afterwards.

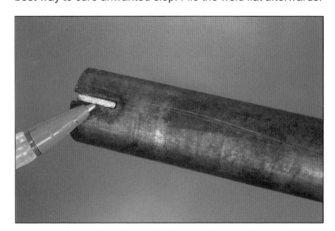

Series 3 gearchange rod components (right) use a plastic bush with a larger hole than series 2 for the rod, a large ring bush with a lip on it, and plastic (two types) rather than bronze 'olive' bushes for supporting the pulley end of the gearchange rod.

Because the clutch cable moves as you change gear it can get damaged as it rubs inside the headset. For this reason Dean at Rimini Lambretta Centre spends some time smoothing off the hole through which it passes.

Dean puts a smooth radius on the headset which helps the cables last longer.

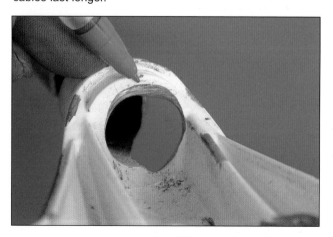

The headset clamp bolts to the headset from inside, with the nuts facing down. Do not forget the aluminium wiring bracket that fits to the front bolt.

Both a plastic bush and a thin metal ring fit between the headset and gearchange casting.

Another plastic bush should be tapped inside the headset end.

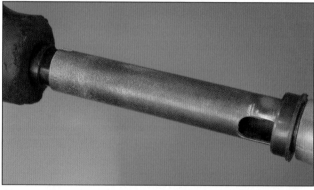

For a really pernickety restoration the screws which hold the metal arches and olives should be black Phillips heads with wavy washers. Note the position of the cable support brackets – which is facing up from the screws.

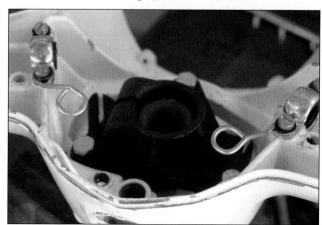

On early headsets the gearchange rod has a splined end, and the gear wheel is brass (or aluminium on Spanish machines) with a pinch-bolt arrangement. Later versions changed to plastic gear and throttle wheels, which are located on the rods by press-in roll-pins.

Most racers prefer this older-type arrangement which is less liable to ever come loose on the rod. Use thick grease – which won't easily be displaced by careless jet-washing – to lubricate all moving components.

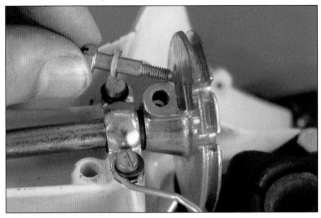

After fitting the gear wheel, pull the gearchange casting away from the headset. If you have a gap like this it can be solved by fitting shims to the gearchange rod.

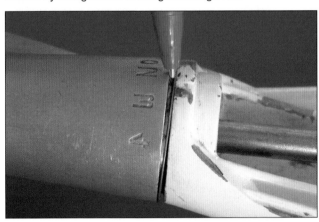

It may take more than one shim to take up all the play without making the gearchange difficult to turn. If it is too tight without shims it could be that the plastic bush needs filing down. First make sure that rust inside the gearchange itself is not the problem. Stainless shims in 0.5mm and 1mm are available from MB Developments.

 **Occasionally the U-shaped bracket can distort the olive enough to make the gearchange stiff. In that instance simply place a washer underneath the bracket to relieve the pressure a little.**

The switch housing fits to the headset with two short screws. Ensure that these screws are not so long that they foul on the wiring. Note that later Indian GP housings are cast considerably fatter than Italian ones.

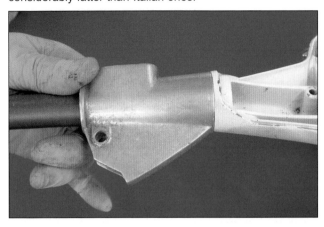

Feed the wiring from your light switch through the headset, then fit the two different-sized metal shims (smaller one goes on first) and throttle tube. Lastly fit the throttle rod and throttle pulley. This may need shimming in the same way that the gear side did in order to take up any slack.

 **Des from Gran Sport found that a good lubricant for fitting handlebar grips is spray paint. It slides when wet, but acts as a light adhesive once it dries. Hairspray also works.**

Grease inside the steering lock mechanism before fitting the lock itself.

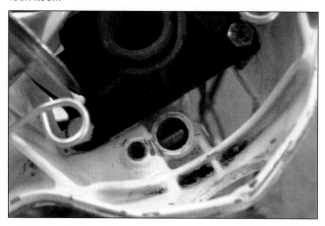

Pattern steering lock kits are available and do work adequately (though never rely on one to prevent theft). A grub screw retains the lock and a metal cap covers the other hole once assembled.

The ignition switch fits with a thin metal shim outside the headset and a knurled ring which should be fastened with a dab of Loctite. Some Indian switches have a second shim inside too. The wiring from the switch is held down with the aluminium tab as shown.

**Dean makes up a round terminal with two 8-inch earth wires to fit to the screw shown (right). One end has a bullet connector which plugs into earth terminal on the bulb holder. This connection is more reliable than the original earth through the headlight rim. The other wire is left bare to act as an earth for the important speedo light bulb (see Electrical Chapter) and simply fits inside the speedo housing before the speedo light bulb holder is pushed in to trap it.**

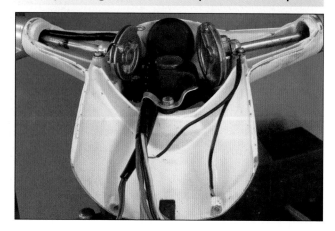

## Locks

Do not throw away original steering or ignition locks just because you have no key. Each should be stamped with a three figure number and Weston Scooter Parts can supply replacement keys from that code.

Toolbox locks fit from inside the toolbox door and are secured by special rivets.

## Legshields

It will be impossible to detail here all the numerous changes to legshields during production in respect to badge holes etc. With original legshields now rarer than honest politicians, it should suffice to find a good condition set of the right type (i.e. 'chrome ring', 'non-chrome ring', 'GP' etc) and drill or fill badge holes to suit. Remember that this is best done before you get them painted!

The very first sort of legshields (early chrome-ring type) is identifiable by nuts welded to the outside of the bracket which bolts to the frame.

On the brackets for later chrome-ring (and subsequent) machines the nuts were placed on the back of the bracket.

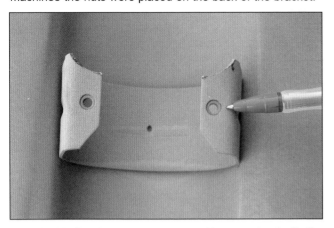

Legshields for chrome-ring type machines are basically flat up the centre of the spine.

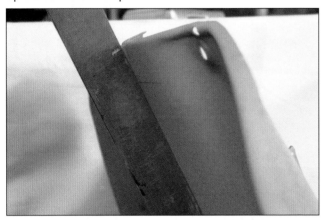

Later, non-chrome ring legshields are visibly flared backwards.

Italian chrome-ring type legshields have this sharp 90-degree lip at the top.

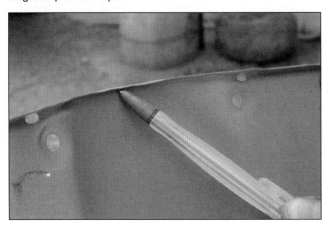

Serveta legshields (below) have a flat spine like the Italian chrome-ring type, but the lip is folded over completely.

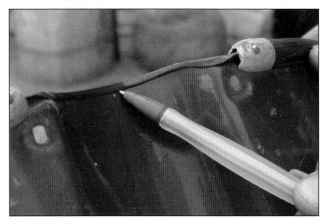

GP legshields are shorter than all the other types to match the shorter frame. They are more smoothly curved at the top, and narrow noticeably just ahead of the outer floor running strip.

# Front Mudguards

LI 125/150 and many Spanish models use a rounded mudguard though slight differences exist between the two types.

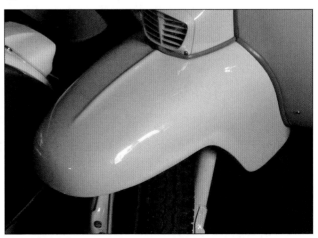

TV 175/Special/SX models use a shapely, more pointed metal mudguard. Most SX 150s had a chrome metal crest on the front mudguard as standard. TV 200s have this shape of mudguard but they are made from fibreglass as standard.

GP models have a sleeker metal mudguard with slimmer sides.

## Toolboxes

Early toolboxes were all manufactured from pressed steel. LI series 1 and LI series 2 type are identified by having very shallow cut-outs in the top mounting bracket (left). Series 1 type also have a rubber bung in the bottom. Series 3 toolboxes look virtually identical but the top mounting bracket has a much deeper cut-out (right).

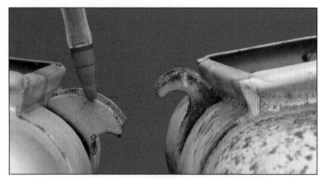

Grey plastic toolboxes (below) were introduced into late LI/Special/SX and early GP production. Later GPs used black plastic. Toolboxes featuring air filter housings are Serveta.

## Sidepanels

All LI-series sidepanels are interchangeable provided the correct panel clips are fitted to the rear of the frame. Early models with panel handles secure onto a thick wire W-clip. Italian machines made post-1969 – and subsequent Indian models – use thin wire spring clips that hook into the curved-up lip at the rear of the panel.

- Panels with a raised centre pressing running their entire length. Those with handles were fitted to LI series 3 125/150 and early TV 175/200 models. Similar ones without handles were fitted to late LI series 3 125 (which had frames stamped LI-4). The very earliest Italian type is marginally wider to accommodate the wider series 2-type fuel tank. Many Spanish models were also fitted with this style of panel and are clearly identified by noticeably wider pressings on the top of the panel where it fits to the frame.
- Panels with a rectangular indent pressed into the lower rear section and using '3-finger flash' ('knuckleduster') badges. These were fitted to later TV 175, TV 200, 125 and 150 Specials and SX 150.
- Panels pressed with an arrow-headed indent in the lower rear section and using a pointed '200' badge. This is a panel that is unique to the SX 200.

Panels with a triangular indent in the lower front and a recess for a plastic grille. These were fitted to all GP models. They were only ever produced in 'clip-on' form and originally featured 'speed stripes' running the length of the panel.

Below are the three early sorts of Slimstyle panel: SX 200 (left), early TV and LI 125/150 (centre), and late TV, SX 150 and LI 125/150 Specials (right).

## Rear Frame Grilles and Badges

Early machines used an aluminium housing containing various types of Perspex badge depending on model and year of production.

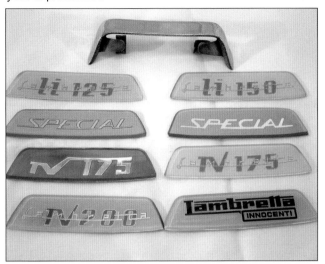

The first Italian GP models (below) used metal grilles painted the same colour as the scooter. Later, Innocenti converted to black plastic; which was used for all Indian GP production too.

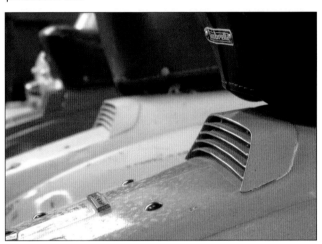

## Choke Lever Repair

Starting a Lambretta without a functioning choke can be quite tricky. Failure is sometimes due to a problem within the lever mechanism and often this can be simply repaired.

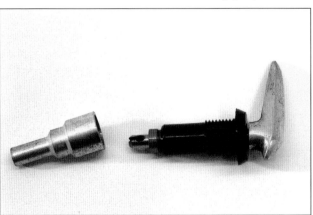

First pull back the brass cap. This uncovers a pin which should be removed to disassemble the mechanism.

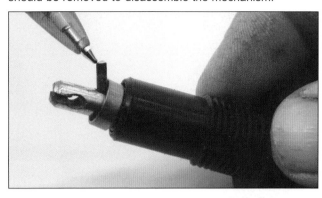

The most common fault is that the pin further up the lever – which works in a spiral slot – has become worn through use. Often it is possible to tap this pin through a little further – so it protrudes like the one shown – to get the mechanism working again.

## Cylinder Head Cowlings

LI series 1 (left) had a short cylinder, so Innocenti used a short cowling to match. Series 2 has a similar shaped – but longer – cowling with a small cutaway for the inlet manifold.

With the LI series 3 the cowlings got the addition of a spot-welded scoop. On later versions (right) the size of the inlet cutaway was increased. Serveta 125/150s tend to use the early type with small cutaways.

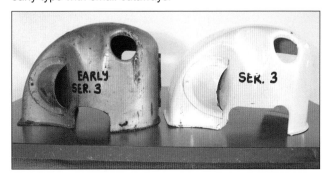

As series 3 (LI-SX-TV) production progressed the size of the exhaust cutaway was also increased (but still with straight edges) to give better access to the fixing studs and ease removal. Serveta 200s tend to use this mid-series 3 type cowling on the right.

Later series 3 and early GP production had an even bigger exhaust cutaway that was no longer flat along the top. This type allows the fitting of many performance pipes without modification.

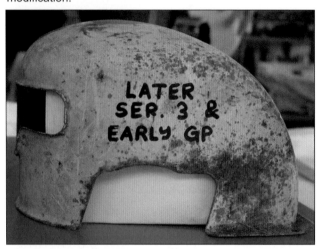

As production continued to the late GP models (right) the scoop was abandoned.

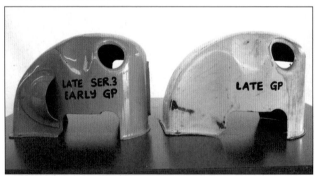

Late GP cowlings have an air divider welded inside.

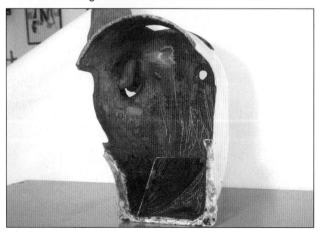

The reason that many people have rattling cowlings is that they don't fit the three fibre (not rubber) pads which are supposed to be glued inside the cylinder head cowling. Two of them are visible below.

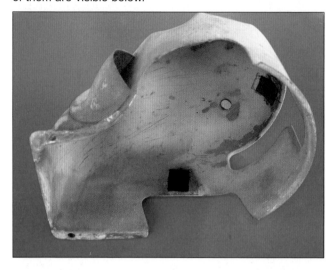

The third fibre pad is fitted above the inlet cutaway.

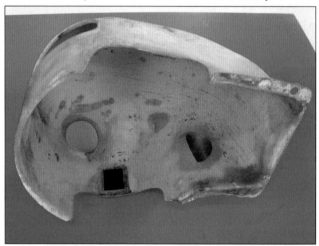

## Flywheel Cowlings

Early cowlings for LI series 1 and 2 are shallower and have no holes around the rim for rubber grommets. The pressing features 2 concentric rings around the centre and a welded tag for the air hose overflow pipe.

Series 3 cowlings are visibly similar but taller and feature four holes to take rubber grommets.

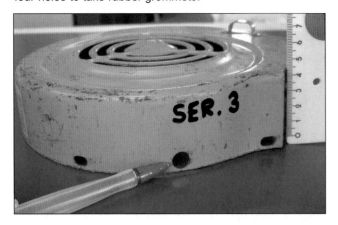

Early TV 175 series 3 cowlings are unique. Instead of grommets there are pressed indents to grip the mag housing.

GP cowlings are similar to LI series 3 ones, but only have a single ring in the pressing. Later ones have no tag for an overflow pipe. On the very last Italian production (GP Electronic etc.) the rubber grommet holes were abandoned once more.

Late Indian GP Electronic machines have taller fins on the flywheel and the cowling is taller to suit. There is also a matching wide cylinder head cowling for these machines.

Serveta cowlings only have a single ring in the pressing like GP, but it is more to the outside whereas a GP one is central.

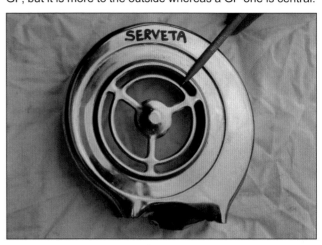

## Air Filter Boxes

The air filter box may seem an innocuous part, but if your carb set-up breathes through one then the different types can make a massive difference to performance and jetting. Innocenti regularly revised their construction through various models as you can see in the following pictures.

**Spanish machines used different air filter systems to the Italian type. From the early 1970s they located the air filter in the toolbox and allowed it to breathe through a louvered toolbox door. At the time of writing filters for these systems have only recently been remade after many years of unavailability.**

For the Lince (Lynx) model of the 1980s Serveta did away with the conventional toolbox altogether and had a different type of filter box breathing through the conventional hole but with no air scoop.

On series 1 and 2 machines the air filter and elbow are retained by a long stud and wing-nut arrangement (left and centre), but this was changed to a spring clip for series 3 machines (right) and subsequent models. As you can see, all air filter boxes are not made equal. The wide 41mm neck on the late LI series 1 and TV 175 series 2 (left) breathes much more freely than the restricted 18mm neck on the LI series 2 (centre) airbox. The last series 2 airboxes (not shown) still have the small 18mm neck, but feature a spring clip fitting for the filter and elbow like that of the Series 3 airboxes (right).

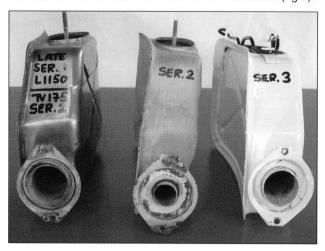

The early series 3 airbox (fitted to LI, TV 175 and even some TV 200) has a concave side that faces the fuel tank. This sits right up against one side of the filter and effectively blocks air flow through it.

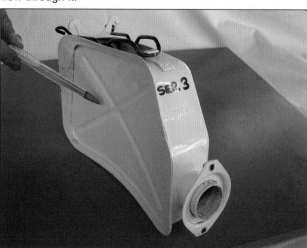

In later production of series 3 machines, Innocenti improved the airbox pressing with a bulge that allowed air to get all round the filter.

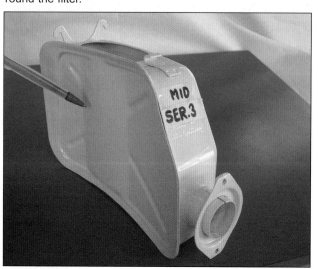

On the last series 3, late SX and GP models (right) strengthening ribs were pressed into the flat side of the airbox.

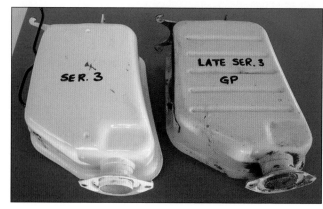

There is a curved baffle inside series 3 airboxes which restricts airflow if you intend to run larger carbs through an original air filter system. Some tuners suggest drilling holes in the airbox to improve flow (which was done as standard to some Indian GPs supplied to Turkey) but this allows the carb to breathe dirty, warm air from under the panels. A better solution is to chop off the top of the box, cut out the baffle and then weld the neck back on (right). Note that this makes a drastic change to airflow so you will need to fit a larger jet than normal to suit.

**The small grinding disc attachments for Dremel drills can usefully be employed to cut out this elbow without the need to remove the airbox neck.**

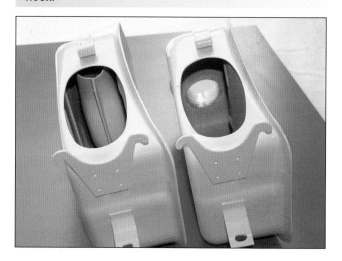

## Air Scoops

Typically Innocenti made several changes to the air scoop under the seat to match the different airboxes. The early scoops are short in length. The restrictive Series 2 type also uses a restrictive slotted scoop (left). The earlier wide necked LI series 1 and TV 175 airboxes are matched with a gaping scoop (right).

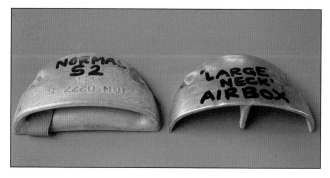

Series 3 machines with 18 and 20mm carbs (left) feature a longer scoop with a restrictive baffle cast into it. This baffle was removed for the GP machines using the larger 22mm carb as standard.

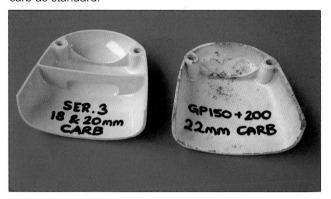

If you want to run a 22mm or larger carb on your scooter then you would do well to fit either a GP air scoop or modify the earlier type by removing the baffle.

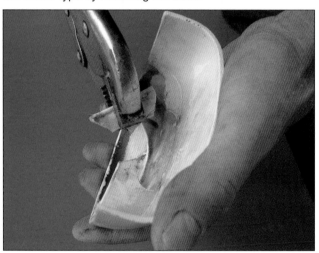

# Air Filter Elbows and Rubbers ('Hoses')

Early series 2 air filter elbows (not shown) have a large hole for the stud and wing nut arrangement that mounts them. Later 'spring clip' series 2 type (and subsequent) have this smaller hole for the bolt that holds in the air filter. When the series 3 type was introduced (right) the casting was simplified.

The GP air filter elbow (right) is longer – because it uses a shorter rubber - and features a flat section which we have marked with an outline.

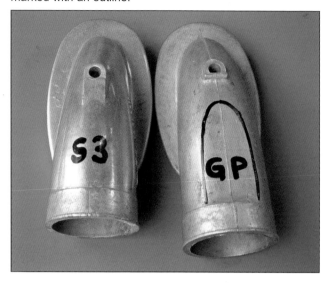

Note the change in inlet rubbers through the series of GP production as the overflow pipe was abandoned.

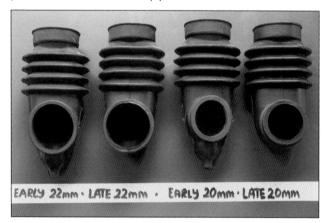

Series 3 inlet rubber with drain valve (left). Late non-frame-breather series 1 and all series 2 use the longer thinner version (right).

The drain valves are prone to leaking, so it does no harm to seal them to the rubber with Loctite when rebuilding.

## Fuel Tanks

Most LI-series fuel tanks look externally similar, but typically there are important differences between them.

Early LI series 1 tanks have this open tube at the bottom which acts as a breather to prevent vacuum build-up as the fuel level goes down.

Later series 2 and 3 models abandoned the breather pipe in the tank and instead had a vent drilling in the tubular handle of the fuel cap (left). Always check that this is clear and free to breathe, and never fit an early type cap (right) to a late tank unless you are fond of heat seizures.

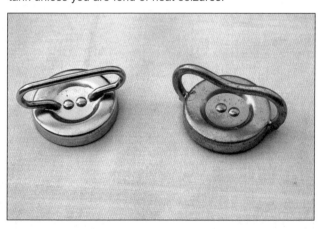

Series 2 and very early series 3 tanks (left) are difficult to distinguish from later series 3 ones (right). Look closely though and you will see that the series 2 tank is actually wider (taller in this pic) by about 1cm. This extra width can cause clearance problems with the sidepanels if fitted to a late series 3 machine by mistake. Early series 3 models had slightly wider sidepanel pressings to compensate.

**The pressings for the fuel tanks got more and more worn out over the years with the later GP type often showing visible ripples in the metal. If you want to chrome a tank then mid-series LI ones are normally better.**

Serveta fuel tanks (upper) do not taper in at the top like Italian series 3 ones and actually hold slightly more fuel.

Rusty fuel tanks can be re-used if all the loose rust has been dislodged and the surface is then treated with a proprietary sealing compound such as Petseal. Weston Scooter Parts built this rig to clean old fuel tanks. Firstly the tank outlet is fitted with a sealed nut, then special polishing stones and a mixture of water and detergent (e.g. washing-up liquid) are placed inside. A cap with a soldered-up breather hole is fitted. The tank is strapped into the rig which slowly rotates it for an hour or two to dislodge all the loose rust. Only once the stones are removed and the contents washed clean is the tank dried and treated with Petseal.

# WHEELS, BRAKES, STEERING AND SUSPENSION

## Front Wheel Removal

 Before removing your front wheel from the forks, test for bearing wear. Grip the tyre and rock it side to side between the fork legs. If there is any noticeable side-play at the wheel rim then the bearings should be renewed.

First disconnect the front brake cable by undoing the adjuster nut and detaching the outer cable. Also unscrew the speedo cable nut and remove the cable. On drum brake models (except TV series 2 drums) once the 21mm-head nuts (spark plug socket size) are loosened and the locating washers pulled away from the links the wheel will drop down and the brake back-plate can be pulled away from the locating peg on the fork link. On disc brake hubs, where the brake back-plate is located by stud and nut to a slot in the fork link, this nut must first be loosened before the wheel can be removed.

 Occasionally if the threads are in poor condition you will find that the spindle nut on one side does not undo. In that instance you need to find a spanner (such as from a bicycle toolkit) that will fit the other spindle nut behind the link. If you tighten that it should hold the spindle enough to remove the outer nut.

 If one of the nuts won't move, tighten the loose one and this should grip the spindle enough to undo the tight one.

 Removing Lambretta disc brakes which have been converted to hydraulic operation can prove a problem because it is better not to dislodge the hose connection. In this case place a box or milk crate near to the front of the scooter so that the wheel can be placed on it while still attached to the hose. On some conversions it may be possible to unscrew the hydraulic slave cylinder from the back-plate. Later conversions using external brake calipers have no such problem since it is easy to remove the caliper from the hub.

## Wheel Studs

On all but the earliest models, the wheel studs are screwed into the hub using a left-hand thread and have a very thin 12mm hex-head (or 13mm on the remade versions). The idea is that these are replaceable in the event of damage, but in practice they are very hard to remove. The recommended removal method is to hold the head of the stud in a quality vice and turn the hub CLOCKWISE to undo the left-handed thread.

 It is worthwhile modifying a six-sided socket especially to remove wheel studs 'on the road'. Use a grinder to take the last 2mm off the end of the socket so that the thin 'head' of the stud is gripped properly. Heat the hub and if there is any useable thread remaining 'double nut' it and use the lower nut to assist in loosening the stud. Do not forget that these have a LEFT-HANDED THREAD.

 M8 bolts may be used in place of proper studs in an emergency but check for clearance at the bolt head when used on the rear hub and grind down a little as necessary.

## Front Drum Hub Strip

Remove the spindle nuts and location washers, followed by the lock-nut from the back-plate side of the hub. If the spindle turns while trying to undo the nut, then apply the brake by pushing on the brake arm.

 TV 175 drum brake hubs have a shouldered spindle like a disc brake hub so there is only one lock-nut on the hub side to undo.

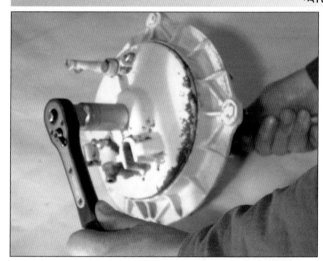

Lift the brake back-plate off the spindle. The front brake of our LI was covered in grease indicating a problem with the central grease seal.

The lip of the grease seal had been turned inside out and damaged when the hub was last rebuilt, or more likely by over-filling the speedo drive grease nipple.

Remove the circlips, spring plate and flat plate holding the shoes in place. A small screwdriver can help to lift off the circlips once the pliers have opened them. GP drum brakes use single piece wire 'W'-clips instead of separate circlips and plates. These are only interchangable as a unit.

Turn the brake arm so the shoes are as wide apart as possible. Lever one shoe up, one end at a time.

 **If the shoes are seized on the pins then cut the spring and apply heat to each shoe to encourage it to come loose from the pin. The pins are cast into the hub and should not come loose.**

Lever out the front hub oil seals.

There is a spacer bush inside the inner seal which must be kept safe before the seal is removed.

You can rest the hub on a stack of two wheels to knock the bearings out. A 3/8-drive extension bar will shift the bearings, but throw them away afterwards. Any bearing knocked out by the middle of the race may reasonably be regarded as knackered.

With the inner bearing and spacer tube removed you can now remove the circlip so that this outer bearing can be drifted out from the other side.

# Front Wheel Hub Identification

Late LI series 1 and LI series 2 (also some early series 3) front drum hubs are basically circular in outer profile.

Serveta Front wheels are circular like Series 2 but generally have no grease nipple fitted to the hub.

Later series 3 (LI-SX-TV) drum hubs have a pointed profile, but still use grease nipples on the speedo drive and brake cam.

For later models (e.g. GP) the front hub was simplified and the fitting of grease nipples was abandoned. All drum hubs (apart from TV) locate onto a peg on the fork link.

TV175 series 1 drum hubs featured stud and nut location into disc-type fork links, and this unique position for the grease nipple. The wheel studs are also splayed at the rear rather than having nut heads.

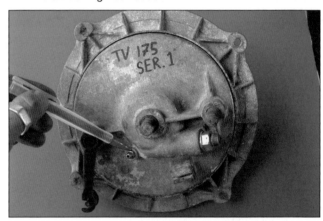

TV 175 series 2 drum back-plates are still stud and nut fixing, but the grease nipple position has been revised.

Disc brake back-plates. Early type TV-SX ones (left) have a large hole either side of the operating mechanism and a speedo drive grease nipple. Later ones (right) have smaller holes and the grease nipple point is blanked off.

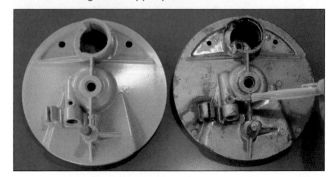

# Speedo Drive

Unscrew the speedo drive retaining nut from the back-plate. These are often hard to get out and are vulnerable to damage so use a six-sided socket.

Check that all the helical teeth on the speedo drive are in good condition, otherwise renew.

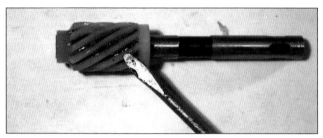

Also check the condition of the drive on the hub.

 **Getting reliable speedo drive components can be a problem. MB Developments have recently had metal drive gears remade which can be fitted to series 3 hubs.**

If you need to change the drive gear on the hub it must first be ground flat on one side.

When the drive has been ground thin enough it will crack and may be lifted off with a screwdriver. The replacement may be warmed in boiling water and tapped into place. Loosely fitting replacements should be Loctited into place.

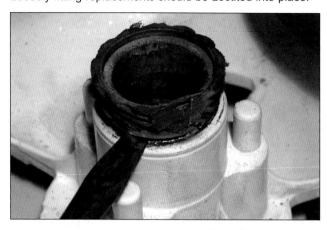

# Front Drum Rebuild

Getting everything clean is the most important thing to do when rebuilding brakes. Remove the front brake cam and grease the shaft so it moves freely before continuing.

**When restoring it is tempting to zinc or chrome-plate the wheel spindle. Do not do this because a plated spindle will be fractionally fatter and can get stuck inside the wheel bearings. Always check that your spindle will slide through the bearings before building your hub. No force should be required.**

The large seal in the back-plate locates with its flat side facing towards you.

Unless they are badly worn or contaminated with grease then old brake shoes can be reused – particularly old Innocenti ones which contain asbestos and often work better than many modern replacements. Thoroughly clean with brake cleaner and then sand the top layer of the shoe just enough to remove any shiny high-spots.

**Beware of brake dust from original brake shoes – it contains asbestos which is harmful if inhaled.**

**To minimise the chances of brake locking, lightly chamfer the leading and trailing edges of each shoe. Also polish the pivot pins and apply a very sparing amount of copper grease to the pins before the shoes are fitted.**

**When fitting new brake shoes cover over the friction surfaces with masking tape to keep them clean until the hub goes back together.**

 **Rebuilt brakes should be run-in by keeping heavy braking to a minimum for around 100 miles of urban use.**

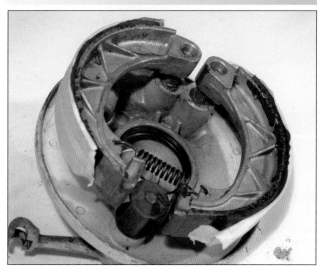

Tap new, thoroughly-greased wheel bearings into place using a socket or drift that rests on the outer track of the bearing.

 **Many re-builders now used sealed or semi-sealed bearings (with the seals facing out) in Lambretta front hubs.**

 **Specific drifts for these bearings and seals are now available from scooter tool specialists.**

Next fit the retaining circlip

There is some argument about the way the outer seal fits. The old Home Workshop Manual suggests it should be with the spring side facing out so that any excess grease forced in via the grease nipple can escape past the seal. On later machines with no grease nipple and using sealed or semi-sealed bearings it is pointless to do this, so most people now build these with the spring side of the seal facing in.

Thoroughly grease inside the bearing recess and fit the inner spacer tube.

Fit the inner bearing. Do not hit it in too far or the bearings will become tight on the spacer tube. Align the tube with the centre of the bearings using a screwdriver.

**A fork link bolt pushed up through the outer bearing will help to align the spacer tube and inner bearing as they are fitted.**

**Never knock a bearing in without a speedo drive ring being fitted, because doing so invariably cracks the hub.**

A spark plug socket can be used to knock the oil seal in, again with spring side facing out. Again there is some disagreement about this and many modern builders now fit the inner seals with the spring side facing the bearing. Since there are greased components on both sides of this seal, this isn't really too important.

Make sure the inside of the hub is clean and remove any surface rust with wet and dry paper. Do not forget to fit the plain or 'top hat' steel spacer bush inside the oil seal before continuing.

 **If your freshly painted front hub grates when assembled because the coating is too thick then a 12mm gear arm shim can be added to the spacer bush to give a little more clearance.**

Fit the back-plate to the hub and push the spindle through before doing the inner spindle nut up against its washer (if fitted).

On the other side fit the steel 'top hat' spacer over (and into) the oil seal before doing up the nut. On later models only a plain tubular steel spacer was fitted here.

It is vital that these axle threads are in good condition. If not, then clean-up the thread with a thread file.

If you haven't already greased everything during assembly then do so now with a grease gun, but take care not to over-fill.

## Disc Brake Front Hubs

The Lambretta cable-operated internal front disc brake was a huge technological advance during its day, but many British buyers were initially unimpressed by its efficiency. As a result softer, grippier pads were fitted to machines destined for the UK. Nowadays there are many more effective front brakes available including hydraulic conversions to the original cable disc hub or full external disc brake conversions.

The original disc brake features a thick steel disc which 'floats' (is free to move) on three pins mounted into the main hub, allowing it to centralise between the pads and adjust for pad wear. The brake back-plate is cast to accept a 'ball and ramp' actuator which pushes one pad against the surface of the disc when the arm is pulled. The back-plate casting extends around the disc opposite the moving pad to contain the 'static pad'; which must be adjusted through windows in the hub to sit in the correct position.

Removal of the disc brake is the same as for a drum, except the right-hand suspension damper must be dismounted to allow access to loosen the brake plate retaining nut on its stud. Disc brake spindles do not use a tightening nut on both sides. The disc brake is dismantled by undoing the lock-nut on the hub side of the wheel spindle.

Knock the spindle out with a copper or nylon-faced hammer.

The back-plate and hub will not come apart until the disc comes off the three pins cast into the hub. If the brake disc is seized onto the pins then first push in the disc 'windows' and remove them. Spray some freeing oil onto the pins and then begin to tap the disc down the pins using a drift, alternating between each of the four hub 'windows'.

 Do not rest the drift on the polished brake surface itself, but instead rest it on the raised boss area in the centre of the disc.

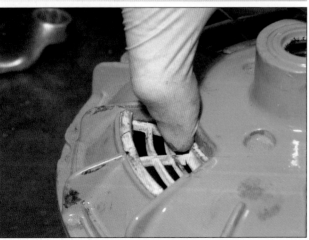

This hub is typical of a badly restored machine. Everything – including the oil seals – has been spray painted without being disassembled or masked.

Remove the seals and bearings from the hub as described for stripping a drum hub.

**If you plan to have your front brake painted (or particularly powder coated) by someone who isn't a Lambretta specialist then it may be best to mask up vulnerable parts yourself to prevent them being coated. Lambretta rubber engine bump stops are the ideal size to protect the centre of the hub where the bearings fit. On disc hubs also take care to mask up the entire area where the disc slides, including the three pins.**

Standard machines are fitted with a large anti-rattle circlip inside the disc. This must be in excellent condition and not worn if viewed through the three pin holes. If it does appear worn you can just tap it round a little to a part of the circlip that is still in good condition.

**Improved braking performance can be obtained by removing the anti-rattle circlip. The disc will centralise better between the pads, but it will also rattle on its pins at walking pace, which does sound terrible.**

Most aftermarket disc brake pads are painted to a slightly larger diameter than will actually fit in the hub, so the pad edges must be carefully cleaned up first. The minimum acceptable thickness of used pads is 3mm. Note: Using a bench grinder with bare hands is not advised.

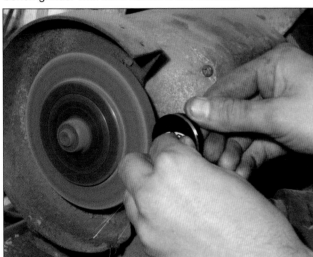

With the edges of the pads cleaned up, the static pad should first be located in its housing.

Rusty or glazed discs can be bead blasted or cleaned-up with emery cloth to leave a matt surface. Fit the disc into the groove in the back-plate so that it holds the static pad in position. Note that the raised boss in the disc faces away from the back-plate.

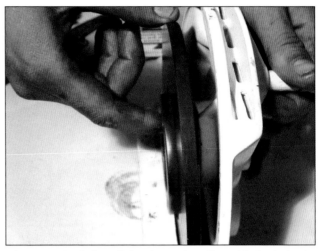

Now turn the hub until the three pins align with the holes in the disc. These pins are unevenly spaced and will only fit into the disc in one position.

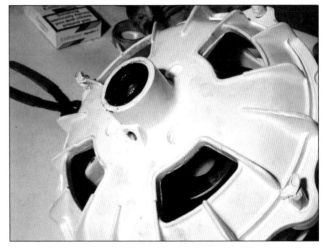

Fit the spindle. This is shouldered so that it can only be fitted from the back-plate side. Ensure that the hub turns correctly if it has been repainted.

Now fit the floating pad, which can be given a light coating of brake grease (or copper grease) on its back surface to prevent brake squeal.

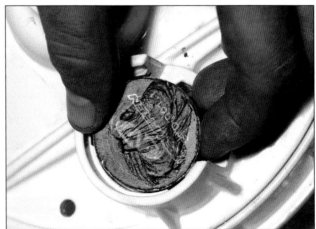

The balls and ramps of the actuator mechanism can be lubricated sparingly with high melting point grease or a very tiny amount of heavy oil before fitting.

When fitting the actuator it is vital that the groove cut into the casting is in perfect condition. The circlip should be fitted securely into the groove of the casting. Tap it round a little to ensure it is firmly seated.

A pressed steel 'I'-cap covers the actuator mechanism. A drop of Loctite will keep it in place.

Before a cable or hydraulic disc conversion is put into service the static pad must be adjusted. The assembly comprises of an Allen-headed grub screw, a locknut and a tab washer. Many re-builders now use a shake-proof washer as an alternative to the tab washer.

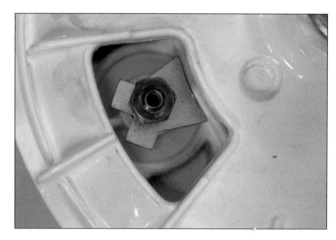

Wind the grub screw in until it locks on the disc, then wind it back half a turn. Hold the grub screw in position while the lock-nut is tightened. If you don't have a suitable cranked spanner then this can be done by holding a socket in a pair of Mole grips and using that to tighten the nut.

Once the lock-nut is tight, bend up the tab washer to secure it. Fit and lubricate all grease nipples as required.

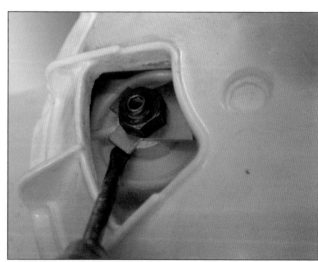

## Rear Wheel Removal

A Lambretta 'jack' stand is a good thing to keep in your toolbox since it allows you to change the rear wheel without putting your scooter on its side. The stand can also be used from the other side unless you use oversized tyres or rims.

On our LI the wheel rim nuts were 14mm-head nylocs, while those that held the wheel to the hub were 14mm-head dome nyloc nuts. Unless you want a perfect restoration there is nothing wrong with using 13mm-head nuts, but it is still a good idea to use nylocs for the rim nuts and dome nuts for the hub nuts with split or wavy washers underneath. By using different types it is easier to undo only the wheel nuts and not the rim nuts by mistake.

 **Before removing the wheel, feel round the back of the hub for the heads of the studs to make sure you are about to undo the correct nuts.**

On this early machine the panel handle clip is held in an upright position by a small bracket near the rear mudguard. This isn't very helpful since it means the rear tyre must be deflated a little to fit the wheel. As such many people chose to remove the bracket for an easier life. On later models with handle-type panels this top retaining bracket was omitted and the clips were free to move enough to get the wheel in and out while still inflated. The last sorts of panels (without handles) had wire spring clips (fitted using a simple bracket) that simply hook into the lip at the bottom of panel.

A Phillips screwdriver pressed into the valve will let a tyre down, if required. Alternatively you can purchase a special tool to unscrew the valve core to let the air out more effectively.

 **Some specially-moulded valve caps can be turned around and used to unscrew the valve core to deflate a tyre.**

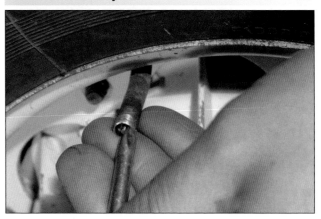

The back wheel can now be withdrawn.

## Rear Hub Removal

First undo the Allen screw which holds the hub-nut locking plate.

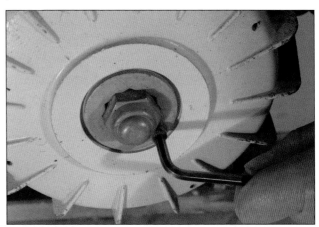

 **Pattern Allen screws are very often of poor manufacture and a sloppy fit on the key; which can make them hard to shift: particularly if Loctited into place. Should this be the case then use an Allen bit on a socket wrench and also grip the head of the screw with a pair of Mole grips. Combined turning of both the ratchet and the grips should shift even the most stubborn screw.**

The traditionally recommended way to hold the hub while the nut is undone is to put a ring spanner onto the end of the brake arm and lever the brake on hard while the nut is loosened.

 **In practice locking the brake is hard to do on your own and may not be successful if the shoes are worn or the rear hub oil seal has leaked. A more effective method is to construct a holding tool by welding or even bolting some box-section metal to an old wheel rim as shown below. This tool can be rested against the floor, frame or engine casings to hold the hub while the nut is undone or fastened.**

If you are using the commonly available three-bolt pattern hub puller it is wise to use an M7 thread tap to clean the bolt holes or at least spray brake cleaner into them.

 **Note that some Indian and pattern hubs only have M6 locking screw threads rather than M7.**

 **Discard the supplied puller bolts and instead replace them with longer, fully-threaded bolts ('set screws') and nuts. These can be wound to the full depth of the holes to take advantage of every available thread. Tighten the nuts against the puller before doing up the centre bolt.**

Once the centre bolt gets tight, give it a sharp tap to shock the hub off. Continue alternately tightening and tapping until the hub comes loose.

**Really tight hubs require removal with a workshop type tool: either the type shown below, or one which bolts to the four wheel studs.**

**The (inadvisable) bodger's way to get the hub off is to fit the rear wheel, put a piece of wood against it and hit that with a large hammer. Turn the wheel and hit the wheel on different sides to shift it off the shaft. The problem with this method is that it risks distorting the wheel or hub.**

## Identifying Rear Hubs

Lambretta rear hubs used three different cone angles and it is imperative that the hubs and cones match. The sharply-pointed 20 degree cones of stearly hubs are easily distinguishable. This was later changed to 11 degrees (hub part numbers starting 1904 or 1994), and finally 8 degrees for the GP type (part numbers starting 1954). As a rule replacement hubs are normally supplied with new cones and these should always be used.

Series 1 and early Series 2 rear hubs only have two holes and will need a modified locking ring if desired as none was originally fitted.

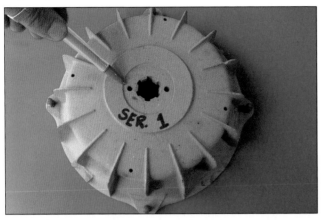

Early Series 1 hubs have the studs peened over at the back rather than the removable ones with a hexagon head.

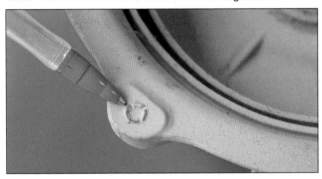

Series 3 hubs have three threaded holes and a recess for the locking plate.

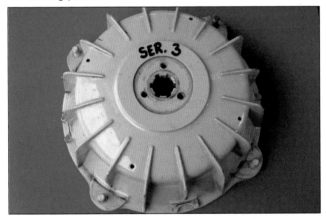

Serveta hubs (right) look similar to series 3 ones, but have a noticeable lip where they are thicker around the brake lining. They are also heavier. In good condition Serveta hubs are the best available.

Later SX and GP type hubs do not have a recess around the locking ring, and have a double lip around the brake lining.

## Top Tips for an Effective Rear Brake

- Use a thick rear brake outer cable (Indian ones are fine) with a good quality inner. The outer cable has to be exactly the correct length (65cm) for optimum efficiency.
- The problem with old hubs is that very few are actually round. If you take the rear wheel off, spin the hub and look from the back, most old hubs demonstrate a kink or warp where they have been whacked off with a bit of wood or lump hammer at some time in the past. As far as replacements go Serveta hubs were the best available, but are now hard to find. Genuine SIL Indian GP rear hubs and brake shoes do actually work pretty well and are strong, but not all Indian hubs are to the same standard. On the pot-holed roads of Ireland for the Euro Lambretta rally it was those with Indian hubs that had the least trouble. At the time of writing Italian remade FA rear hubs are the most commonly supplied spare, but these are usually fitted with very poor quality studs and are not highly regarded. Also check the fit with pattern rims which may need to be centralised on FA hubs.
- Use good quality brake shoes. The best are New Old Stock (NOS) Innocenti ones which were made with asbestos. It is possible to clean up old shoes if not too worn or oily with brake cleaner and careful sanding but DO NOT BREATHE THE DUST. Of the remade ones Ferrodo and Adige are good quality. Not all other Italian brands are so good.

## Rear Brake Reassembly

First ensure you have the correct brake shoes for the cam you are going to fit.

There are three common types of rear brake cam. The LI/TV/SX type (left) is thick and uses brake shoes part no. 15044040. The GP type (centre) has a narrower cam face and uses brake shoes part no. 22044040. The offset type (right) is from a Serveta and uses the same brake shoes as LI/SX.

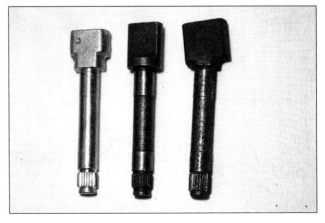

Clean, assemble and grease the shaft of the rear brake cam. A washer sits under the head of the cam before it is inserted into the casings. At the other end an O-ring is fitted first, then the brake lever followed by a washer and finally the circlip.

 **TOP TIP** **If you assemble with a fatter 12x2.5 or 12x3mm O-ring and leave out the washer under the circlip, you can seal the shaft better against the elements.**

When assembling your rear hub and brake shoes, ensure that the brake shoe cam is in the correct way round. Some cams are punched with a dot, and this dot must face upwards with the engine in place.

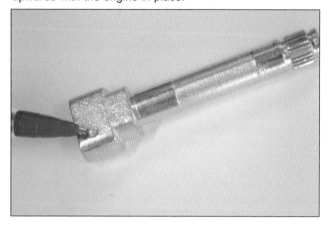

There are even differences between the fat LI-type cams. The one with the wider face (below) is preferable to the narrow one.

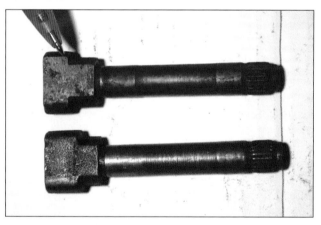

Clean and grease the brake cam before fitting it to the casings. Very lightly grease the pivot pins with copper grease. If you use too much it can get onto the linings and reduce braking efficiency, so clean off any excess.

Connect the tension spring between the shoes, place the ends over the cam and then pull the shoes apart at the pivot ends until they can be slid over the pins. Tap them down into place.

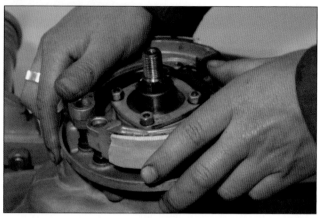

The shoes are held in place first by a flat bridge plate, then a wavy pressure plate, and finally by the circlips. On later models the use of separate circlips was abandoned and a single 'W'-shaped wire clip was used instead. The W-circlips fit onto specifically machined pivot pins and do not use either the bridge or wavy plates.

## Rear Hub Refitting

Fit the thin shim before fitting your rear hub cone. Make sure the split in the cone is located above one of the splines rather than over a gap.

Fit the hub. Original rear hub nuts are nyloc. They fit over a wavy washer and are held in position by a locking ring. It is worth renewing the hub nut after regular use to keep the nyloc fresh.

Make sure the wavy washer used is not wider than the nut otherwise it will prevent the locking plate from sitting flat. Also ensure that it is not of the thicker Series 1&2 type since these sit the nut up so high that the nut can come undone even with the locking ring in place. MB Developments produce a thicker stainless steel locking ring that eliminates this problem.

Stop the rear hub moving with a holding tool or force on the rear brake arm. Tighten the hub nut up to a torque setting of 15 – 16.5 kg-m (110 - 120 lbs-ft) for 8 or 11 degree cone hubs or 20.7 kg-m (150 lbs-ft) for early 20 degree cone hubs. Tighten to the lower figure to begin with.

If you are lucky one of the holes in the locking plate will be in line with the one in the hub. If not turn the plate until it is as close as possible to a hole and then tighten some more until it lines up and the Allen locking screw will fit. Never loosen the nut to align the holes. Never use a worn locking plate that is a sloppy fit on the hub nut. Add a little Loctite Screwloc to the Allen screw before fitting it and torquing to 1.4 – 1.5 kg-m. The locking plate should sit flat against the hub when everything is correct.

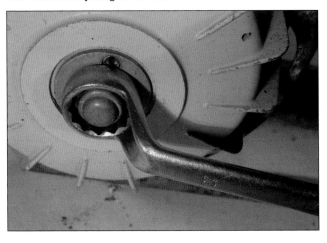

## Wheel Rims

The elusive quality you should be looking for in wheel rims is for them to be perfectly circular. All I can say is good luck. Original Innocenti ones tend to be the best. These are identified by the Innocenti stamp and dimples pressed in to the back of the fixed studs of one rim half (see following pic) on all but the very last GP production. Indian rims tend to be strong and true, but sometimes look like they have been finished using someone's teeth.

You can check the true of rims by resting their flat side against glass or a similar flat surface, or resting them back to back.

At the time of writing remade Italian rims vary in quality from poor to dire. One common problem is that the centres are slightly oversized and don't locate properly on the hub. If you want your wheel to run concentric then these may have to be positioned by hand. Also watch out for studs made from cheese, flaky chrome and powder coating on the threads because they couldn't be bothered to mask them up. Apart from that they are perfect!

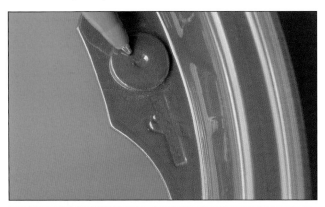

Some pattern rims were produced with the valve hole too far out. These can be dangerous when used on the front wheel with certain inner tubes because the valve can touch on the fork link bolt and deflate at high speed. It is important to always check you have clearance here.

Wide rims are available and these can enhance road-holding when used on the rear wheel.

Plastic powder coating is a popular finish for wheel rims because it is highly resistant to corrosion and will last much longer than paint or chrome. If you do have your rims powder coated though, ensure that the threads of the studs are properly masked and also insist that the coating is not laid on too thick. If a thick coating is used this will sag in use, causing your wheel nuts to come loose with potentially dire consequences. You have been warned.

## Changing Steering Bearing Cones

Notchy steering is a very common cause for MoT test failures on scooters because the bearings – particularly the top ones – aren't particularly beefy and are often insufficiently lubricated or poorly adjusted. In many cases it is sufficient to loosen the bearing cups, re-pack the bearings with grease and adjust them properly. In a slightly worse scenario the bearings themselves may need to be replaced, but if the owner has been particularly negligent and the bearings have eaten into the cones then the whole lot needs replacing. Steering bearing and cone sets are available with everything you need to sort out the problem, but getting the old cones out is not that easy.

If you want to get the bearing cones out prior to painting the frame then you won't mind heating the frame, but owners of pristine paintwork may want to avoid use of a blowlamp.

A useful tool to get out the steering cones can be made by welding a length of 16mm steel rod to an early Series 2-type engine frame cone. These frame cones are hardened and the outer lip is ideal to put through the centre of the headstock tube and be used as a drift to knock out the steering cones.

**The best technique Rimini Lambretta Centre have found to remove lower bearing cones is to use two hammers. Rest the shoulder of the first hammer on the edge of the cone and hit the rear of it with the other hammer.**

**Do note that it is not regarded as good practice to hit one hammer against another, so wear eye protection. This method is still better than smashing your fingers when trying to use a hammer and chisel though.**

**Really stiff bottom frame cones may be removed by welding a plate or bar across the bottom of the cone and hammering down on it with a bar through the headstock.**

Alternate the blows from side to side and the cone will eventually come out. Those looking to keep their paintwork in good condition may want to gaffer tape around the area to protect it. Getting cones out this way will wreck the shiny metal dust cover, but these are cheap to replace.

The top bearing cones are best shifted with a large steel bar or thick-walled tube. Stuff a screwdriver down through the top of the headstock to keep the bar in contact with the lip of the bearing track.

**Be careful not to rest your bar against the fork steering stop welded inside the headstock tube because they are fairly easy to knock out by accident.**

There are different top frame cones depending on the age of the machine. Early LI/TV/150-Special ones use a narrower cone (left) to fit inside the chrome ring – which is secured in the frame by a grub screw. Later ones have a fatter cone (right) which fits directly into the frame.

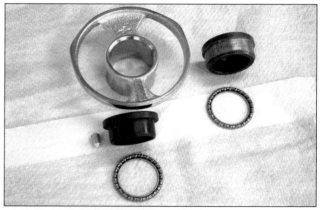

**If you are trying to change the bearing cones ('tracks') on an early machine NEVER try and remove them by hitting the chrome ring because these are easily damaged and replacements are hard to find. First knock the cone out of the chrome ring from below, then undo the grub screw and knock out the chrome ring.**

Check the inner bottom fork bearing race for pitting and replace if required. This one is fine.

There are holes in most forks that allow a pin-punch to be used to shift the bottom bearing race. Alternate blows from one side of the race to the other. The thin metal dust shield will usually be wrecked by this process and should be renewed before the new bearing track is tapped into position.

 **If you have difficulty shifting the track with a skinny punch, drill the holes out a little and use a thicker punch.**

## Fork Stripping

Lambretta forks are simple in the extreme, but on all early models they are almost impossible to strip without a fork spring compressor tool. In recent times these have been remade as pattern tools in various degrees of quality. Poor quality ones aren't really worth having.

Undo the two bolts (on early models) holding in the lower fork link buffer in each leg. Remove any grease nipples. Compress the fork link with a large ring spanner over the end of the fork link and use a pair of pliers to withdraw the buffers. On later models with clip-in buffers use a wide-bladed flat screwdriver to lever them out.

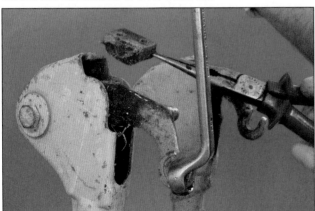

Before the compressor can be used, the fork link pivot bolts must be removed. This can sometimes be a challenge in itself if the bolts are seized. Removing seized bolts is best achieved by soaking with an anti-seize oil such as Plusgas. Then put a deep socket over the head of the bolt, wind the nut off until it just covers the last thread of the bolt and put the whole lot in a vice. With one jaw resting on the nut and the other jaw on the socket, you should be able to tighten the vice and the head of the bolt should move into the socket. If it is still stiff when the nut bottoms out on the fork apply more oil to the exposed part of the bolt and push it back the opposite way. Keep repeating until the bolt is free enough to be pushed all the way through once the nut has been removed.

**If the forks look very rusty and the bolt doesn't look like moving, then it can be better to take the forks to a specialist dealer rather than attempting bolt removal yourself. There is a scope to cause considerable damage if this process goes wrong.**

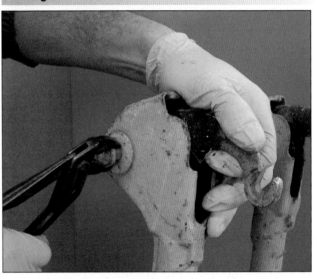

Wind the bolts of the spring compressor into the pivot bolt holes of the fork and push down to compress the spring. This should give enough clearance to remove the link. Later GP-type forks – using a loose ball and cupped fork rod – can often be disassembled without need for a spring compressor.

Early fork rods are only punched to keep the ball ends in place so it is not unusual for them to come apart. This is not reason to throw them away provided the rods themselves are still straight. Simply reassemble and centre punch the rods to get them to grip the ball ends again.

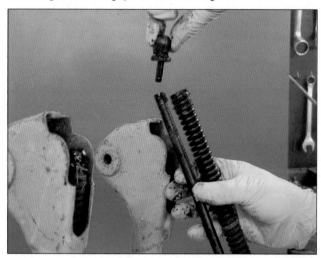

Next remove the top ('compression') buffers from the fork legs.

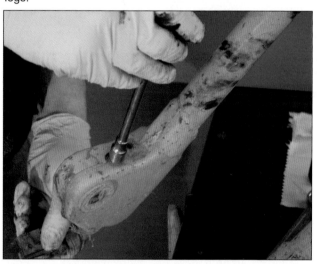

Use a hooked rod to pull out the old spring stops. There are several different types of spring stop.

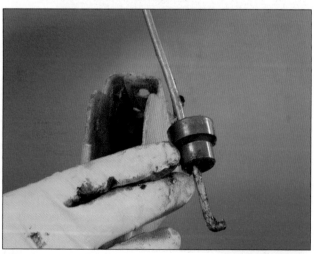

# Fork Links

Many different sorts of fork links were used over the years. As such, if you are building a set of forks from bits found from various sources always hold the links back to back and check that they align properly at the fork bolt, wheel spindle mount and also at the buffer stops. It is a good idea to file the buffer stop positions on pairs of links so that they are flat and match perfectly.

Disc brake fork links – which locate the hub back-plate by a stud and nut rather than a simple peg – are highly sought after by people converting their drum machines to hydraulic disc brake operation and mounting front fork dampers. Even these 'stud and nut' links were available in several types. The most highly prized are TV175 series 1 and 2 links (originally for drum hubs). These links are less acutely angled than regular disc links, which gives greater clearance to the fork leg when a disc hub has been converted with a bulky hydraulic slave cylinder. The TV series 2 links (right) are also supposed to offer better handling for race use. These are identified by a noticeable gap between the spindle mount and the damper stud hole.

**The demand for disc brake conversions to older models has caused high demand for disc-type fork links. Stoffi's Garage in Austria and MB Developments are among the firms who offered converted drum links that were modified to suit disc-type hubs. More recently disc-type fork links have been remade to a high standard so modified ones are no longer required.**

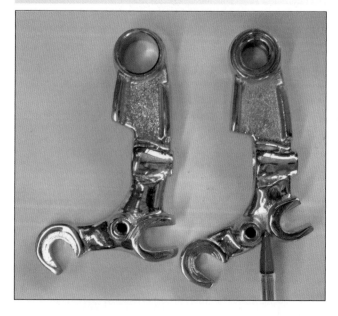

Three types of damper-mount fork links are shown below. The late Italian 200cc type (top) is defined by the lug to take the screw-in damper mounting. They have a shallow cup for the loose ball of the GP-type fork rod shown alongside, and can sometimes be assembled without a compressor tool depending on the fork spring used. The earlier 200 type (centre) has a deeper cup and thread for a grease nipple, and these are used with the fixed ball-type fork rod. The late Serveta link (bottom) works with a fixed ball fork rod, but the 9mm thread on the damper mount means that it will only accept fat Serveta dampers. These links are only available with drum-brake fittings.

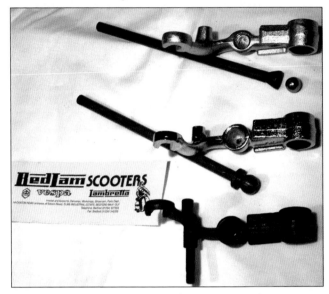

Special drifts have been manufactured recently to remove worn-out fork link bushes.

## Fork Rebuild

 **If you have any doubt of the straightness of your forks then they can be checked for alignment and even straightened. Grand Prix Scooters in Leicester offer this service.**

For Lambretta forks to work properly it is vital that the fork springs are the same length, and also that the fixed spring stops welded inside the fork legs are at the same depth. Very often they are several mm different. Use a steel rule to measure the fork stop depth and note which one is deeper. Steel spacers (e.g. piston shims or front axle retaining washers) can be added to the spring on the deeper fork leg in order to shim it to the same overall length to compensate.

**Before going any further make sure that your fork pivot bolts fit through the forks, particularly if they have just been painted or powder coated. File the holes until the bolts are a push-fit.**

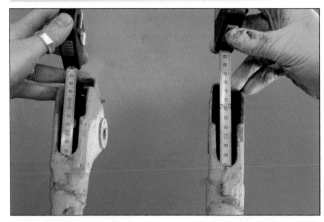

Fork buffers. Later machines use the clip in buffers (left) which just slot into a formed metal holder welded into the fork leg. Earlier types (right) fit with two M6 bolts. The remade Italian Casa Lambretta buffers are of good quality.

Some reproduced early-type fork buffers are poorly made with rubber filling the screw threads. In that case simply run an M6 tap through to clean them out.

Put the forks upside down in a vice to work on them. The first step is to fit the top (thin) fork buffers.

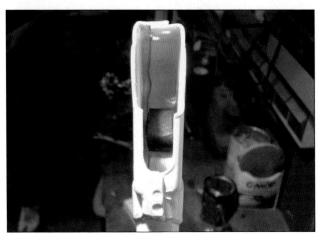

Various loose spring stops have been used through the years. Series 2 and early series 3 had steel 'top hat' stops with separate inner bushes, later replaced with nylon 'top hats' and finally this type which are like flat nylon discs. Always check with a torch to see that no old spring stops remain in the forks before rebuilding.

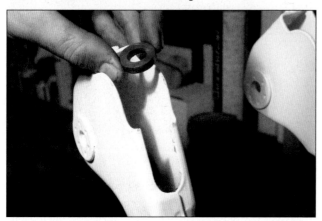

 **For optimum performance always ensure your fork springs and rods are the same length. Polishing the balls of the fork rod will do no harm either.**

 **It is possible to change the behaviour of your fork by fitting aftermarket 'dual rate' fork springs or increasing the pre-load of the springs by fitting double-height nylon washer type spring stops. In practice double spring stops are probably unnecessary unless you are particularly heavy or often carry a passenger and luggage.**

 **Indian fork springs are best avoided since quality inconsistencies mean one may be softer than the other.**

Fit the springs, rods and spring stops in one go – along with any washers between the spring and stop that are required to compensate for uneven welded stop depths. Use really heavy duty grease on the fork components to resist jet-washing and so it doesn't drip out like oil when it gets hot. Too much grease is not enough.

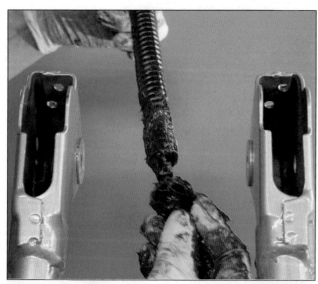

 **US firm West Coast Lambretta Works pioneered the development of a roller bearing conversion for fork links which should be vastly superior to plastic bushes.**

Early links have a bronze bush that lasts forever if lubricated correctly. Later models use a plastic bush which regularly wears out. It is worth fitting new ones if there is any slop.

 **If your links are the bronze bush type then it is imperative to use the early type pivot bolt with grease nipple, along with the matched drilled inner bush and the correct steel centre bush.**

Sometimes plastic bushes can be too tight so an adjustable reamer can be employed to slightly enlarge the hole. It is the right size when the inner bush can be fitted with firm thumb pressure.

Grease the inner steel bush before fitting inside the plastic one.

Use grease to hold the two steel shims in place before fitting the link.

Use of a fork compressor is essential with non-GP set-ups in order to get enough space to slot the fork link into place. Later GP-type fork rods have a loose ball at the bottom – and sometimes these can be assembled without need of a fork compressor – but these rods must only be used with 'shallow cup' GP links.

With the link in place, fit two well-greased fork bolts from the outside. Later models require a cable holder bracket to be fitted to the left leg before the link nuts go on. A shake-proof washer is used under the right nut.

 **Certain remade fork link bolts are slightly longer than required, and this increases the chances of your front wheel valve cap coming into contact with them – with potentially dangerous consequences. Possible 'workarounds' are to add washers to the bolt before it is fitted until the thread is totally flush with the (half-height) nut, or to fit the bolt and nut as normal and then hacksaw off any excess thread beyond the nut.**

 **Stainless steel fork link bolts and bushes are available which should improve bush life considerably and make future rebuilds much easier.**

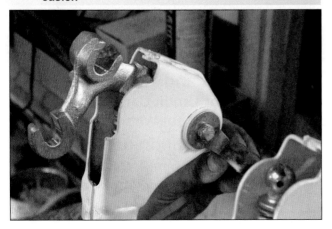

Use a ring spanner hooked over the end of the fork link to allow room to fit the lower (fat) fork buffers.

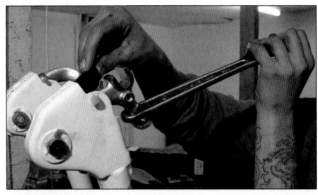

Finally fit a grease nipple in the bottom of the fork link and screw in any damper mount studs that may be fitted.

# Front Fork Dampers

Front fork dampers were fitted as standard to all 175cc and 200cc models, and greatly improve the handling. It may be of advantage to fit these to smaller capacity machines, particularly if upgrading the engine performance. This may be achieved by several methods.

**Top Damper Mount:**
- Fit 175 or 200 series forks which have the correct damper bracket welded on. Note that GP 125/150 can only accept GP 200 forks.
- Fit a clamp-on damper bracket kit.
- Weld original type damper brackets to your forks. These are now available as a spare part and should be positioned 23.5cm from the lower point on the fork leg as shown below.

**Make sure the forks are stripped before the brackets are welded on or you will melt plastic spring stops with potentially dangerous results.**

**Bottom Damper mount:**

- Fit 175 or 200 series fork links. Note that these usually come with stud type (as opposed to peg type) front hub fixing suited to the use of front disc brakes or TV175 drum brakes. Spanish links are available with damper mounts and pin-type drum hub fixings.

- Fit normal drum links and Indian damper bracket converters which simply bolt on using the main spindle nuts.

- As an improved alternative to bolt-on Indian brackets MB Developments can adapt drum links with a TIG-welded damper mounting.

 **Late Spanish machines used fat double-action dampers fitted onto unusual 9mm studs at both the link and fork end. These dampers are no longer available, which is a shame since the handling provided was excellent.**

 **At this time good quality Indian front dampers are available that are more effective than the stainless/chrome or Sebac Italian dampers previously available.**

## Rear Shock Absorbers

Rear shocks absorbers were initially supplied in two lengths. Early Series 1 and 2 types were 13mm longer than the later series 3 type. The earlier type will provide greater exhaust and bodywork clearance for aggressive cornering on a Slimstyle machine, but may cause clearance problems around the cylinder, particularly with the use of TS1 kits. All the aftermarket shocks are supposed to conform to one length or the other, but in practice can vary from brand to brand and will often be found to be an intermediate length.

It is possible to remove the springs from old shocks but generally this is pointless (unless for chroming) since the dampers themselves are not repairable and no longer available as a spare part. Complete units are relatively inexpensive, and even cheap ones (Escorts from India and Sebac from Italy) can perform quite well. More expensive race shocks with adjustable damping and spring pre-load are available from British and Italian firms. Bitubo gas shocks had a habit of blowing seals in the past. The British ones sold by Taffspeed and the like have proved very popular.

**Rear shocks can be fitted upside down. The correct way up is with the spring nearest to the frame mounting point.**

**Later Spanish machines used a rear damper with an extra-wide mounting. These can't safely be used on Italian or Indian machines, but Italian-width dampers may be fitted to Spanish frames/engines provided that spacers are fitted to hold the narrower shocks firmly in place.**

# SCOOTER 'in Style'

## from Import to Full Restorations, Spares & Repairs

## Large amount of New and Second hand parts in stock

# CHASSIS REBUILDING

## Before We Begin

Lambrettas were a mass-produced item and not always built to the world's tightest tolerances, so don't expect everything to go together easily. New pattern parts are rarely a perfect fit so be prepared to file, bend or adjust everything to get it to fit correctly. You are working with the best that is available, but that isn't always up to much!

## General Chassis Tips:

- If you aren't fussed about a 'perfect' restoration then change all the 14mm nuts used on early models (wheels, cylinder head etc.) to 13mm so you only need to carry one socket.

- If you want a really perfect restoration then you should use the 'blackened' studs and washers that were originally fitted to the scooter. The problem is that these have virtually no resistance to corrosion so if you wash your scooter or ride it in the rain then the fasteners will go rusty. That looks pretty grim on a restoration. The options are plated or preferably stainless steel fasteners.

 **IMPORTANT NOTE: The photos for this section were taken at different times and occasionally show components fitted that haven't already been mentioned in the captions. Please ignore this and fit parts according to the sequence suggested in the text.**

## Fit Stand

Grease and connect the stand spring before offering the stand up to the frame. Original offset-type stand springs have recently been reproduced and are a better fit than the common concentric type.

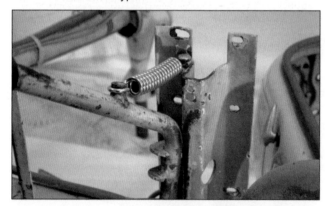

 **All good dealers use and supply stand support brackets to stop the stand bolts distorting the frame. These are an essential fitment. Thicker ones are better since they are less liable to distort.**

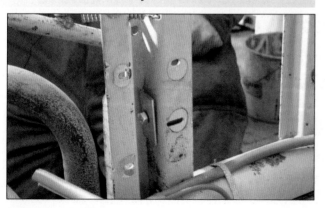

## Fit Rear Mudguard

Italian machines used metal mudguards while Indian models introduced plastic ones during early production. Spanish rear mudguards have a simpler single piece metal pressing. These bolt on through brackets either side of the main frame tube, and via a single hole at the rear of the frame.

## Fit Bearing Cones 'Cups' and Forks

Use paint stripper to clean off any over-spray inside the frame so that the steering bearing cones can be fitted.

**A Dremel or similar tool can be used to remove any paint so that the steering cones will fit properly, but be careful not to remove any metal.**

Grease the outside of the upper and lower bearing cones and hammer them into place using a suitable drift.

Thoroughly grease all the bearings before fitting the forks.

**One racer trick to improve steering action is to not use caged bearings (as originally fitted) but loose balls. The increased number of contact patches gives a much better 'feel' to the steering. These can be a struggle to install since you have to rely on grease to hold them in place while the forks are fitted.**

Do not over-tighten the top fork bearing nut because this can actually dent the races. Tighten until the forks can be turned without feeling any resistance. Then fit the tongued washer and lock nut.

Test that the steering hasn't become stiff once the lock nut has been done up. If it feels stiff then the bottom nut must be loosened a little. If you can grip the fork legs and feel any forward-backward movement then the nuts are too loose.

 If the fork bearings feel stiff in only one direction, this can be a sign that the fork tube or frame is bent.

 If new frame cones have been fitted, these may only settle down with use and the forks may need to be re-tightened after a few miles.

 The way to test for correct steering tightness is to put a brick under each stand foot and align the forks to the front. They should be hard to balance with the steering straight and if you manage it then a tap to the rear of the frame should be enough to make the wheel drop to one side.

## Fit Speedo Cable

 We initially installed the wrong speedo cable by accident to our LI, not realising that the early speedo on this machine only accepts a smaller type of inner cable. Some Indian GP speedos also use this smaller cable, so make sure you get the correct type for your machine.

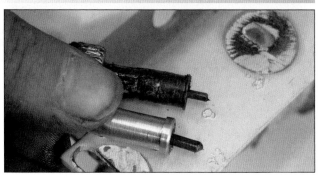

The quick way to fit a complete speedo cable is to start by pushing the inner cable (hub end first) up from the bottom of the forks through the angled drilling provided.

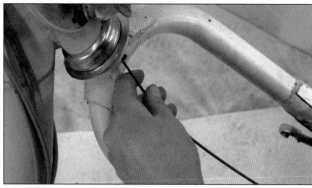

Then simply thread the outer cable down over the inner and use it as a guide to get the outer through the correct hole at the bottom of the forks. Once in place, withdraw the inner cable, wipe it clean, grease it and slide it back into the outer from the top.

When you finally attach the speedo cable to the front hub, first slide the knurled fixing nut and sleeve over the outer cable, then clamp the brass 'olive' around the bare last 10mm of the outer cable. This olive holds the outer cable in place when the knurled nut is tightened into the speedo drive housing.

Occasionally the speedo will not work when a new cable is fitted, usually because the outer cable is too long. Trim 5mm off the lower end of the outer cable and trim back the plastic sleeving by the same amount until the speedo functions correctly. You need a sharp cutter or a grinder to do this correctly. Do not leave any sharp edges on the outer cable which will cause the inner cable to fray.

## Fit Front Wheel

On drum brake models the hub back-plate locates onto a peg on the fork link before the wheel spindle is pushed into position.

It is vital that the special front fork spindle washers locate properly into the recesses in the fork links before the domed spindle nuts are tightened.

## Fit Headset Bottom

Fit the headset to the forks with the Allen clamp bolt, which is secured by a shake-proof washer.

 **One favourite racer's trick is not to over-tighten the headset clamp bolt. Competition riders prefer to set it so they are only just able to move the headset with the front wheel clamped tightly between the legs. This has two advantages: firstly you can finalise your headset alignment with the scooter fully built, and secondly it means that the headset is more likely to twist on the forks rather than break during a crash. Do note that this is not acceptable for an MoT as the test requires the headset to be firmly fixed.**

 **Since the headset is a clamp fit on the forks you have some leeway over its vertical positioning. On early 'chrome ring' machines it should be sufficient to locate it as close as possible to the chrome ring without touching. On later machines the headset should be positioned as low as possible without the casting touching the steering lock lug welded to the headstock tube.**

 **Check the operation of your steering lock before fitting your legshields. You may need to run a file through the pin hole if paint has entered during a respray. If the pin doesn't release properly it could be a problem when you park up!**

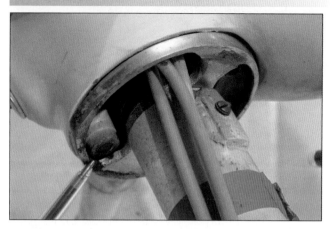

## Cable Tips

Correct cable routing is one of the most sought-after bits of information for anyone rebuilding a Lambretta. The scooter will be much nicer to ride if the cables all follow the intended path without being tensioned by headset or engine movement. The routing shown here is that used by Innocenti HOWEVER even machines coming out of the factory may have had slight variations as to which side one cable crossed over another one. Don't panic about such tiny details as long as the main run of cables is correct.

 **On original machines the cables and wiring were retained by foldable aluminium ties which make it difficult to change an outer cable without removing the horncasting. If you want a proper restoration then you should use these ties, but if you aren't fussed about originality then using releasable plastic cable ties is a better idea. At least then you have a better chance of changing a damaged outer cable without stripping your scooter down.**

 **If you are cabling for a TS1 or Imola kitted scooter - or even anything with an oversized carb – be aware that you will need a longer throttle cable and it may well need to follow a different route to meet a carb on the other side of the scooter.**

 **In the words of one of our advisers 'there is no excuse nowadays for not fitting Teflon/nylon-lined cables to a scooter.' These simply have such an improved action and longevity that saving a few pence with standard cables is a false economy. Nylon-lined cables are available from numerous sources, and even the recent Indian original ones are good quality.**

 **In practice it is almost impossible to replace outer control cables (except the rear brake) if all the cable ties are still in place. Some dealers suggest cutting the ties after the machine is fully assembled but this can cause problems around the front tyre and brake pedal. Fitting releasable plastic cable ties is a good compromise.**

**TOP TIP** If you have released some ties to allow an outer cable change then the easiest way to proceed is to thread a length of garden wire through the new outer cable and the old one. Once through both outers knot the wire at both ends and pull the wire from the old cable end. This should pull the new outer cable into position.

**TOP TIP** It is easier to fit the rear brake cable to the adjuster first rather than at the pedal end. Curl one end of the inner cable 180 degrees and clamp it into the adjuster. Pass the inner cable through the engine casing from the rear and then slide over the 'top hat' and outer cable. Leave it this way until the engine and brake pedal have been fitted.

**TOP TIP** Train spotters who want to fit a grease nipple set to complete an original-looking restoration can either cut Teflon-lined cables in two to fit them into the in-line grease nipples, or a better way is to drill through the grease nipples at 5.2mm (which is the diameter of most outer cables) and thread the Teflon-lined outers right through. Make sure you superglue the balls of the grease nipples in place before drilling the centres out.

## Cable Routing

Start by fitting your two gearchange cables. Locate them into the headset clamp and use insulating tape to hold them in position on the frame while adding the other cables.

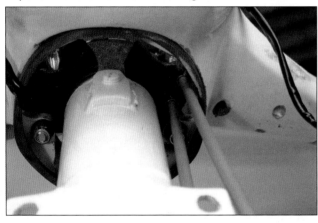

The gearchange cables follow the left side of the headstock tube before wrapping around the front of the main frame tube behind the forks.

**ONE TO WATCH** It is important to have enough slack in the gear cables at the point shown that you can get a finger underneath them. This slack is needed for steering movement.

The clutch cable runs from the gearchange casting, through the support hoop in the headset, and down the right side of the headstock tube. Put the gearchange into the 3rd gear position while doing this to ensure there is enough slack in the outer clutch cable.

**TOP TIP** If possible, don't fully tighten the headset clamp bolt until the cables have been routed. That way the headset can be moved from side to side to check the cable slack without moving the forks and unbalancing the machine.

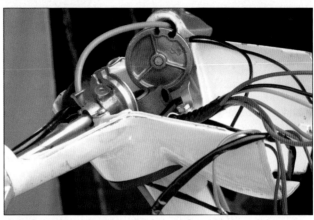

It is important that the clutch and front brake cables route down the correct way through the headset, which is just in front of the clamp bolts.

The clutch cable then runs down to meet the gear cables, and runs along the top of them at the frame tube.

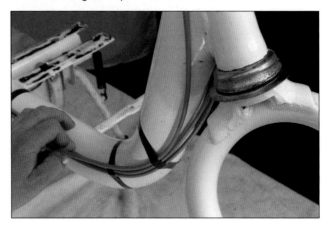

Next fit the throttle cable. This crosses the clutch cable just below the headset.

The throttle cable then follows along on top of the clutch cable until it diverts across the frame tube just before the stand support strut. It is important to leave enough slack for headset movement.

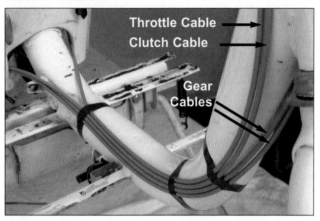

If you intend to fit grease nipples and a support bracket, this is the position in which they should sit.

Fit the wiring loom which starts off running down the left of the headstock tube.

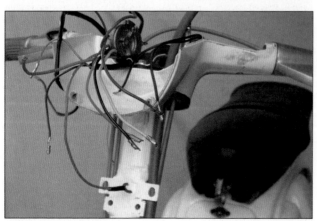

The wiring will be held in place inside the headset by this aluminium tab. Also fit the front brake cable which crosses BEHIND the clutch cable (i.e. closer to the rider) inside the headset and down through the other hooped guide. Note that this very early headset uses a metal bracket instead of wire hoops to keep the cables away from the speedo.

The front brake cable runs down ahead of the wiring loom and the gear cables. On a standard machine, one of the cable ties is positioned here. Note how a plastic cable tie is employed to hold the cables in position while the metal ties are done up.

**If you want to be able to change your outer cables without the need to remove your horncasting then it may be better to omit the tie at this position, or at least leave it loose.**

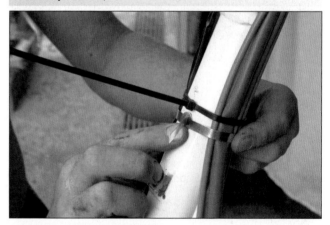

The wiring loom crosses the gearchange cables before it comes to the second cable tie position; which is at the top of the main frame tube. From here the front brake cable peels off under the forks and through the guide on the right fork leg.

The wiring loom follows the flywheel side of the frame tube and is secured by the tie between the floor struts. The brake light switch wiring crosses over the top of the frame tube.

 **The tie just ahead of the seat arch only secures a rubber guide for the throttle cable and nothing else.**

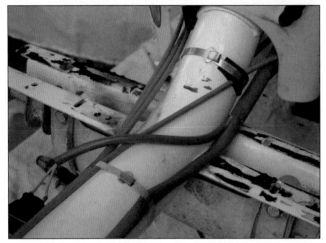

Routing of the wiring varied from the factories but it is better if it follows up and over the air box bracket. This prevents the petrol tap split-pin from damaging the wiring loom.

The wiring loom also follows up and over the rear running-board support strut – as does the stator plate wiring on a standard machine.

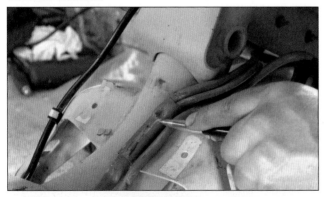

The loom has a fat piece of sleeving to protect it where it passes under the tank. The wiring splits just afterwards in several directions behind the tank strap.

The wiring for the rear light then passes under the rear frame support and up over the standard ignition coil position. Normally the wiring is not retained by any ties here, but you may want to add one if your coil is positioned elsewhere.

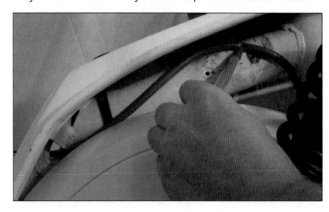

Original aluminium-type cable ties are threaded through the slots, folded back and the end is folded back again.

An extra (non-original) cable tie can be added just ahead of the floor struts to keep the cables clear of the anti-splash bracket on the brake pedal.

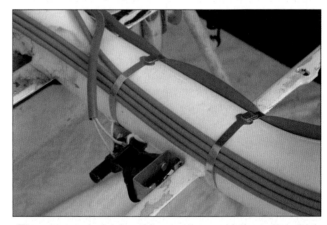

The gear and clutch cables are grouped through a thick piece of sleeving as they travel under the seat arch. They then travel around the outside of the casing but BELOW the engine mounting. It is better to keep this amount of slack in them. The clutch cable has been coloured light green in this photo to identify its route.

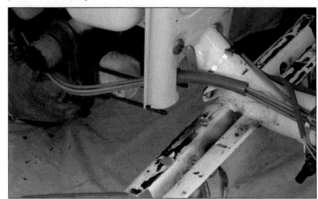

Fit the choke cable through the tubular bracket and attach it to the lever. A cable guide is connected to the choke lever control to keep the cables away from the head cowling and HT cap. A wire type (shown) is used on early models. A pressed steel or plastic version is fitted to later machines.

Four remaining ties are used under the seat arch to secure the wiring loom and the rubber guide for the HT ignition cable.

Before you can do the cables up properly you will have to fit the levers. As standard a spring and cap were fitted to the levers to stop them rattling. Ensure everything is liberally greased with heavy duty grease.

 **Instead of using the original star washer and round nut, it can be better to use an M5 nyloc nut and M5 plain washer on the lever pivot bolt. You can also add an M7 plain washer to take up any slack. This will hold the bolt more securely and prevent the holes in the housing from becoming ovalised.**

When you fit the front brake cable clamp make sure the inner cable turns 180 degrees around the bolt and sits within the fingers of the pinch plate. Also ensure that it is fitted in such a way that the adjuster is in the middle of its range.

## Fit Seat and Seat Catch

Under both seat brackets of our LI were four thick metal washers to space the bracket away from the paintwork.

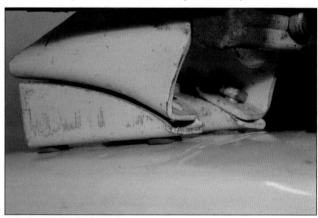

On models fitted with dual seats there are fat plastic washers between the seat catch and the frame. More plastic washers are fitted underneath the frame followed by a wavy metal washer and the nut.

# Fit the Rear Frame Badge Holder or Frame Grille

The frame badge holders locate into large holes at the rear of the frame using special U-shaped brackets. Be very careful with ones containing Perspex badges since these need to be slightly curved and are easily fractured or scratched. The first Italian GP models used alloy grilles painted the same colour as the scooter. Innocenti later converted to black plastic, which was used for all Indian GP production too.

# Fit Back Light

You may need to glue the light housing gasket into place to get it to stay in position while the housing is being fitted. GP models do not use a gasket under their plastic light housing.

**The original earth wire from the bulb holder runs to one of the light housing bolts, but this does not always provide the best electrical connection. On AC Electronic systems with regulators mounted in the original coil position it might be better to extend the wire and earth it directly to one of the regulator bolts.**

# Fit Panel Clips and Mudflap

Different arrangements are fitted depending on whether the panels are 'handle' (below) or 'clip-on' type. The later clip-on types improve accessibility for rear wheel removal.

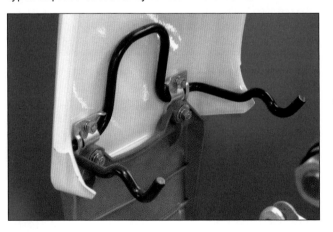

# Fit Frame Cones

Before fitting check that the cones slide freely on the engine pin. If not, tap a flat screwdriver into the gap to open them up a little, but not too much. Hold them into position in the frame with grease.

**Two types of frame cones were used. The taller, chamfered ones are for later machines with 'wide' engine mounts. The narrower cones are for use with narrow early engine mounts.**

# Fit the Engine

It is easier to fit the cowlings before you fit the engine.

Fitting an engine is really a two-man job because it is difficult to keep everything aligned while the bolt is pushed through. It helps to rest the engine on something like a block of wood to keep it level and then to lower the frame into position. Give the engine bolt a generous coating of grease before fitting.

**Remember to refit the rubber engine bump stop.**

With the main engine bolt in place, next fit the shock, making sure to liberally grease the mounting points. Only wavy washers and plain nuts hold the shock, but half-height nyloc nuts might reasonably be preferred. Heat the rubber gear arm cover in hot water to soften it, dry it and slide it up the tie rod. Fill the cover with grease and slide it into position when the circlip and shim are in place.

Don't forget to fit the gaskets to the top of the casing before fitting the cable adjuster and gear arm brackets. A Lambretta gearchange will only work properly when the gear arm bracket is mounted this way round (so it overhangs the gasket face).

Use an open-ended spanner to tension the clutch arm enough to hook the cable in. Note that it is important that the clutch arm should sit at roughly 90 degrees to the cable. In any other position the lever action will feel heavier than it really needs to. The lever can be moved on the splines of the shaft if it is in the wrong position.

 **The rubber cable gaiters supplied on some Indian machines were so stiff that they could cause the machine to jump out of top gear.**

## Fit the HT Coil

Note the thick insulator used on this early machine to protect the HT coil when it is mounted in this position. The mounting was revised when plastic coils were later introduced.

## Fit Fuel Tank

**On a restoration be sure to run the stator wires up through last two cable ties before fitting the tank. Several different types of tank rubber were used during production, but the later slotted GP-type ones (not shown) are best because they stay in place. These are slightly fatter, and GP-type tank straps are approx 10mm longer to suit. The large rubbers on our early tank locate into holes in the frame.**

**Bend new tank straps around your knee to shape them prior to fitting. Stainless steel ones are now available.**

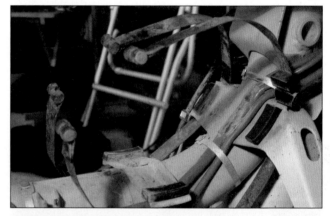

The neck of the tank faces backwards as you insert it into the frame.

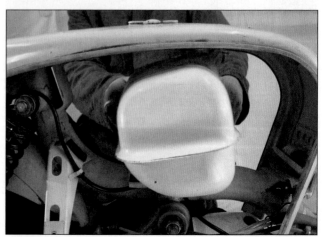

Loosely do up the tank strap bolts over the top front corner of the tank.

 **It is best to fix the fuel tap to the tank before final fitting so that both can be adjusted together. Ensure that the tap doesn't stick out of the frame too far and the filler neck sits central to the recess. Remember that both fuel tap and tank threads should be started at the same time.**

Insert the remaining rubbers before tightening the strap bolts.

 **Later models use a drip tray and fibre collar around the tank neck to stop fuel/oil spilt during refuelling from covering your engine. These may reasonably be fitted to earlier models too. The drip tray is best inserted from the top after the tank is correctly positioned.**

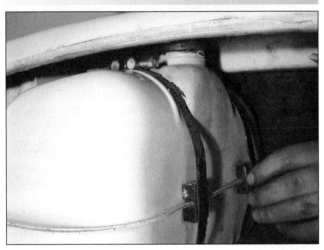

## Fit Toolbox

Fit the toolbox door first using the special split-ended pin. The original fixings use a plain nut and tab washer, but a modern M5 (8mm head) nyloc nut and plain washer would be preferable in anything but the most fastidious restoration. Soak the toolbox rubber in hot water to make it easier to fit. The join in the rubber should be next to the toolbox door hinge.

 **Several types of fixing screw were used with the later ones having a kinked dogleg in them. It is easier to fit the toolbox on earlier machines if the top fixing is kinked backwards a little.**

The lower fixings hook into slots in the frame. On some models plastic bungs were used to hold them in position. If you do not have these then simply push some M8 bolts down alongside the heads of the fixings to hold them into place while the nuts are fastened.

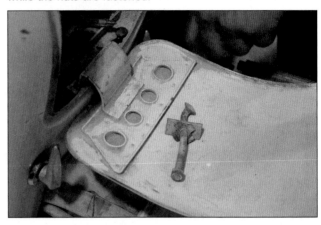

## Fit Air Filter Box and Scoop

These fit in reverse of the removal procedure from Chapter 10.1. Don't forget any of the gaskets.

**Only use the special square-head bolt in the fixing to the frame tube. A normal hex-head bolt may never come undone.**

## Fit Flywheel Cowling and Earth Wire

These wires are essential for good earthing with every sort of wiring or ignition system.

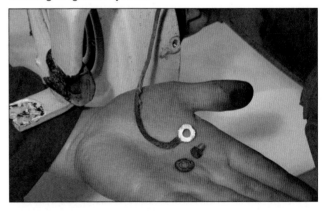

## Fit Carb

Make sure the carb is pushed fully home onto the manifold and sits at the correct angle. Do not hammer it into place!

## Bodywork Assembly – Which Order?

**As you may imagine it is possible to assemble Lambretta bodywork in many different orders during a full restoration. According to Rimini Lambretta Centre there is only one correct way to do it if you are fussy about the fit and alignment of the various components. Ideally you should have already carried out a 'dry run' of bodywork fitting before any paint was applied so that the fit could be 'tweaked' where necessary.**

1. Fit the L-shaped running board support leg (kickstart side) and ensure alignment with the main floor cross-members.
2. Fit the sidepanel rubber buffers to each running board support strut.
3. Fit the rubber sidepanel beading around the lip on the seat arch after first applying a coating of impact adhesive (e.g. Bostik) to ensure they stay in place. Don't use 'Superglue' as this will melt the paint.
4. Loosely fit the rear running boards with all the correct rubber spacers underneath.
5. Fit the sidepanels and ensure they are fully seated into position on the beading. Since these are the only component which can't be adjusted for position, all the other components must follow their alignment.
6. Adjust the positioning of the rear running boards so that they do not touch the sidepanels and there is a small gap of a few mm all around them. Do not fit the footboards too close to the sidepanels, as all the bodywork components will 'move' around due to vibration in use and will damage the paintwork if it rubs. Once you are satisfied with their position firmly fix down the footboards.

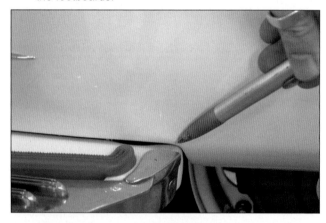

7. Fit and adjust the legshields so that there is a small, even gap to the running boards at the rear, and to the headset (or chrome ring) at the top.

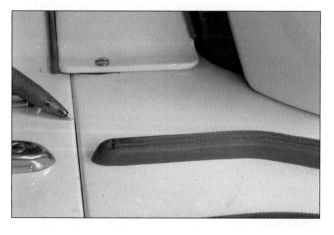

## Before Fitting Legshields

Many restoration specialists are now able to supply complete legshield and runner fixing kits. It will be easier and cheaper to buy one of these kits than try to assemble the parts yourself. Some of the rubbers are specially shaped.

The rubbers can be held into position on the struts with clear silicone instant gasket which will allow the rubbers some movement if the holes aren't perfectly aligned.

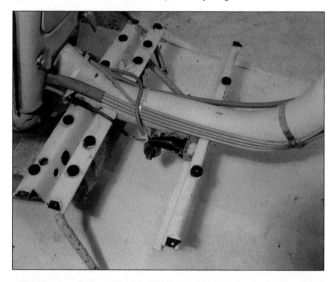

On these original legshields there is a rubber spacer glued into the legshields between the bottom screw holes for the horncasting.

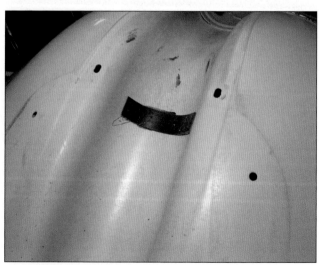

## Fitting Legshields

Slide the legshields down & over the frame and struts from the top. This is best done by two people, one either side of the scooter. If you have already cabled up the scooter, turn the handlebars to one side and gently pull the outer cables & wiring loom back behind the legshield fixing bracket by the steering column. Then turn the handlebars to the other side and repeat the process with the outer cables on the other side of the steering column.

 **On later non-chrome-ring frames be extremely careful that the bottom of the handlebars does not rub on the top of the legshields when turning the handlebars from one side to the other.**

Fix the front legshield bracket to the frame using the two 5mm bolts and relative washers. A drop of 'Loctite' on these bolts is advisable. Before tightening ensure that there is an even gap of 1- 3mm between the top of the legshields and the bottom of the actual headset on late machines. Turn the handlebars SLOWLY from side to side to check that this gap remains uniform as the headset is turned.

 **If the gap between legshields and headset changes as the handlebars are turned, then it's likely that the headset clamp is bent. Substitution of the clamp is the only cure for this.**

On chrome-ring type frames, simply ensure that the top of the legshields fits right up against the underside of the chrome ring.

The foot-well area of the legshields can now be fixed down using the outer floor strips. Ensure that the rear edge of the legshield sits squarely against the running-boards leaving a small, even gap.

 **If there is a wedge-shaped gap between the runners and the legshields then the rear footboard struts may need to be bent inwards or outwards.**

## Fit Mudguard and Horncasting

Loosely bolt the mudguard and horncast together with the rubber gasket between them. The holes are slotted to allow some latitude in fitting.

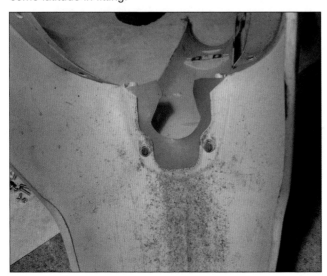

Check everything under the horncasting is positioned correctly e.g. the horn has been wired up. Turn the headset to one side and then fix the horncast loosely using the top two screws.

With the screws loosely fitted it is possible to slide the horncasting gaskets up into position. Cutaways for the lower screws show whether the gaskets are fitted the right way round or not. Also slide the mudguard rubber gaskets into place before fitting the remaining screws.

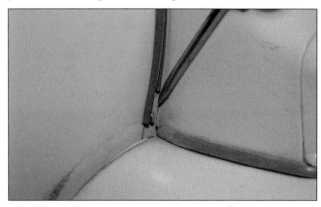

Tiny serrated-centre washers were originally used on the mudguard bolts, but flat washers and nylocs would work just as well nowadays.

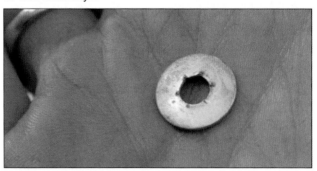

**Check to see that the bottom of the headset does  not rub on the top of the horncasting when the bars are turned from side to side. Insert a piece of paper between the two parts before moving the headset. Turn the handlebars slowly from one side to the other, whilst gently moving the paper as you do so. If the paper suddenly becomes stuck, stop and carefully remove the horncasting & mudguard and realign the legshields. It's possible that the top legshield fixing bracket has become bent and therefore the legshields sit further forwards pushing the horncasting up against the underside of the headset. Adjust as required and then try again. The trick with the paper saves your paint from being scratched off.**

# Fit Floor Channels and Rubbers

The floor strips can't go on until after the mudguard because the lower fixing screws would be covered over before they could be fastened. New aluminium floor channels are never perfectly formed so position and bend them on top of a rag to ensure that the paint isn't marked.

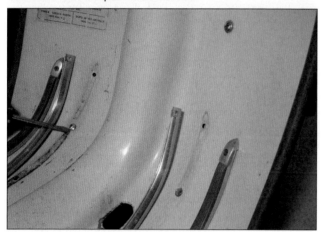

Heat the floor channel rubbers in water from the kettle and 'roll' them into place. The screws holding the channels down makes it impossible to slide them into position.

 **Some floor channel rubbers are less pliable than others. Stiff ones must be pushed in at the sides with a screwdriver.**

Be careful not to over-tighten the aluminium end caps because they are thin and brittle. Make sure they fit correctly over the floor strips before tightening and bend in the ends of the floor channel if required.

These special fasteners are used to secure the outer front end caps, which do not have a spacing lump under the casting like the others.

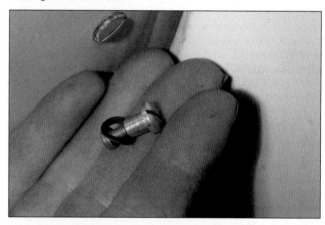

**Once you are satisfied with the positioning of the legshields and floor channels remember to go back and tighten the mudguard to horncasting screws.**

# Fit Bridge Piece

The central bridge piece and its two rubbers can now be fitted. Remember to fit the two round or rectangular rubber spacers below the screw holes.

**For easier access in the future, longer than standard bridge-piece screws can be employed.**

# Fit Rear Brake Pedal

Slide the inner brake cable into the clamp bolt before fitting the pedal to the frame. Then hook the return spring over the pedal being careful not to let it spring back and damage the stop light switch.

# Adjust the Cables

Push the rear brake arm forward before pinching up the clamp bolt on the brake pedal. Adjust the gear cables so that neutral is in the correct position on the headset and the throttle cable so that the carb slide isn't pre-tensioned. The clutch cable also requires a small amount of slack so that there is a gap of 1.5mm between the lever and the housing before the cable becomes tensioned.

## Fit Exhaust Downpipe ('Manifold')

- Always use a new gasket whenever the exhaust has been removed.
- On most original exhausts you can't fully fit the exhaust downpipe until the cowling is in position.
- The manifold is best retained by new spring or wavy washers and brass 11mm head nuts as originally fitted. Do not over tighten these since they are easily rounded or stripped.
- Do up the flywheel-side nut first since this is the one that is most restricted.

 **Special exhaust gaskets are available with larger ports to suit tuned cylinders. Be sure to fit one if your exhaust port has been opened otherwise your power output will be restricted.**

 **Make sure the exhaust gasket goes on the right way up since they can fit in different positions. When improperly fitted the gaskets partially mask the port resulting in reduced performance.**

## Fit Exhaust Body

Once the manifold and cowling are in place, fit the main exhaust chamber. Some tuners specify the use of heat resistant exhaust paste or silicone sealant on performance pipe joints, but with the difficulty of removing standard exhausts, copper grease is probably a better bet on the down pipe joint. On standard series 3 systems remember to bolt the bracket underneath the engine as well as fastening the visible ones through the main bracket and the tailpipe.

## Fill With Oil

Fill the gearbox with straight SAE 90 grade oil. Many people now only use 0.5 litres of oil in their engines when the original specification was 0.7 litres for a 'dry' engine. You can use the level plug at the front of the side casing to set the correct amount with the scooter parked on a level surface.

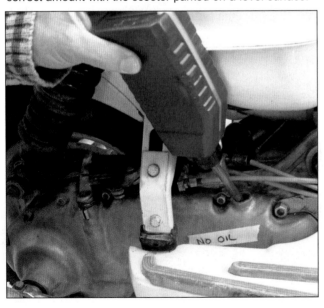

## Check Spark

Before fitting the spark plug or the headset top, check all your electrical connections are good and turn on the ignition switch, if fitted. Fit the plug to the HT cap. Rest the plug against the engine and press the kickstart pedal. Only once you see a decent spark is it worth fitting the headset top. Hopefully you should now be able to fit the plug, add some fuel/oil mixture and start the engine.

## Test Riding

 **Before test riding the scooter go around every visible nut and bolt to check they are tight. You wouldn't be the first person to set off down the road with the rear shock nuts undone or the brake cables disconnected. You soon learn from your mistakes though!**

After a short test ride to warm up the engine you should adjust the tick-over and mixture screw settings. Take it easy for the first 100 miles to bed in any new brake and engine parts and check again for anything that needs tightening up. The most important thing is to enjoy riding your Lambretta!

# SPECIAL PARTS

For many people, owning a Lambretta doesn't stop at restoring a standard machine. With huge potential for tuning and customising the Lambretta is the ideal tapestry for expressing your individuality.

So many different firms make parts for Lambrettas and production stops and restarts so often that it is impossible to produce a definitive list. Below are simply some of the more commonly available parts to give an indication of what is possible.

## Common Cylinder Conversions

In the quest for more power, various tuning conversions have been developed. These are the most popular ones:

- 125/150 to 175cc using 150 series 3 cylinder bored out to accept a Lambretta '175 Conversion' piston.
- 125/150/175 to 186cc 'Suzuki 185' using 150/175 series 3 cylinder bored out and shortened to accept a Suzuki TS 185 piston.
- 125/150/175 to 175cc Scooter Restorations iron-lined alloy SR175 kit.
- 125/150/175 to 186cc plated alloy 'Mugello' piston-ported kit.
- 125/150/175 to 186cc iron-barrelled 'Gran Turismo' reedvalve kit.

**Above: The British-made Gran Turismo 186cc kit. This is the only reedvalve conversion that allows the use of a carb in the original left-hand position.**

- 125/150/175 to 186cc 'Imola' plated alloy reedvalve kit.

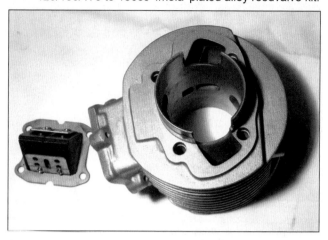

**Above: The Mk2 Imola cylinder kit with bolt-on reedblock, improved porting and a much larger gasket face for greater tuning potential.**

- 200 to 200cc 'Stage 4' - tuned original cylinder bored out to accept a thin-ring Asso or Vertex piston.
- 200 to 205cc 'Honda 205'. Tuned original cylinder bored out to accept a Honda MTX200 piston.
- 200 to 200cc plated alloy 'Mugello' piston-ported kit.
- 200 to 200cc plated alloy 'Monza' reedvalve kit.
- 200 to 200cc plated alloy AF 'TS1' reedvalve kit.
- 200 to 225cc plated alloy AF 'TS1' reedvalve kit.
- 200 to 200cc iron-lined alloy AF 'Rapido' Classic/Race kit.
- 200 to 225cc iron-lined alloy AF 'Rapido' Classic/Race kit.
- 200 to 230cc 'Kawasaki 240' conversion using 200cc cylinder bored out and modified to accept a Kawasaki H2 750 piston.
- 200 to 250cc iron-lined alloy AF 'Rapido' kit (requires 60mm crank and bored-out crankcase mouth).

If you are increasing the performance of your engine you will need to alter the carb jetting – or more likely fit a bigger carb – and alter your gearing to suit.

## Inlet Manifolds

Over the years many different inlet manifolds have been produced to fit carbs from 24mm-38mm onto tuned original cylinders.

- MB Developments: produced a range of inlet manifolds that will allow the fitment of a huge range of carbs to standard, tuned or kit cylinders.

**Above: MB Developments TS1/Imola manifolds not only allow for the use of different carbs but also position them nearer the cylinder so that carb holes do not need to be cut into panels with most configurations.**

- ScootRS (Vietnam): inlet manifolds to fit various Mikuni and Keihin-type carbs onto Lambretta cylinders.

**Above: A ScootRS conversion manifold for Mikuni carbs with flange and stud fitting.**

## Cylinder Heads

- Centre plug and water-cooled head conversions: Taffspeed, Readspeed, Worb5, MB Developments, Chiselspeed, RS Tuning and PM Tuning.

## Transmission Parts

- Rear sprockets ('crown wheels' or 'outer clutch bells') have been produced in 45, 46, 47, 48 and 49 tooth versions. The most recent development has been extended ones that are designed for 6-plate (or more) clutch conversions.

**Above: Taffspeed's lightweight, hardened rear sprocket for 6-plate clutch conversions. A 6-plate clutch is pretty much essential in engines producing over 25hp at the rear wheel. These are available from many of the major tuning shops.**

- Uprated top chain guides

**Above: Many different firms now produce versions of the MB nylon top chain guide as seen in the Advanced Engine Building chapter. This Scooter Time/Rimini Lambretta Centre one is a different take on the subject since it is sprung loaded and thus self-adjusting.**

## Brake Conversions

- MB Developments: external hydraulic conversions, hydraulic slave cylinder conversions for original disc hubs, switch housings incorporating hydraulic master cylinder mountings.
- ESP Scooters: external hydraulic conversions using motorcycle parts.
- Jahspeed: external hydraulic conversions.
- Lambretta Laboratory/PM Tuning: twin outboard disc and anti-dive brake conversions.
- Stoffi's Garage (Austria): Anti-dive external hydraulic disc conversions.
- Taffspeed/MB/Chiselspeed and many other shops: hydraulic slave cylinder conversions for original disc hubs.
- West Coast Lambretta Works (USA): Solid rod rear-set brake conversion.
- ScootRS (Vietnam)/Saigon Scooter Centre (Vietnam): Economical external hydraulic conversions, switch housings incorporating hydraulic master cylinder mountings.

**Above: A ScootRS outboard disc brake conversion which features an entirely re-cast hub and still incorporates a speedo drive.**

## Electronic Ignitions

● SIL Indian types: faults as listed in previous chapters, particularly on 'pattern' versions, but can be corrected to produce a reliable kit.

● AF Rayspeed: renewed production of lightweight electronic flywheels in India soon to start (at time of writing)

● Tino Sacchi Varitronic: lightweight Italian-built electronic ignition with advance/retard. Production soon to start (at time of writing).

● MB Developments: lightweight European-built system with optional advance/retard. Production soon to start (at time of writing).

● PM Tuning: Race spec computer-programmable advance/retard digital multi-map CDI box to fit with AF/Indian ignition systems.

● Scooter Loopy: CDI/Regulator fitting kit adaptors.

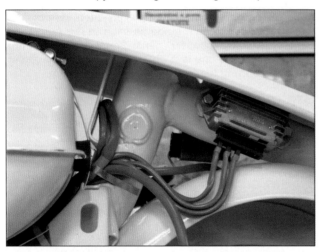

**Above: One of the many electronic CDI and regulator mounting kits now available.**

## Long-Range Fuel Tanks

● Rimini Lambretta Centre: 18-litre baffled fibreglass tank
● Diablo Moto Nuneaton: 18-litre curved-sided steel tank, battery versions available
● Burns Scooter Services: 18-litre flat-sided steel tank
● ESP Scooters: 18-litre flat-sided aluminium tank, tool recess in front.
● Saigon Scooter Centre (Vietnam): Long range tanks, twin tank conversions and legshield fuel tanks.
● ScootRS (Vietnam): twin tank conversions.

**Above: Rimini Lambretta Centre's 18-litre job is the only long range fuel tank moulded in fibreglass.**

## Main Re-manufacturers:

● Casa Lambretta (Vittorio Tessera): Masses of Lambretta frame and engine bits remade, mostly to a high standard.

● MB Developments: Remade, performance and accessory parts manufactured in the UK and Asia. Many components available in stainless steel versions.

● Saigon Scooter Centre: Many remade standard, performance and accessory parts made in Vietnam/Far East.

● ScootRS: Many remade standard, performance and accessory parts made in Vietnam/Far East.

● Scootopia: UK-based re-maker of period Lambretta accessories.

● AF Rayspeed: Re-manufacturer of engine, body and tuning components in India, Italy and Spain. Producer of AF TS1, Rapido and AF electronic kits.

● Scooter Restorations: Re-manufacturer of components in India and producer of the SR kit.

● Tino Sacchi: Re-manufacturer of various Lambretta engine parts and producer of the Imola/Monza/Mugello kits and Varitronic ignition system.

## Remade Body Parts

● Tino Sacchi: TV/SX/GP-type complete cable front disc brakes (not to original quality), Fibreglass SX/TV/Special mudguards and other body parts.

● Lambretta Body Bits: Remade Serveta Jet (like LI/SX/TV) type steel legshields, SX150/SX200 'handle type' sidepanels, steel rear mudguards, rear running boards.

● Saigon Scooter Centre Vietnam: hand-beaten SX metal mudguards and legshield toolboxes.

● ScootRS Vietnam: various remade bodywork components including legshield toolboxes, mudguards and sidepanels.

● John Churchill: fibreglass remade parts including SX 200 sidepanels.

● PM Tuning: a selection of remade body parts in carbon fibre or fibreglass including rear mudguards and toolbox doors.

● MB Developments: most Lambretta GP body parts remade in carbon fibre. Carbon/Kevlar high-strength cylinder and flywheel cowlings.

## Suspension:

● Taffspeed/AF Rayspeed/Chiselspeed: adjustable British rear suspension units in steel or billet aluminium.

● Bitubo (Italy): adjustable gas shocks. Known for seals blowing if overloaded or over-pumped.

● West Coast Lambretta Works (USA): Daytona adjustable steering dampers re-valved to suit use as Lambretta fork dampers. Adjustable fork spring pre-load kits.

## Other Custom Parts

- Cambridge Lambretta Workshop: fuel level sensor light conversion.
- Aluminium stand feet available from various manufacturers.

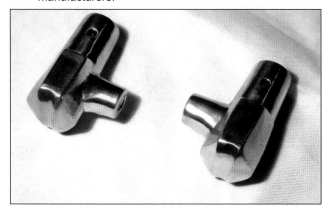

- ScootRS Vietnam: Various stainless steel custom components.

**Above: ScootRS tidy-looking stainless steel floor runner conversions.**

**Above: Many people have expressed an interest in tubeless wheel conversions for Lambrettas because tubeless wheels deflate much more slowly than tubed tyres when punctured. At the time of writing ScootRS in Vietnam are the first firm to put these into production; both in plain painted steel and in stainless steel as shown.**

## we manufacture cool

**scootRS.com**

From top left, clockwise:

- ☼ **PWK D-slide carb and manifold, TS1**
- ☼ **Hydraulic disc brake, ss dampers**
- ☼ **Dual tanks, ss straps, PWK and filter**
- ☼ **SS tubeless rim (no rust or blowouts!)**
- ☼ **SS tuned exhaust and protector trim**
- ☼ **Electric start, hydraulic disc, ss trim**
- ☼ **Glovebox, race seat, dropbars**

## at world best prices!

# CARB JETTING FOR STANDARD MACHINES

| MODEL | Carb | Bore | Slide | Atomiser | Main Jet | Pilot Jet | Starter Jet | Float Weight |
|---|---|---|---|---|---|---|---|---|
| ●LI III 125 | SH1/18 | 18mm | 5914 - 1 | 5899 - 1 | 99 | 45 | 50 | 5gms |
| ●LI III 150 ●Serveta LI 150 (18mm carb) | SH1/18 | 18mm | 5914 - 2 | 5899 - 1 | 105 | 45 | 50 | 5gms |
| ●LI 125 Special | SH1/20 | 20mm | 5914 - 2 | 5899 - 4 | 99 or 103 or 105 or 107* | 45 | 50 | 5gms |
| ●LI 150 Special | SH1/18 | 18mm | 5914 - 1 | 5899 - 2 | 101 | 45 | 50 | 5gms |
| ●SX150 ●Serveta LI 150 (20mm carb) | SH1/20 | 20mm | 5914 - 2 | 5899 - 5 | 102 | 45 | 50 | 5gms |
| ●GP 125 ●Serveta Lince 125 | SH1/20 | 20mm | 5914 - 1 | 5899 - 4 | 98 | 45 | 50 | 5gms |
| ●GP 150 | SH2/22 | 22mm | 7895 - 2 | 5899 - 4 | 118 | 45 | 50 | 5gms |
| ●GP 150 Indian 'Mikarb' | | | | | 85 | 25 | 50 | |
| ●TV 175 III | SH1/20 | 20mm | 5914 - 1 | 5899 - 2 | 106 | 50 | 50 | 5gms |
| ●TV 200 | SH1/20 | 20mm | 5914 - 1 | 5899 - 2 | 108 | 48 | 50 | 5gms |
| ●SX200 ●Jet 200 ●Lince 200 | SH1/20 | 20mm | 5914 - 1 | 5899 - 2 | 103 | 48 | 50 | 5gms |
| ●GP (DL) 200 | SH2/22 | 22mm | 7895 - 1 | 5899 - 2 | 118 or 123** | 45 | 50 | 5gms |

* Innocenti tried various main jets from '99' to '107' in the Special 125 model during production.
** Some GP200 carbs came fitted with '123' main jets as opposed to '118' listed in most books. The '123' jet was also used on later Indian machines running the 42mm 'big bore' exhaust and is an advisable minimum on a standard GP200 fitted with a performance pipe.

# COMMON COMPONENT IDENTIFICATIONS

This appendix lists parts that may commonly be purchased from non-specialist shops if required. Sometimes specialist bearing shops can offer very good value for money on such items. When it comes to bearings it always pays to have the best available, particularly when over-stressing your engine by tuning.

## OIL SEALS

**The most commonly recommended (and supplied) brand is Rolf. There are probably better seals available, but there are plenty worse ones too. The complete oil seal sets for Lambretta engines that come in packets are generally reasonable quality. Seals often have a fourth number (i.e. 33 – 50 – 6 ….'5') which relates to the strength of inner spring. These fourth numbers normally run up to '10'. Do not use seals with a fourth number less than '5'.**

Kickstart shaft: 22-32-5.5
Mag housing outer: 25-42-6
Mag housing inner: 33-52-6
Rear hub: 32-45-6
Drive side main oil seal: 33-50-6 *(those with a suffix of 'AS' or 'RP' have a double lipped seal which is preferred by most dealers. Those with a prefix of 'FPM' are high specification Viton seals which are highly resistant to unleaded fuel)*

## BEARINGS

**When buying bearings try to avoid Indian, Chinese or Eastern European bearings where possible. This may sound like unreasonable prejudice in 20 years time, but at the moment there is too much rubbish produced there to take a risk in the hope of finding a good source. Most people prefer 'branded' bearings from SKF, FAG, INA, Torrington or NSK. An old maxim that still holds true for most parts (or tools) is: 'if they aren't proud enough to put their name on it then don't use it.'**

Drive side main bearing: 6305 - C3
(Alternatively use 'RS' – which has a single rubber seal - or '2RS' which has two seals and remove one of them on the sprocket side.)

Flywheel side main bearing [LI-SX-TV-GP]: NU205
(specify a plastic cage hi-load bearing)

Flywheel side main bearing [GP200 crankshaft]: NU2205
(specify a plastic cage hi-load bearing)

Gear cluster needle bearing (casing): 16-22-12

Endplate gear cluster bearing: 6004

Endplate layshaft needle bearing: 20-24-10

Rear sprocket needle roller bearings: 24-28-10
(Use 2 only in early riveted type sprockets. Alternatively use the later bronze bush in any type of sprocket)

Front hub bearing: 6201

# IGNITION TIMING

Piston Travel (mm) vs Crankshaft Rotation (°BTDC)

## 58mm Stroke Crank

|      |   | 107mm rod | 110mm rod | 116mm rod |
|------|---|-----------|-----------|-----------|
| 15°  | - | 1.25mm    | 1.25mm    | 1.23mm    |
| 16°  | - | 1.42mm    | 1.41mm    | 1.40mm    |
| 17°  | - | 1.60mm    | 1.59mm    | 1.58mm    |
| 18°  | - | 1.79mm    | 1.79mm    | 1.77mm    |
| 19°  | - | 2.00mm    | 1.99mm    | 1.97mm    |
| 20°  | - | 2.21mm    | 2.20mm    | 2.17mm    |
| 21°  | - | 2.43mm    | 2.42mm    | 2.39mm    |
| 22°  | - | 2.66mm    | 2.65mm    | 2.62mm    |
| 22°  | - | 2.90mm    | 2.89mm    | 2.86mm    |

## 60mm Stroke Crank

|      |   | 107mm rod | 110mm rod | 116mm rod |
|------|---|-----------|-----------|-----------|
| 15°  | - | 1.30mm    | 1.30mm    | 1.28mm    |
| 16°  | - | 1.48mm    | 1.47mm    | 1.46mm    |
| 17°  | - | 1.67mm    | 1.66mm    | 1.64mm    |
| 18°  | - | 1.87mm    | 1.86mm    | 1.84mm    |
| 19°  | - | 2.08mm    | 2.07mm    | 2.05mm    |
| 20°  | - | 2.30mm    | 2.30mm    | 2.26mm    |
| 21°  | - | 2.53mm    | 2.52mm    | 2.49mm    |
| 22°  | - | 2.78mm    | 2.76mm    | 2.73mm    |
| 22°  | - | 3.03mm    | 3.01mm    | 2.98mm    |

## 61mm Stroke Crank

|      |   | 107mm rod | 110mm rod | 116mm rod |
|------|---|-----------|-----------|-----------|
| 15°  | - | 1.33mm    | 1.32mm    | 1.31mm    |
| 16°  | - | 1.51mm    | 1.50mm    | 1.49mm    |
| 17°  | - | 1.70mm    | 1.70mm    | 1.68mm    |
| 18°  | - | 1.91mm    | 1.90mm    | 1.88mm    |
| 19°  | - | 2.12mm    | 2.11mm    | 2.09mm    |
| 20°  | - | 2.35mm    | 2.34mm    | 2.31mm    |
| 21°  | - | 2.59mm    | 2.57mm    | 2.54mm    |
| 22°  | - | 2.83mm    | 2.81mm    | 2.79mm    |
| 22°  | - | 3.09mm    | 3.07mm    | 3.04mm    |

## 62mm Stroke Crank

|      |   | 107mm rod | 110mm rod | 116mm rod |
|------|---|-----------|-----------|-----------|
| 15°  | - | 1.36mm    | 1.35mm    | 1.33mm    |
| 16°  | - | 1.54mm    | 1.53mm    | 1.52mm    |
| 17°  | - | 1.74mm    | 1.73mm    | 1.71mm    |
| 18°  | - | 1.95mm    | 1.94mm    | 1.91mm    |
| 19°  | - | 2.17mm    | 2.15mm    | 2.13mm    |
| 20°  | - | 2.40mm    | 2.38mm    | 2.36mm    |
| 21°  | - | 2.64mm    | 2.62mm    | 2.59mm    |
| 22°  | - | 2.89mm    | 2.87mm    | 2.84mm    |
| 22°  | - | 3.15mm    | 3.13mm    | 3.10mm    |

*Notes*
**LI/SX/GP/TV200 CON ROD = 107mm**
(Figures also suit Kawasaki 106mm Rod)

**TV175 CONROD = 116mm**
(Figures also suit Yamaha RD400/Rotax 115mm Rod)

**YAMAHA RD350 = 110mm**

# CRANKSHAFT SPECIFICATIONS

## Italian Crankshafts (all measurements in mm)

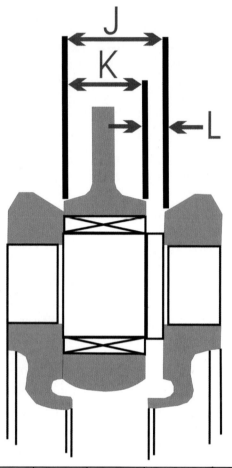

| MODEL | (J) - Gap Between Crankwebs (mm) | (K) – Con-Rod Big End Width (mm) | (L) Sidefloat on Assembly (mm) | (L) Maximum Permissible Side float |
|---|---|---|---|---|
| LI 1, LI 2, LI 3 (Early), TV 175, TV 200 | 14.0 | 13.8 | 0.122-0.275 | 0.40 |
| Later LI, Special, SX and GP using gudgeon pin shims | 14.0 | 12.8 | 1.100-1.275 | 1.50 |

## SIL Indian GP 150/200 wide con-rod type

**Assembly tolerances and Wear limits between crank shaft and con-rod big end.**

| With of Crank shaft boss in mm (C) | With of Con-Rod big end in mm (A) | Roller Cage width in mm (B) |
|---|---|---|
| +0.1 15.8 -0.05 | + 0 15.5 - 0.5 | -0.2 15.7 -0.55 |

### Assembly Clearances

|  (C-A) |  |  (C-B) |  |
|---|---|---|---|
| **Min** 0.25 | **Max** 0.45 | **Min** 0.25 | **Max** 0.75 |

## Original Type Crankshaft Notes

- TV 175 con rods have flats machined into the webs and a 116mm (centre-centre) length con-rod. All other standard cranks use a 107mm rod.
- Early TV 200 crank was replaced by part 42912150 which is noticeable by the flats on the crankwebs. The later cranks are intended to be used together with a revised piston and gudgeon pin shims.
- SX 200 crank part 19612150 identified by 19.5mm balance holes in the webs. Should be used together with tapered gudgeon pin (19612018) for optimum engine balance.
- GP 125 and 150 cranks have thick flywheel taper and balance holes. GP200 has thick taper and plain webs. Both are intended for use with shimmed pistons. Some GP 150s came fitted with GP 200-type cranks.
- Original SIL Indian GP 'wide big-end' type cranks supplied since the mid-90s. Identified by the rod being 15.5mm wide at the big end bearing, but having no big end shims. These cheap cranks have proved popular as spares for standard machines since no gudgeon pin shims are required, but the bearing and rod are not suitable for use in high-performance motors. These well-made crankwebs can be fitted with Italian 'race'-type rods and bearings with good results.

| PART NUMBER | MODELS | PISTON SHIMS | CRANKWEB FEATURES | COMMENTS |
|---|---|---|---|---|
| 19912140 | LI125/150 ser. 3 Early Special 125/150 | NO | no flats | Replace with 19912190 |
| 19912190 | Later Special 125/150, SX 150 | YES | no flats | |
| 19212140 | TV 175 ser. 3 | NO | 2 flats | 116mm con rod (non-TV175 are 107mm) |
| 42012140 | TV 200 | NO | 2 flats + 2 small holes | Replace with 19612150 |
| 42912150 | Spare for TV 200 & early SX 200 | YES | 2 flats + 2 small holes | Replace with 19612150 |
| 19612150 | Late SX 200 | YES | 2 flats + 2 19.5mm holes | Use with tapered gudgeon pin |
| 22012020 | GP 125/150 | YES | no flats 2 holes 19.9mm stepped crankpin | Thick flywheel taper. 13mm wide flywheel oilseal shoulder. |
| | Late Indian GP 150 | YES | no flats no holes 22.9mm crankpin | Thick flywheel taper. 13mm wide flywheel oilseal shoulder. |
| 43012020 | GP 200 | YES | no flats no holes 22.9mm crankpin | Thick flywheel taper. 10mm flywheel oilseal shoulder for wider NU-2205 flywheel bearing |
| | Late SIL Indian GP 200 | NO | no flats no holes 22mm crankpin 15.5mm con rod big end width. No big end shims | Thick flywheel taper. 10mm flywheel oilseal shoulder for wider NU-2205 flywheel bearing |

## Original-Type Pattern Cranks

- Pattern Omega GP cranks were produced in 58mm and 60mm stroke. No longer in production but identified by 'Ω' symbol on con rod. These crank webs are of good quality and are suitable for Jap con-rod conversions.
- Pattern Mazzucchelli original GP-type cranks in 58mm and 60mm stroke. Identified by MMC on the con rod. Since the mid-1990s production has not been to the high standards of earlier versions.
- Pattern MEC Eur (MDP) original GP-type cranks in 58mm stroke. Identified by MDP or the Innocenti 'i' mark on the con rod. These can be prone to twisting in powerful engines if the crankpins aren't Loctited.

## 'Race' Type Pattern GP Cranks

- As pioneered by AF Rayspeed but now available from many sources.
- Various levels of quality depending on batch.
- Identified by 0.5mm big end shims and 22mm crankpin.
- Available with 107mm (LI/SX/GP) or 116mm (TV175) rods.
- Available in 58, 60 or 62mm stroke.
- Certain batches can be prone to 'twisting' if web to big end pin fit is too sloppy. Some dealers strip and rebuild these with Loctite retaining compound before sale to prevent twisting in most applications.

## 'Jap Conversion' GP Cranks

- Usually identified by wider-than-standard big end but using a 22.9mm 'stepped' crankpin.
- No big end shims fitted in early conversions. Later versions used 0.5mm or 1mm big end shims.
- Conversions available in rod lengths from 106-125mm.
- Conversions available to suit 18mm small end bearing Jap pistons (e.g. Suzuki)

## 'Balanced' Race Cranks

- Small batches of full-circle cranks (which are drilled and plugged with metal weights to balance them) are being tested to try and alleviate the twisting problem of other designs. These are currently being produced by MB Developments and Tino Sacchi (at the time of writing). So far these have been made in 58, 60, 62 and 64mm stroke versions.

# ENGINE SHIM IDENTIFICATION

Simply lay the shim over the page to identify it.

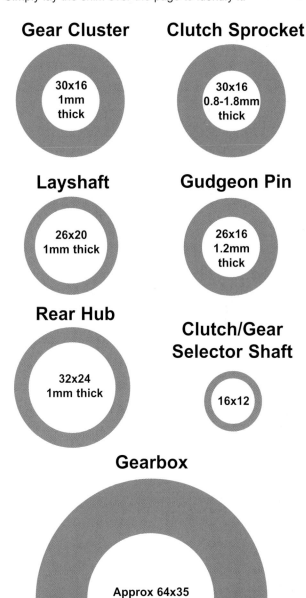

**Gear Cluster**

30x16
1mm
thick

**Clutch Sprocket**

30x16
0.8-1.8mm
thick

**Layshaft**

26x20
1mm thick

**Gudgeon Pin**

26x16
1.2mm
thick

**Rear Hub**

32x24
1mm thick

**Clutch/Gear Selector Shaft**

16x12

**Gearbox**

Approx 64x35
1.8 - 2.8mm thick

# GEARBOX IDENTIFICATION CHART
## ORIGINAL LAMBRETTA 4-SPEED GEARBOXES

These are the gear sets available as standard on production scooter models. In some cases there may be several slightly different gearbox types all using the same ratios. Early gear clusters are likely to be bored down the centre to accept the spindle of early clutch pressure plates. This central drilling was abandoned on later models.

| GEARBOX | GEAR No. | GEAR CLUSTER | LOOSE GEAR | LOOSE GEAR DIAMETER ± 0.2mm | LOOSE GEAR IDENTIFICATION & NOTES | GENERAL GEARBOX NOTES |
|---|---|---|---|---|---|---|
| *LI 150 Special 'Pacemaker' *Late LI 125 (Italian) | 1st 2nd 3rd 4th | 11 13 17 19 | 50 41 39 35 | 115.3 106.5 97.2 92.8 | Late cluster not bored for clutch centre spindle<br><br>3rd across 5 teeth: Early = 33mm, Late = 33.8mm | DO NOT use early type gearbox in a powerful engine because it is too weak |
| *LI 125 S.1 S.2 early S.3 (Italian & Spanish) | 1st 2nd 3rd 4th | 9 12 16 19 | 51 42 39 35 | 119.0 109.5 97.2 92.8 | | Low 1st gear makes this a good box for sidecar use. |
| *LI 125 Special *GP 125 *GP 200 (Italian) | 1st 2nd 3rd 4th | 10 12 15 18 | 50 42 39 36 | 117.5 109.5 111.1 – 100.4 95.3 | | SPROCKETS: 125cc uses 15x46 200cc uses 18x47 Good for clutch life. |
| *GP 200 (late Indian) | 1st 2nd 3rd 4th | 10 12 16 18 | 50 42 38 36 | 115.3 109.5 100.2 95.3 | | Smaller 3rd – 4th gear jump than Italian GP 200 but not built as strong. Good for clutch life. |
| *LI 150 (Spanish) | 1st 2nd 3rd 4th | 11 13 17 20 | 50 41 39 34 | 115.3 106.6 97.2 90.2 | | Biggest 3rd – 4th ratio jump. Dire for most uses. |
| *LI 150 (Italian) | 1st 2nd 3rd 4th | 11 14 17 20 | 50 41 37 34 | 115.3 105.5 96.2 90.2 | 3rd 34.6mm across 5 teeth | Excellent gearbox for general use with correct sprockets |
| *SX 150 *GP 150 | 1st 2nd 3rd 4th | 10 12 15 19 | 50 42 39 35 | 117.5 109.5 111.1 – 100.4 92.8 | | Big 3rd – 4th ratio jump. |
| *GP 150 (Indian Vijay Super) | 1st 2nd 3rd 4th | 10 12 16 19 | 50 42 38 35 | 117.5 109.5 100.2 92.8 | | Different 3rd gear ratio to Italian which reduces 3rd – 4th ratio jump |
| *GP 150 (Indian Vijay Super Mk2) | 1st 2nd 3rd 4th | 10 13 17 21 | 50 41 37 33 | 117.5 106.5 96.2 87.7 – 88.1 | | Oddball late Indian box uses GP 125 1st, Pacemaker 2nd, LI 150 Italian 3rd and SX 200 4th gears. |
| *TV 175 (2 & 3) *SX 200 *Jet 200 *Lince 200 | 1st 2nd 3rd 4th | 12 14 18 21 | 49 40 37 33 | 112.8 104.7 – 104.9 95.6 – 95.9 87.7 – 88.1 | 3rd 34.2mm across 5 teeth | Good gearbox for tuned motor use with correct sprockets |
| *TV 200 (GT 200) | 1st 2nd 3rd 4th | 13 15 19 22 | 47 39 36 32 | 111.1 102.4 93.3 85.3 | | Too tall gearing for use in most tuned engines unless very torquey. |

# SPECIAL LAMBRETTA
# GEARBOX IDENTIFICATION CHART

Most of the gear sets listed below were produced in small numbers, primarily for competition use in the UK.

| GEARBOX | GEAR No. | GEAR CLUSTER | LOOSE GEAR | LOOSE GEAR ORIGIN |
|---|---|---|---|---|
| *LI 150 Rallymaster special (UK) | 1st<br>2nd<br>3rd<br>4th | 9<br>12<br>17<br>20 | 51<br>42<br>37<br>34 | LI 125 early<br>LI 125 early<br>LI 150 Italian<br>LI 150 Italian |
| *MSC (UK) close ratio | 1st<br>2nd<br>3rd<br>4th | 11<br>13<br>16<br>18 | 50<br>41<br>39<br>36 | LI 150 Spanish<br>LI 150 Spanish<br>GP 125 Italian<br>GP 125 |
| *AF (Indian) close ratio | 1st<br>2nd<br>3rd<br>4th | 11<br>13<br>16<br>18 | 50<br>41<br>38<br>36 | LI 150 Spanish<br>LI 150 Spanish<br>GP 125 Indian<br>GP 125 |
| *MRB (UK) LI-150 based close ratio | 1st<br>2nd<br>3rd<br>4th | 11<br>14<br>16<br>18 | 50<br>41<br>37<br>34 | LI 150 Italian<br>LI 150 Italian<br>LI 150 Italian<br>LI 150 Italian |
| *MRB (UK) LI 150/SX 200 based close ratio | 1st<br>2nd<br>3rd<br>4th | 12<br>14<br>16<br>18 | 49<br>40<br>37<br>34 | SX 200<br>SX 200<br>LI 150 Italian<br>LI 150 Italian |
| *MRB (UK) TV 200/SX 200 based close ratio | 1st<br>2nd<br>3rd<br>4th | 13<br>15<br>19<br>21 | 47<br>39<br>36<br>33 | TV 200<br>TV 200<br>TV 200<br>SX 200 |
| *MRB (UK) LI 150/SX 200 based close ratio MK2 | 1st<br>2nd<br>3rd<br>4th | 12<br>14<br>17<br>20 | 49<br>40<br>37<br>34 | SX 200<br>SX 200<br>SX 200<br>LI 150 Italian |

# GEAR RATIO SELECTION

If you have changed the performance of your engine then you may need to revise the gearing to make best use of the new power output. You can do this by replacing the gearbox, by changing the sprocket sizes or a combination of the both methods.

Within most of the Lambretta world, gearing is expressed in terms of a Drive Ratio for top gear (4th), which is calculated as follows:

**(4th gear loose cog) / (4th gear cluster)**
**x (rear sprocket) / (front sprocket)**

For standard Italian LI 150 the drive ratio is:
**35/19 x 46/15 = 5.65 : 1**

In other words the crankshaft must turn 5.65 times to turn the rear wheel once in 4th gear. The drive ratio expresses how tall the overall gearing is, with a higher drive ratio figure actually being lower gearing.

| Drive Ratio | Standard Sprockets | Original Gearboxes |
|---|---|---|
| 6.13 | 15 x 46 | LI 125 Special, GP 125 |
| 5.65 | 15 x 46 | LI 125 (all), LI 150 Special (Pacemaker), SX 150, GP 150 |
| 5.22 | 18 x 47 | GP 200 (all) |
| 5.21 | 15 x 46 | LI 150 |
| 4.82 | 15 x 46 | TV175 (all), SX200 |
| 4.46 | 15 x 46 | TV 200 |

The correct drive ratio for your engine depends on a number of factors.

You should select high gearing (lower drive ratio figure) if:
- your engine/exhaust produces good power at low revs
- you want to cruise at low revs on the motorway
- you ride mostly one-up

You should select lower gearing (higher drive ratio figure) if:
- your engine/exhaust produces most of its power at high rpm
- your engine is not very powerful
- acceleration is more important than top speed
- you often ride with a heavy load

AF Rayspeed produced the following table as a guide for customers when selecting overall gearing for a particular set-up. These are not gospel figures since the final drive ratio you select may also depend on your intended use for the scooter and other factors regarding the tuning of the engine.

| Engine/Exhaust | Drive Ratio |
|---|---|
| TS1 - NK | 5.2 |
| TS1 - Fresco | 4.8 |
| Rapido 250 - Fresco | 4.7 |
| Rapido - NK | 5.2 |
| Rapido - Fresco | 4.8 |
| GP 200 - NK | 5.2 |
| GP 200 - Fresco | 4.8 |
| 175 - Clubman | 4.9 |
| 175 - NK | 5.2 |
| 175 - Fresco | 4.9 |
| Taffspeed pipes | 4.5 – 4.7 |
| PM Tuning pipes | 5.1 – 5.3 |
| MB Dev Tour pipes | 4.8 – 5.2 |
| Kegra KRP2 pipes | 5.2 |
| Scorpion pipes | 4.9 – 5.2 |

## Chain Selection

| Rear Sprocket | F. Sprocket | Chain |
|---|---|---|
| 46 | 14 | No Chain Available |
| | 15 | 80 |
| | 16 | Stretched 80 |
| | 17 | 81 |
| | 18 | Stretched 81 |
| | 19 | 82 |
| | 20 | Stretched 82 |
| 47 | 14 | 80 |
| | 15 | Stretched 80 |
| | 16 | 81 |
| | 17 | Stretched 81 |
| | 18 | 82 |
| | 19 | Stretched 82 |
| | 20 | 83 |
| 48 | 14 | Stretched 80 |
| | 15 | 81 |
| | 16 | Stretched 81 |
| | 17 | 82 |
| | 18 | Stretched 82 |
| | 19 | 83 |
| | 20 | Stretched 83 |
| 49 | 14 | 81 |
| | 15 | Stretched 81 |
| | 16 | 82 |
| | 17 | Stretched 82 |
| | 18 | 83 |
| | 19 | Stretched 83 |
| | 20 | 84 |

## How to obtain the desired Final Drive Ratio

| Final Drive Ratio | Gear Box | Primary Ratio |
|---|---|---|
| 4.6 | Li 150 With | 17 / 46 (81 Pitch) |
| | GP200 With | 20 / 46 (Stretched 82 Pitch) |
| | GP150 With | 19 / 48 (83 Pitch) |
| | SX200 With | 16 / 47 (81 Pitch) |
| 4.7 | Li 150 With | 16 / 46 (Stretched 80 Pitch) |
| | GP200 With | 20 / 47 (83 Pitch) |
| | GP150 With | 18 / 46 (Stretched 81 Pitch) |
| | SX200 With | 16 / 48 (Stretched 81 Pitch) |
| 4.8 | Li 150 With | 17 / 48 (82 Pitch) |
| | GP200 With | 19 / 46 (82 Pitch) |
| | GP150 With | 18 / 47 (82 Pitch) |
| | SX200 With | Standard 15 / 46 (80 Pitch) |
| 4.9 | Li 150 With | 16 / 46 (Stretched 80 Pitch) |
| | GP200 With | 20 / 49 (84 Pitch) |
| | GP150 With | 16 / 46 (Stretched 80 Pitch) |
| | SX200 With | 15 / 47 (Stretched 80 Pitch) |
| 5.0 | Li 150 With | 16 / 47 (81 Pitch) |
| | GP200 With | 19 / 48 (83 Pitch) |
| | GP150 With | 17 / 46 (81 Pitch) |
| | SX200 With | 15 / 48 (81 Pitch) |
| 5.1 | Li 150 With | 16 / 48 (Stretched 81 Pitch) |
| | GP200 With | 18 / 46 (Stretched 81 Pitch) |
| | GP150 With | 17 / 47 (Stretched 81 Pitch) |
| | SX200 With | 15 / 49 (Stretched 81 Pitch) |
| 5.2 | Li 150 With | Standard 15 / 46 (80 Pitch) |
| | GP200 With | Standard 18 / 47 (82 Pitch) |
| | GP150 With | 17 / 48 (82 Pitch) |
| | SX200 With | Not available |
| 5.3 | Li 150 With | 15 / 47 (Stretched 80 Pitch) |
| | GP200 With | 18 / 48 (Stretched 82 Pitch) |
| | GP150 With | 16 / 46 (Stretched 80 Pitch) |
| | SX200 With | 14 / 47 (80 Pitch) |

# TORQUE SETTINGS

Below are listed the torque figures for most Lambretta nuts and bolts. For some components several figures are listed where sources disagree with each other.

- The Indian figures below are derived from the SIL Indian GP 150/200 workshop manual.
- The MB figures are torque settings that MB Developments prefer.
- The UK figures are those from the Lambretta Home Workshop Manual.

Where there are choices of figures my preference would be to use the tighter MB/UK settings; provided quality fasteners are used.

| COMPONENT | KG-M | LBS-FT | NM |
|---|---|---|---|
| Flywheel nut (Indian figure) | 6.9 | 50 | 68 |
| Flywheel nut (MB figure) | 7.6 | 55 | 75 |
| Cylinder exhaust/Inlet nuts (Indian figure) | 0.48 – 0.53 | 3.5 – 3.8 | 4.7 – 5.2 |
| Cylinder exhaust/Inlet nuts (MB figure) | 1.0 – 1.27 | 7.2 – 8.7 | 9.8 – 11.8 |
| Cylinder head nuts (Indian figure) | 1.9 – 2.2 | 14 - 16 | 19 - 22 |
| Cylinder head nuts (MB figure) | 2.0 – 2.5 | 15 - 18 | 20 - 24 |
| Stator plate bolts | 0.48 – 0.53 | 3.5 – 3.8 | 4.7 – 5.2 |
| Gear selector pinchbolt | 0.48 – 0.53 | 3.5 – 3.8 | 4.7 – 5.2 |
| Endplate (flange) nuts (Indian figure) | 1.0 – 1.27 | 7.2 – 8.7 | 9.8 – 11.8 |
| Endplate (flange) nuts (MB figure) | 1.4 – 1.7 | 10 - 12 | 14 - 17 |
| Clutch bell centre nut (Indian figure) | 6.7 – 7.5 | 48.5 – 50.5 | 66 - 74 |
| Front sprocket bolt (Indian figure) | 3.0 – 3.5 | 22 - 25 | 29 - 34 |
| Side casing 10mm head nuts (Indian figure) | 0.48 – 0.53 | 3.5 – 3.8 | 4.7 – 5.2 |
| Rear brake shoe pivot pin (Indian figure) | 0.48 – 0.53 | 3.5 – 3.8 | 4.7 – 5.2 |
| Rear hub bearing flange nut (Indian figure) | 0.48 – 0.53 | 3.5 – 3.8 | 4.7 – 5.2 |
| Rear hub nut (20 degree cone) UK-figure | 20.7 | 150 | 203 |
| Rear hub nut (11 degree cone) UK-figure | 15 – 16.5* | 110 – 120* | 147 – 161* |
| Rear hub nut (8 degree cone) UK-figure | 15 – 16.5* | 110 – 120* | 147 – 161* |
| Rear hub locking plate screw (Indian figure) | 1.4 – 1.5 | 10 - 11 | 14 – 14.7 |
| Fork link bolt and nut (Indian figure) | 5.5 – 5.6 | 40 – 40.5 | 54 - 55 |
| Front axle nut (Indian figure) | 5.5 – 5.6 | 40 – 40.5 | 54 - 55 |
| Wheel to hub nuts (Indian figure) | 2.0 – 2.3 | 14.5 – 16.6 | 19.6 – 22.5 |

\* tighten to the first lower figure first and continue tightening as required to align the locking plate screw

CONVERSION FACTORS

Pounds-force feet (lbs-ft) = kg-m  x  7.233
Newton metres (Nm) = kg-m  x  9.804

# INNOCENTI LAMBRETTA SLIMSTYLE PAINT COLOURS

**The following information was supplied by Rimini Lambretta Centre**

The listed colours use codes that were subsequently utilised by 'PPG', 'Lechler', 'RM', 'MaxMeyer' and several other paint suppliers. For definitive breakdowns of each paint colour (i.e. the various component ratios used to make each specific colour), these can be obtained from the 'Flet Italia' listings using the various four digit paint codes. They are not usually listed under 'Lambretta' or 'Innocenti', nor can they be found using the old Innocenti paint codes.

The names given are direct translations of the Italian colour names. In the main, those listed below are the Italian factory base colours. Additional two-tone shades were often only requested or even applied by the various importers or concessionaires of each country.

In Britain, most of the original Innocenti paint colours were re-named - and others were introduced for the UK-specific two-tone schemes. For example, the SX range additional colour options include such exotic names as 'Polychromatic Copper Pink'. Try finding the colour codes for that one! The commonly seen 'flashes' most owners now put on their side panels were originally introduced and applied by UK Lambretta Concessionaires or even individual dealers to brighten up boringly painted single-colour scooters. Two-toning made them more appealing to the public and thus easier to sell. As such, listing all the possible 'extra' colour options is basically an impossible task. Instead what we have listed are the standard Innocenti colours and their relative codes. Any competent paint supplier should be able to use these codes to produce a reliable colour match for restoration of a scooter.

## Paint Tips for All Models

- Dual seat frames & relative rear bracket were painted gloss black.
- Saddle seat frames were painted the colour of the main scooter body.
- Where fitted, the front shock absorbers were painted 'Fiat 690' metallic aluminium grey.
- Rear shock absorbers were gloss black, except for GP models which were a satin black.
- Where fitted, plastic toolboxes must remain in their natural colour (unpainted).

## Innocenti LI 125

'Iseo Light Green' 8035
'Beige' - not available

All parts should be painted in the same 'Iseo Light Green' or 'Beige' colour – including the handlebar lever housings.

## Innocenti LI 150

'New White' 8059
'New Blue' 8038
'Nile Green' 8015
'Ruby Red' 8047
'Grey' 8068 (also known as 'Grey '61')

All parts painted in 'New White' except for the side panels and front horncasting which can be one of the following colours: 'New Blue', 'Nile Green' or 'Ruby Red'. The very first production LI 150's also used 'Grey' as the base colour instead of 'New White'.

## Innocenti TV 175

'New White' 8059
'Dark Grey' 8071
'Coral Red '62' 8065
'Light Yellow' 8064
'Metallic Light Blue' 8062

*First version:* all parts painted in 'New White'. Alternatively, all parts painted in 'New White' except for the side panels, front horncasting and front mudguard which can be painted in one of the following colours: 'Dark Grey', 'Coral Red '62' or 'Light Yellow'. Only on the very earliest production models were the rear mudguard and side panel insides painted with textured black anti–noise paint.

*Second Version:* All painted in 'Metallic Light Blue' except for the toolbox, air filter box, air filter elbow, rear mudguard, flywheel cowling, cylinder cowling, petrol tank and both petrol tank straps, which were painted 'New White'.

## Innocenti TV 200

'New White' 8059
Side panel colours: choice of White, Green, Blue, Gold, Black or Red.

All parts painted in 'New White'. Alternatively, all parts painted in 'New White' except for the side panels, front horncasting and front mudguard which can be painted in one of the following colours: Green, Blue, Gold, Black or Red. These colours were added to all four separate parts or alternatively just the side panels themselves (basically at the customer's choice).

## Innocenti LI 125 Special

'Metallic Light Blue' 8061 (slightly different shade to the TV 175 'Metallic Light Blue')
'Biancospino' (off-white) 8082

All parts painted in 'Metallic Light Blue' except for the toolbox, air filter box, air filter elbow, rear mudguard, flywheel cowling, cylinder cowling, petrol tank and both petrol tank straps which were all painted 'New White'. Alternatively, all parts painted in 'Biancospino' except for the hubs and wheel rims which were painted in 'Fiat 690' metallic aluminium grey.

## Innocenti LI 150 Special

'Metallic Grey' 8060
'Light metallic Gold' 8063

All parts painted in 'Metallic Grey' (silver) or 'Light metallic Gold' except for the toolbox, air filter box, air filter elbow, rear mudguard, flywheel cowling, cylinder cowling, petrol tank and both petrol tank straps which were painted 'New White'.

## Innocenti SX 150

'Spring Grey' 8070
'New White' 8059
'Apple Green' 8039
'Orange 1967' – not available

All parts painted in 'Spring Grey' or 'New White'. Alternatively, all parts painted in 'Apple Green' or 'Orange 1967' except for the toolbox, air filter box, air filter elbow, rear mudguard, flywheel cowling, cylinder cowling, petrol tank and both petrol tank straps that were painted 'New White' with the hubs and wheel rims painted in 'Fiat 690' metallic aluminium grey.

## Innocenti SX 200

'New White' 8059
Sidepanel colours: choice of Red, Green, Gold, Blue, Black or Purple.

All parts painted in 'New White'. Alternatively, the very last production models had hubs, forks, stand, stand splash-plate and wheel rims painted in 'Fiat 690' metallic aluminium grey (as on the GP range which was about to be introduced).

## Innocenti GP 125 (DL125)

'Turquoise' 8016
'Biancospino' (off-white) 8082

All parts painted in 'Turquoise' except for the air filter box, air filter elbow, rear mudguard, flywheel cowling, cylinder cowling, petrol tank and both petrol tank straps which were painted 'Biancospino'. The hubs, forks, stand, stand splash-plate and wheel rims were all painted in 'Fiat 690' metallic aluminium grey. Alternatively, all parts were painted 'Biancospino' except for the hubs, forks, stand, stand splash-plate and wheel rims which were painted in 'Fiat 690' metallic aluminium grey.

## Innocenti GP 150 (DL150)

'Blue' (code not known)
'Red' (code not presently known but available shortly)
'Biancospino' (off-white) 8082
'Orange' 8037

All parts painted in 'Red' or 'Orange' except for the air filter box, air filter elbow, rear mudguard, flywheel cowling, cylinder cowling, petrol tank and both petrol tank straps that were painted 'Biancospino'. The hubs, forks, stand, stand splash-plate and wheel rims were all painted in 'Fiat 690' metallic aluminium grey. Alternatively, all parts were painted 'Biancospino' except for the hubs, forks, stand, stand splash-plate and wheel rims that were painted in 'Fiat 690' metallic aluminium grey. Alternatively, as previous but with the two side panels and the horncasting painted in 'Red' or 'Blue' (the exact code for the blue is not known but it is very similar to 'English Blue' 8031).

## Innocenti GP 200 (DL 200)

'Yellow Ochre' 8080
'Red' (code not presently known but available shortly)
'Biancospino' (off-white) 8082

All parts painted in 'Red' or 'Yellow Ochre' except for the air filter box, air filter elbow, rear mudguard, flywheel cowling, cylinder cowling, petrol tank and both petrol tank straps that were all painted 'Biancospino', with the hubs, forks, stand, stand splash-plate and wheel rims all painted in 'Fiat 690' metallic aluminium grey. Alternatively, all parts were painted 'Biancospino' except for the hubs, forks, stand, stand splash-plate and wheel rims that were painted in 'Fiat 690' metallic aluminium grey.

# LAMBRETTA SLIMSTYLE ENGINEERS STUDS

**Information for this appendix supplied by Terry White of Rapid Industrial Fasteners.**

The studs listed below are the standard sizes and where possible have been determined by measuring original Lambretta parts, however some dealers have their own interpretation of what is the correct size and some size variation may be encountered.

All of these studs can be supplied in high tensile steel, however stainless steel has become popular for items such as crankcase side studs where tensile loading is not crucial (stainless steel has a low tensile strength and will stretch under load – not good for barrel studs!).

**M6 x 21mm,** Threaded 5mm & 10mm – Rear Hub Plate.

**M6 x 25mm,** Threaded 11mm each end – Mag Flange.

**M6 x 33mm,** Threaded 12mm each end – Crankcase Side.

**M7 x 28mm,** Threaded 10mm each end – Gear Box End Plate.

**M7 x 33mm,** Threaded 12mm & 14mm – Exhaust Port.

**M7 x 34mm,** Threaded 12mm each end – Inlet Port (Short)..

**M7 x 44mm,** Threaded 14mm each end – Inlet Port (Long – 125,150,175cc).

**M7 x 50mm,** Threaded 13mm each end – Inlet Port (Long – 200cc).

**M8 x 47mm,** Threaded 16mm & 19mm – Crankcase Side (Exhaust).

**M8 x 160mm,** Threaded 23mm & 32mm – Cylinder Barrel (also fits Vespa PX200).

**M12 x 1.5P (Fine Pitch) x 60mm,** Threaded 20mm each end – Disc Brake Hub.

Some special sizes have also been manufactured and have become popular additions to the range as follows.

**M6 x 41mm,** Threaded 15mm each end – Crankcase Side (Long).

The above size was originally made for mounting the tailpipe a Clubman type exhaust, however Des at Gran Sport let us know that Lambretta crankcases were generally tapped 15mm deep (a standard chaincase stud is threaded 12mm) and using the extra 3mm of thread will reduce the play in worn casing threads.

**M6 x 38mm,** Threaded 7mm & 25mm – TS1 Inlet Port (Long).

**M8 x 168mm,** Threaded 23mm & 40mm – Cylinder Barrel. The above size is favoured by some of the specialist engine tuners as it allows more secure fixing of the cylinder head.

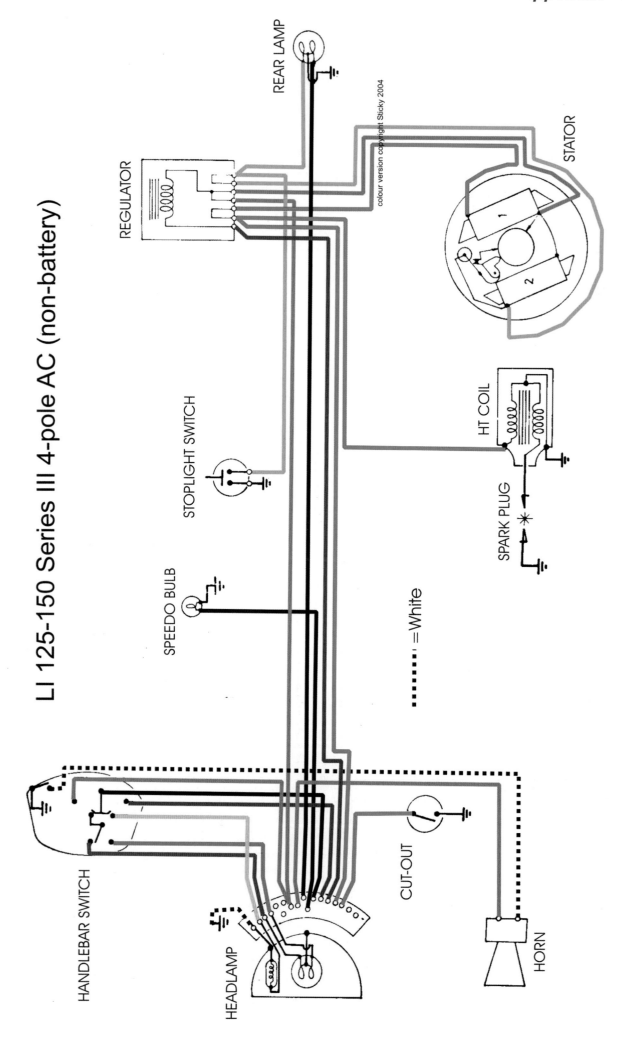

LI 125-150 Series III 4-pole AC (non-battery)

REAR LAMP

STATOR

REGULATOR

colour version copyright Sticky 2004

HT COIL

STOPLIGHT SWITCH

SPARK PLUG

SPEEDO BULB

........ = White

HANDLEBAR SWITCH

HEADLAMP

CUT-OUT

HORN

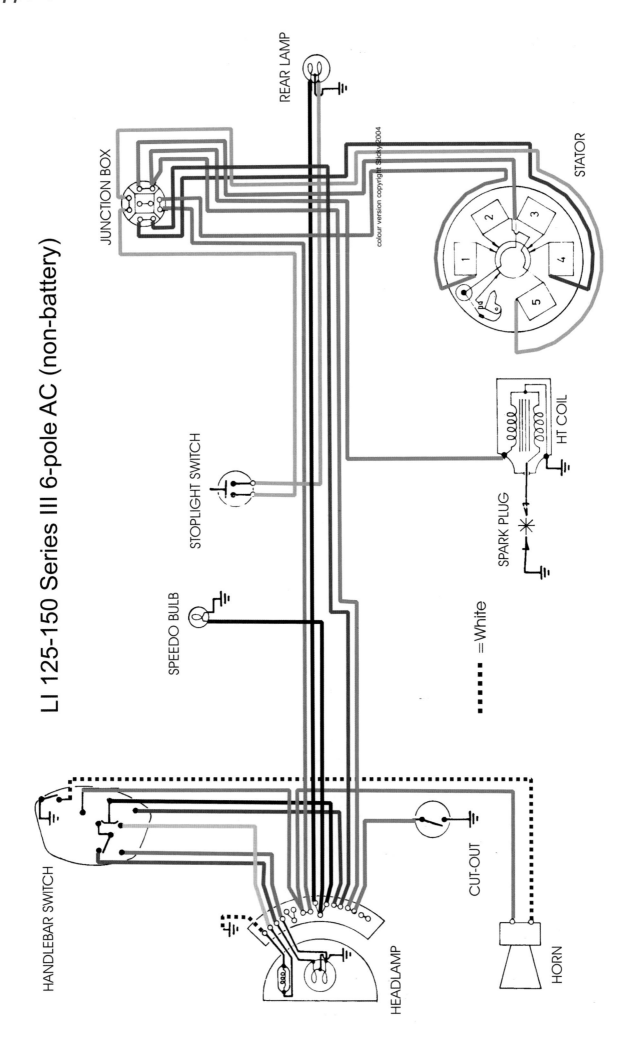

LI 125-150 Series III 6-pole AC (non-battery)

REAR LAMP

JUNCTION BOX

colour version copyright Sticky 2004

STATOR

1  2  3  4  5  p d

HT COIL

SPARK PLUG

STOPLIGHT SWITCH

SPEEDO BULB

= White

HANDLEBAR SWITCH

HEADLAMP

CUT-OUT

HORN

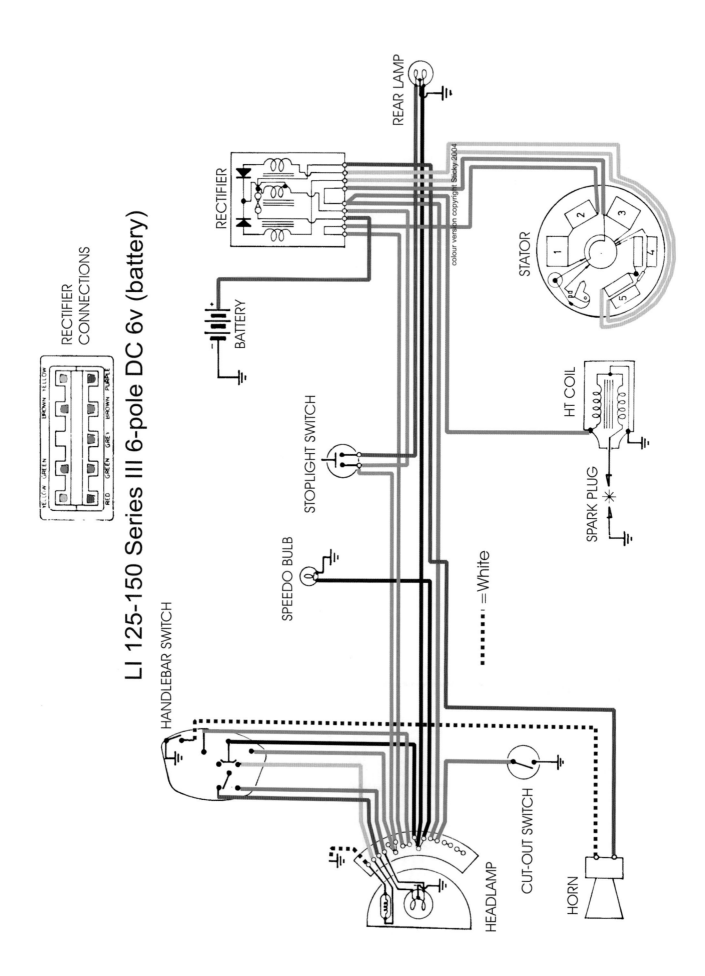

LI 125-150 Series III 6-pole DC 6v (battery)

RECTIFIER CONNECTIONS

RECTIFIER

BATTERY

REAR LAMP

STATOR

HT COIL

SPARK PLUG

STOPLIGHT SWITCH

SPEEDO BULB

HANDLEBAR SWITCH

HEADLAMP

CUT-OUT SWITCH

HORN

••••••• =White

colour version copyright Sticky 2004

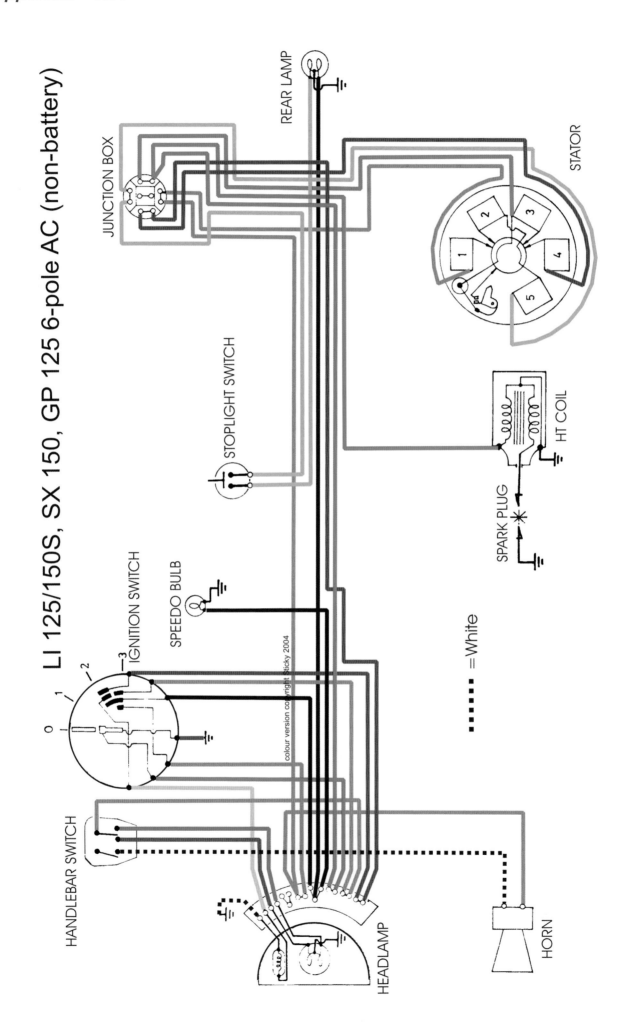

LI 125/150S, SX 150, GP 125 6-pole AC (non-battery)

JUNCTION BOX

REAR LAMP

STATOR

STOPLIGHT SWITCH

HT COIL

SPARK PLUG

IGNITION SWITCH

SPEEDO BULB

colour version copyright Sticky 2004

= White

HANDLEBAR SWITCH

HEADLAMP

HORN

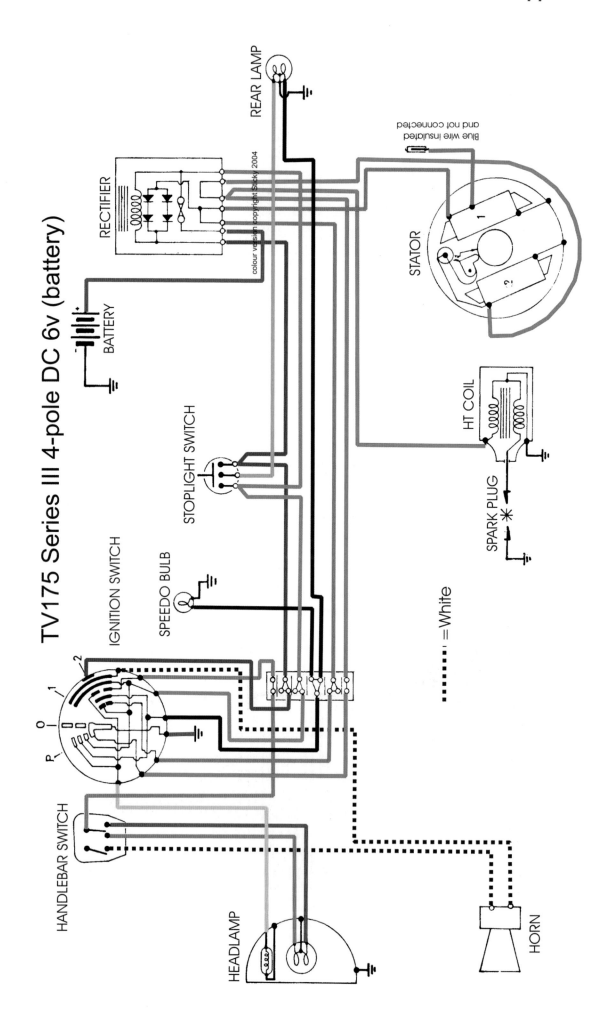

TV175 Series III 4-pole DC 6v (battery)

RECTIFIER

BATTERY

REAR LAMP

Blue wire insulated and not connected

STATOR

HT COIL

SPARK PLUG

STOPLIGHT SWITCH

IGNITION SWITCH

SPEEDO BULB

= White

colour version copyright Sticky 2004

HANDLEBAR SWITCH

HEADLAMP

HORN

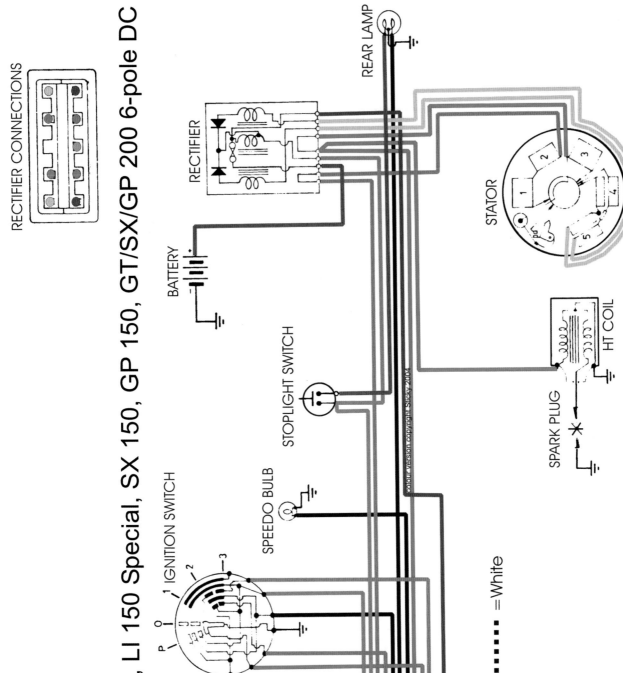

RECTIFIER CONNECTIONS

TV 175 series III, LI 150 Special, SX 150, GP 150, GT/SX/GP 200 6-pole DC

REAR LAMP

RECTIFIER

STATOR

BATTERY

HT COIL

STOPLIGHT SWITCH

SPARK PLUG

SPEEDO BULB

IGNITION SWITCH

= White

HORN & DIP SWITCH

HEADLAMP

HORN

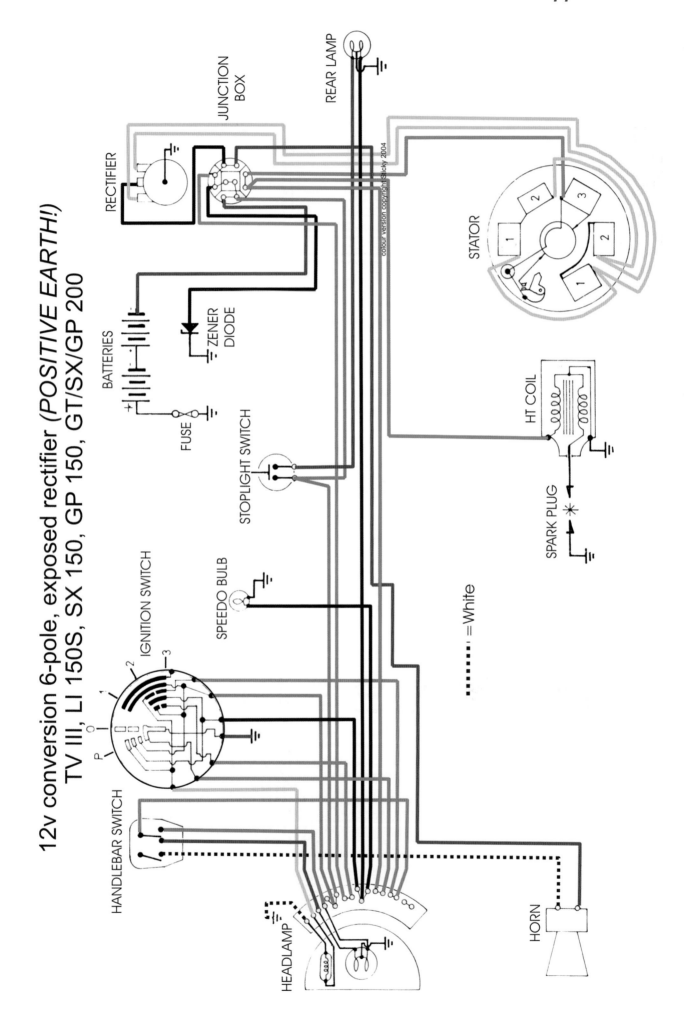

12v conversion 6-pole, exposed rectifier *(POSITIVE EARTH!)*
TV III, LI 150S, SX 150, GP 150, GT/SX/GP 200

RECTIFIER

JUNCTION BOX

REAR LAMP

STATOR

BATTERIES

ZENER DIODE

FUSE

STOPLIGHT SWITCH

HT COIL

SPARK PLUG

IGNITION SWITCH

SPEEDO BULB

= White

HANDLEBAR SWITCH

HEADLAMP

HORN

colour version copyright Sticky 2004

12v conversion 6-pole, enclosed rectifier (*POSITIVE EARTH!*)
TV III, LI 150S, SX 150, GP 150, GT/SX/GP 200

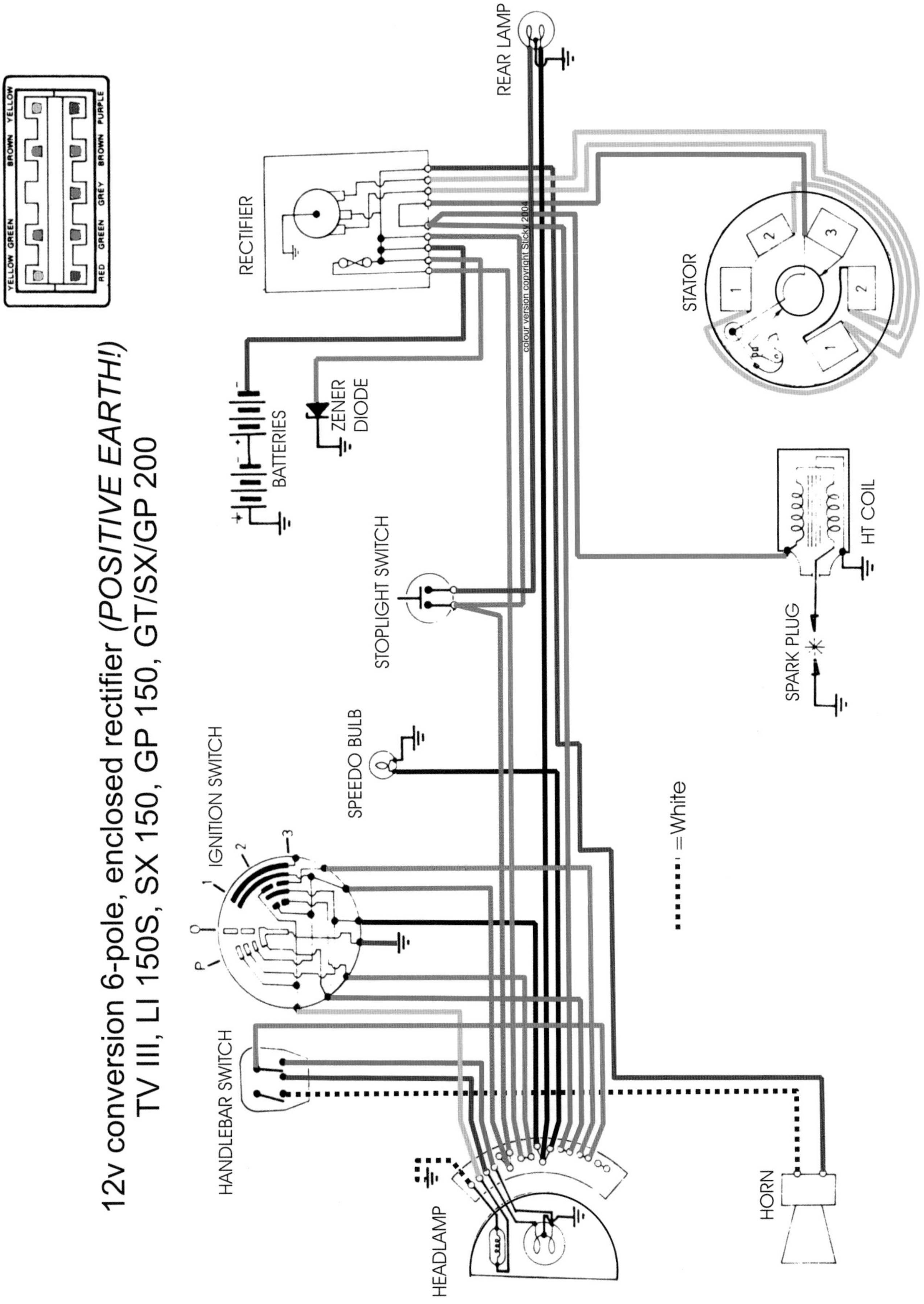

REAR LAMP

RECTIFIER

STATOR

BATTERIES

ZENER DIODE

HT COIL

SPARK PLUG

STOPLIGHT SWITCH

IGNITION SWITCH

SPEEDO BULB

········· = White

HANDLEBAR SWITCH

HEADLAMP

HORN

YELLOW GREEN | BROWN | YELLOW
RED GREEN GREY BROWN PURPLE

colour version copyright Stück 2104

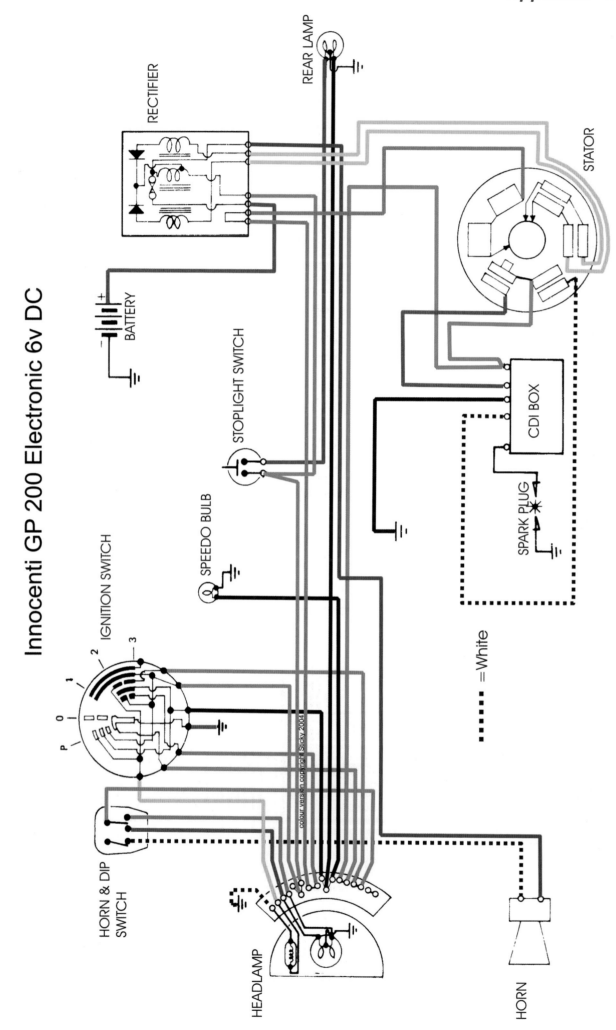

Innocenti GP 200 Electronic 6v DC

RECTIFIER

REAR LAMP

STATOR

BATTERY

STOPLIGHT SWITCH

SPEEDO BULB

CDI BOX

SPARK PLUG

IGNITION SWITCH

= White

colour version copyright Sticky 2004

HORN & DIP SWITCH

HEADLAMP

HORN

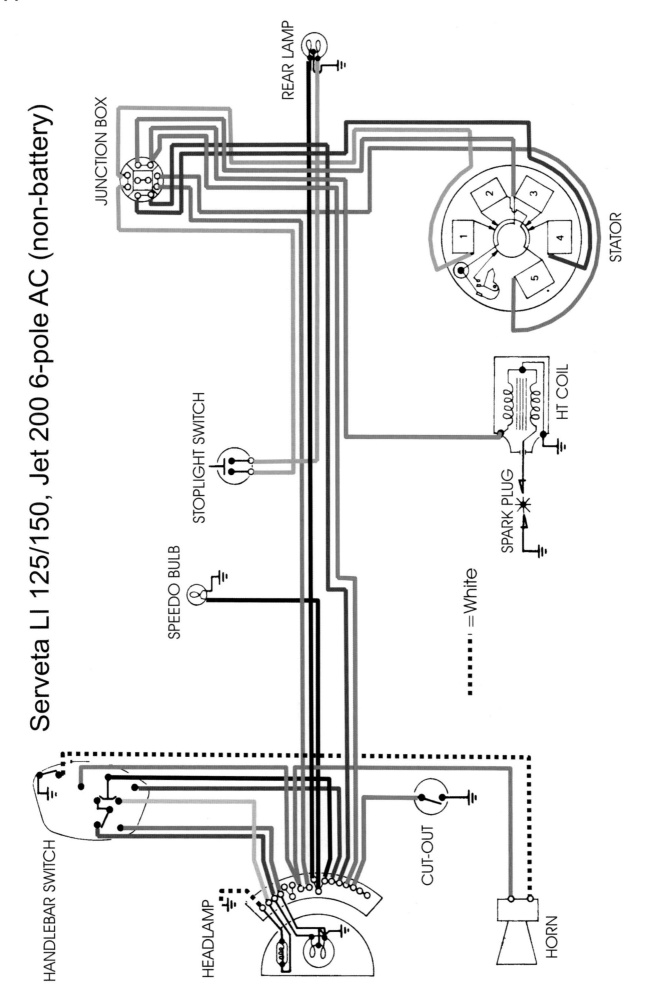

Serveta LI 125/150, Jet 200 6-pole AC (non-battery)

JUNCTION BOX

REAR LAMP

STATOR

STOPLIGHT SWITCH

HT COIL

SPARK PLUG

SPEEDO BULB

······· = White

HANDLEBAR SWITCH

HEADLAMP

CUT-OUT

HORN

Serveta LI 150, Jet 200, 6-pole DC (battery and indicators)

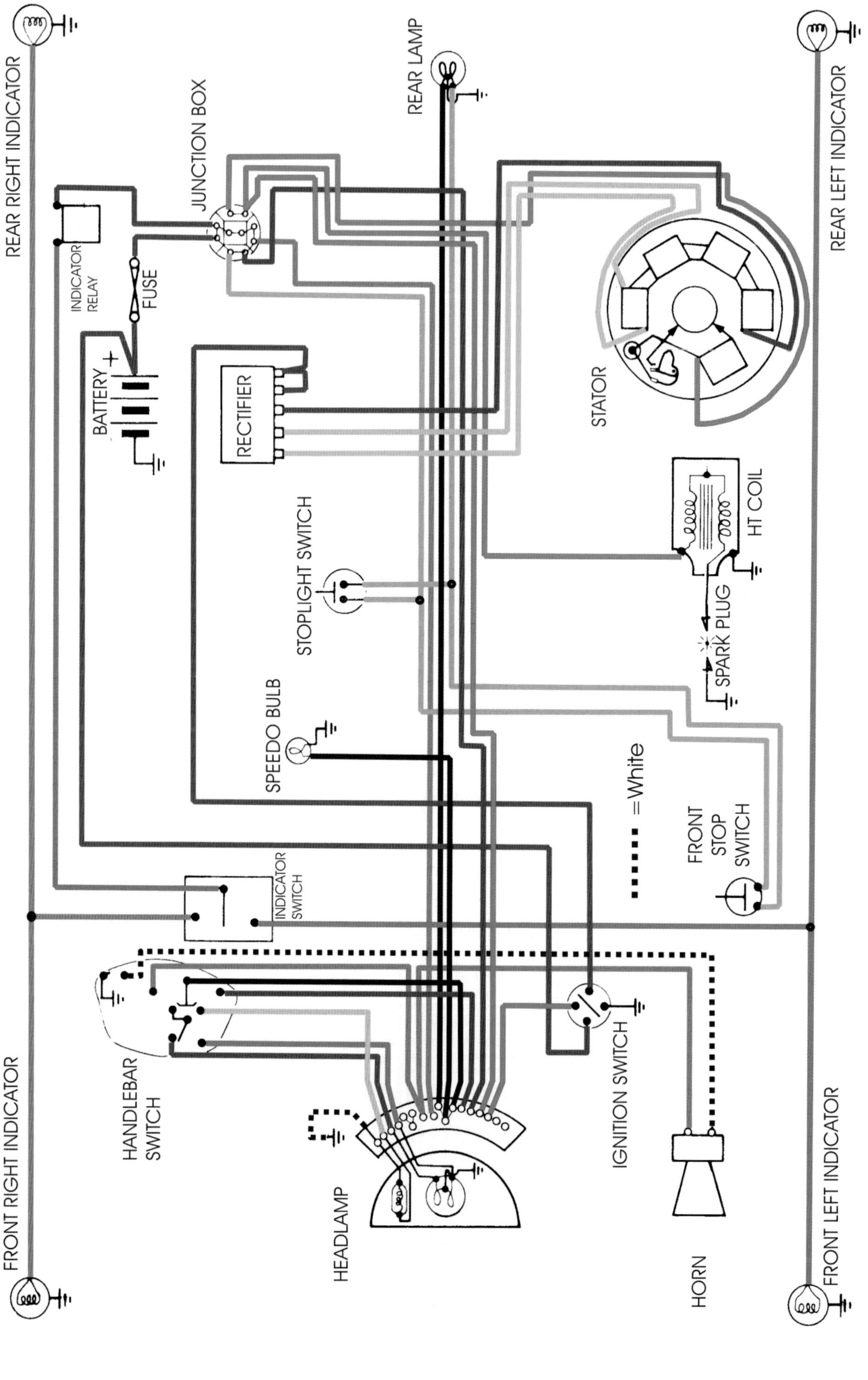

REAR RIGHT INDICATOR

JUNCTION BOX

REAR LAMP

REAR LEFT INDICATOR

INDICATOR RELAY

FUSE

BATTERY +

RECTIFIER

STATOR

HT COIL

STOPLIGHT SWITCH

SPARK PLUG

SPEEDO BULB

FRONT STOP SWITCH

= White

INDICATOR SWITCH

HANDLEBAR SWITCH

IGNITION SWITCH

FRONT RIGHT INDICATOR

HEADLAMP

HORN

FRONT LEFT INDICATOR

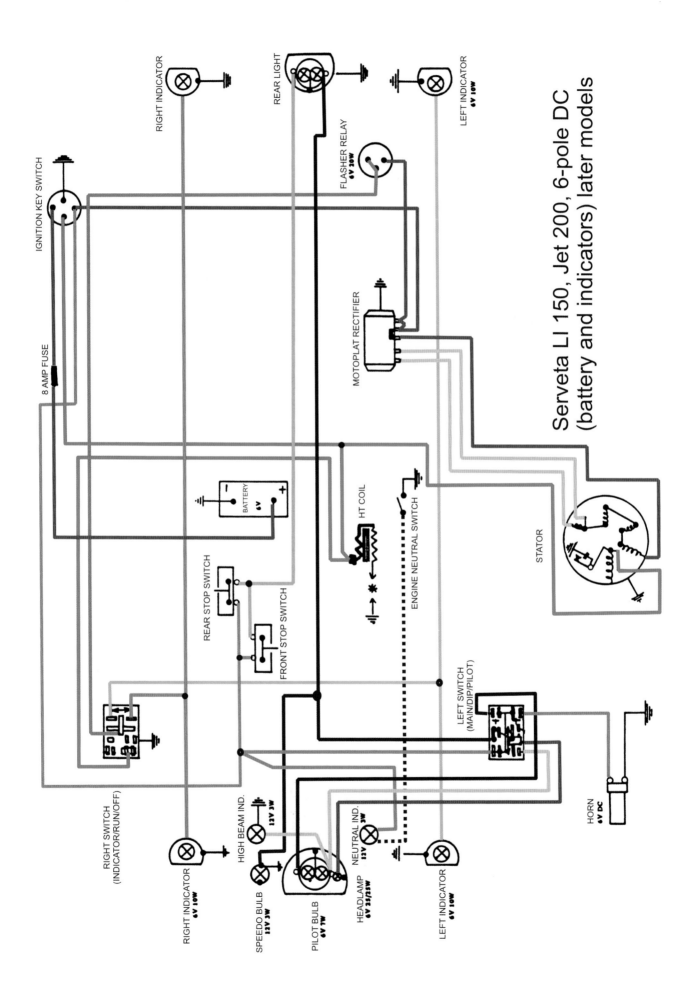

Serveta LI 150, Jet 200, 6-pole DC (battery and indicators) later models

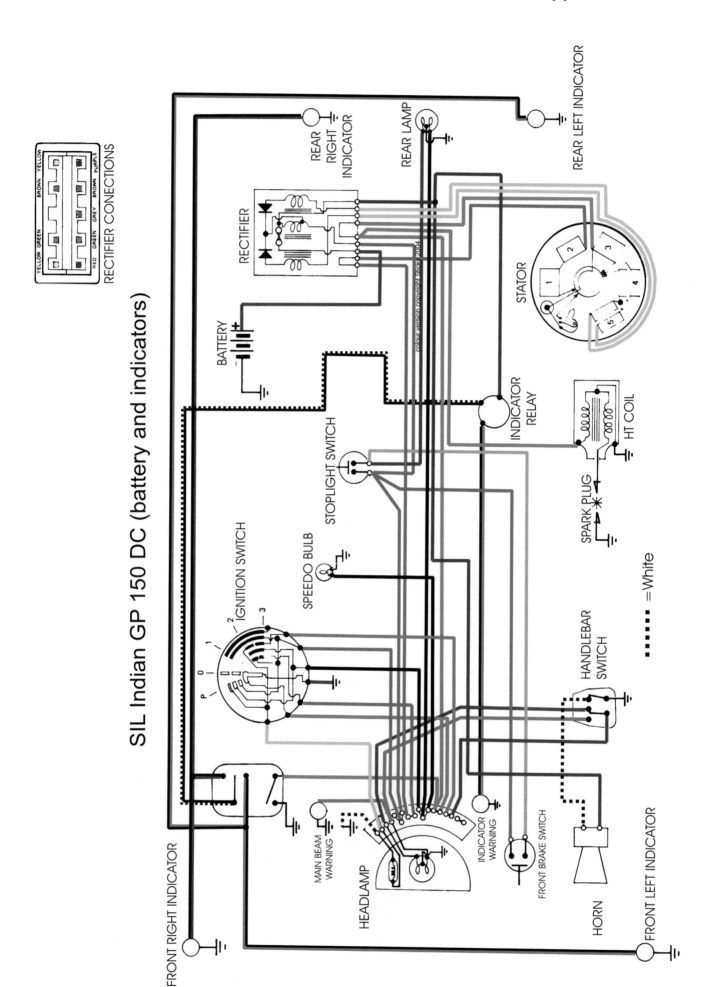

SIL Indian GP 150 DC (battery and indicators)

RECTIFIER CONECTIONS

YELLOW GREEN  BROWN YELLOW
RED GREEN GREY BROWN PURPLE

FRONT RIGHT INDICATOR

REAR RIGHT INDICATOR

REAR LAMP

REAR LEFT INDICATOR

RECTIFIER

BATTERY

STATOR

INDICATOR RELAY

HT COIL

SPARK PLUG

STOPLIGHT SWITCH

IGNITION SWITCH

SPEEDO BULB

HANDLEBAR SWITCH

= White

MAIN BEAM WARNING

HEADLAMP

INDICATOR WARNING

FRONT BRAKE SWITCH

HORN

FRONT LEFT INDICATOR

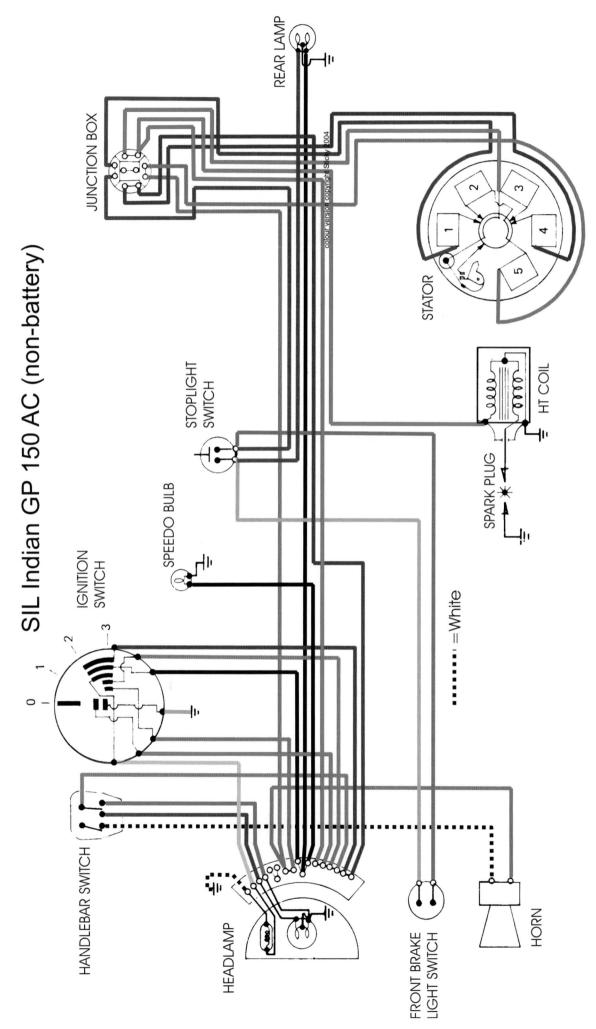

SIL Indian GP 150 AC (non-battery)

REAR LAMP

JUNCTION BOX

STATOR

HT COIL

SPARK PLUG

STOPLIGHT SWITCH

SPEEDO BULB

IGNITION SWITCH

......... = White

HANDLEBAR SWITCH

HEADLAMP

FRONT BRAKE LIGHT SWITCH

HORN

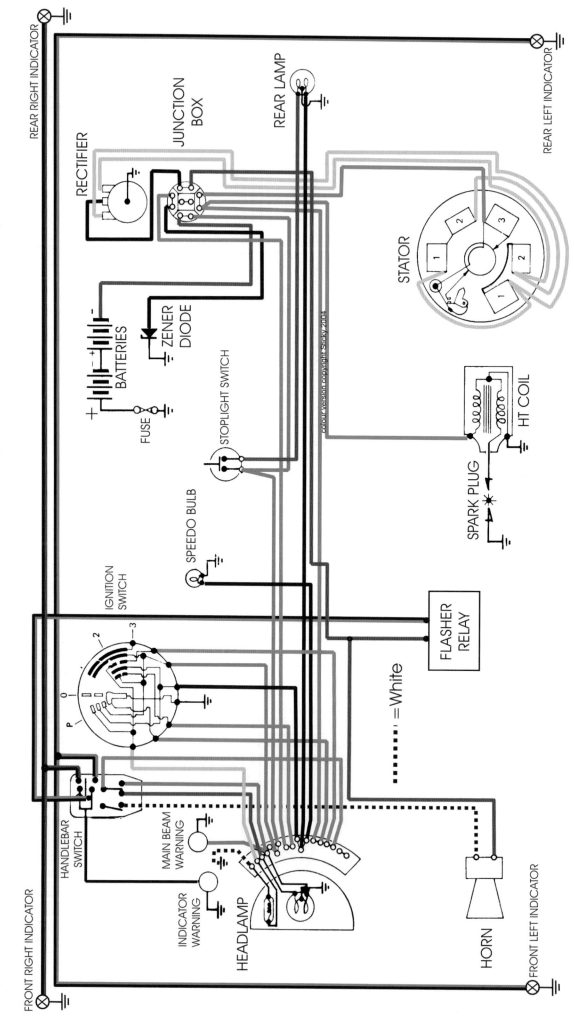

SIL Indian GP-range 12v DC (*POSITIVE EARTH!*)

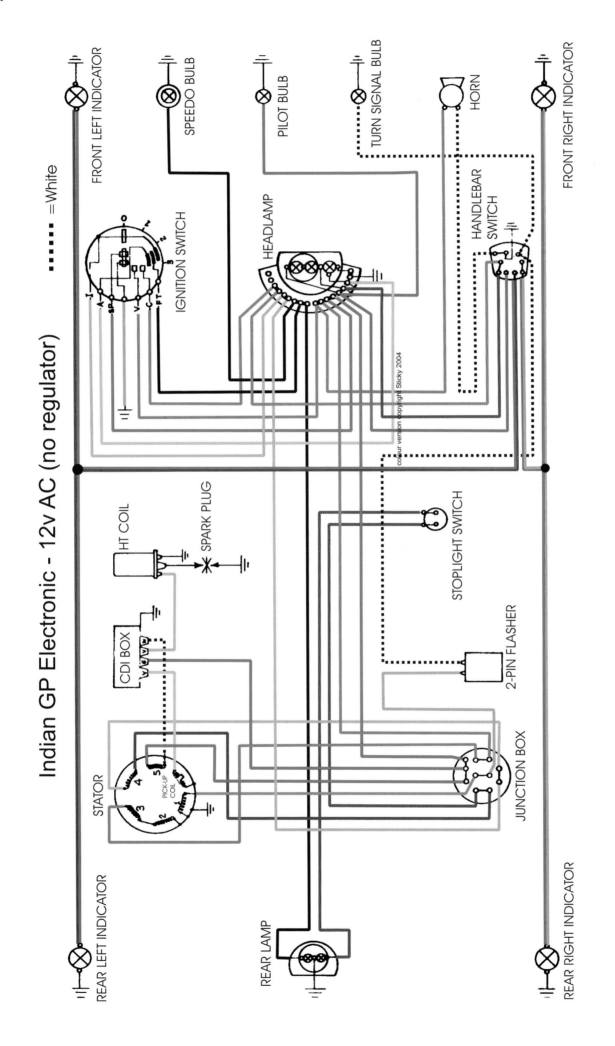

Indian GP Electronic - 12v AC (no regulator)

# SIL Indian GP 12v AC Electronic (with regulator, no indicators, no battery)

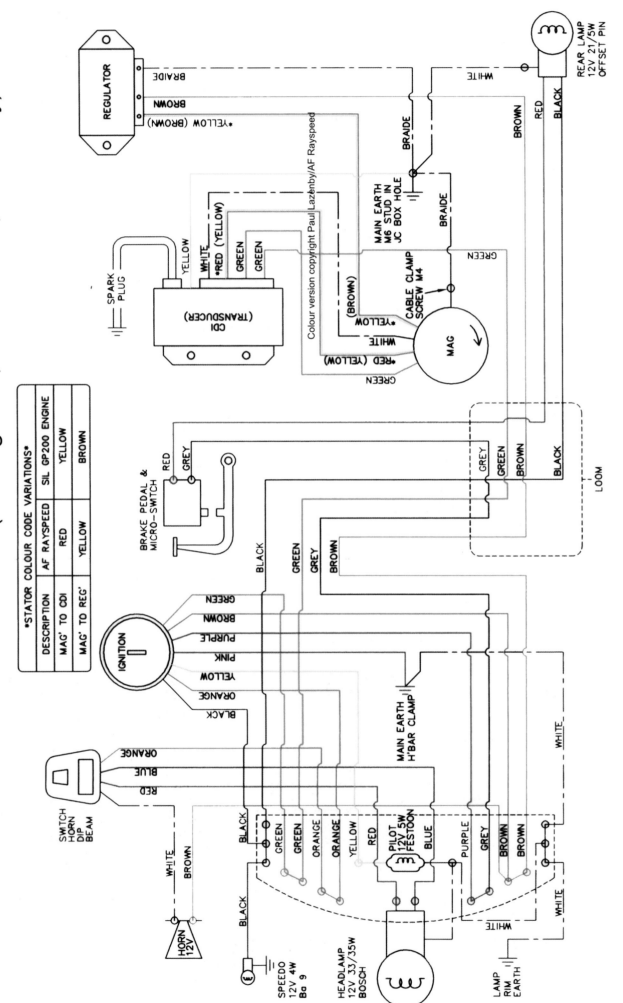

| DESCRIPTION | AF RAYSPEED | SIL GP200 ENGINE |
|---|---|---|
| MAG' TO CDI | RED | YELLOW |
| MAG' TO REG' | YELLOW | BROWN |

*STATOR COLOUR CODE VARIATIONS*

Colour version copyright Paul Lazenby/AF Rayspeed

## SIL Indian GP 12v AC Electronic (with indicators, no battery)

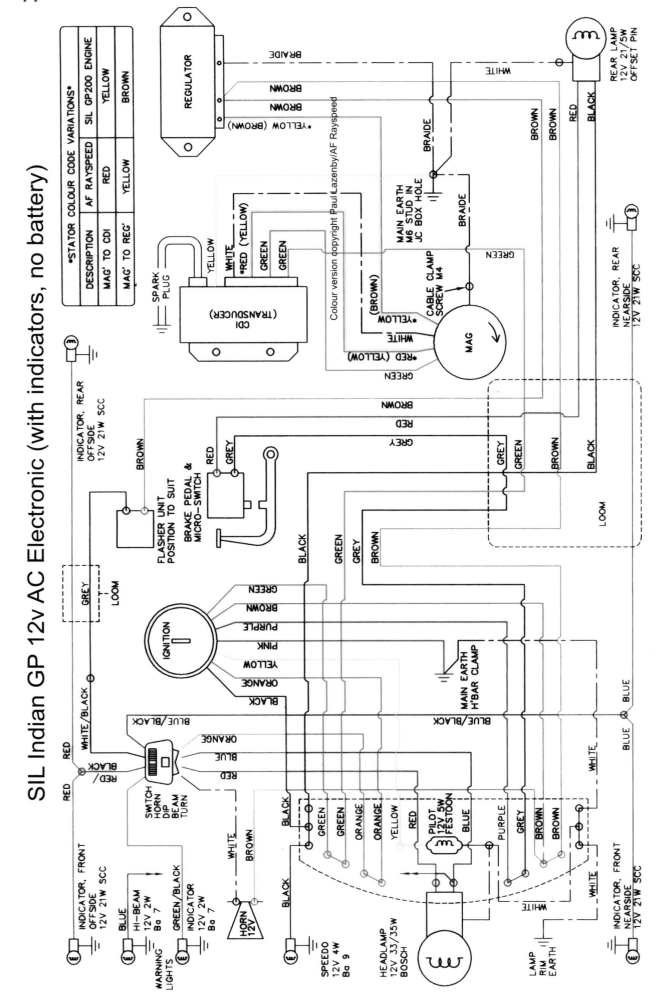

| *STATOR COLOUR CODE VARIATIONS* | | | |
|---|---|---|---|
| DESCRIPTION | AF RAYSPEED | SIL GP200 ENGINE | |
| MAG' TO CDI | RED | YELLOW | |
| MAG' TO REG' | YELLOW | BROWN | |

Colour version copyright Paul Lazenby/AF Rayspeed

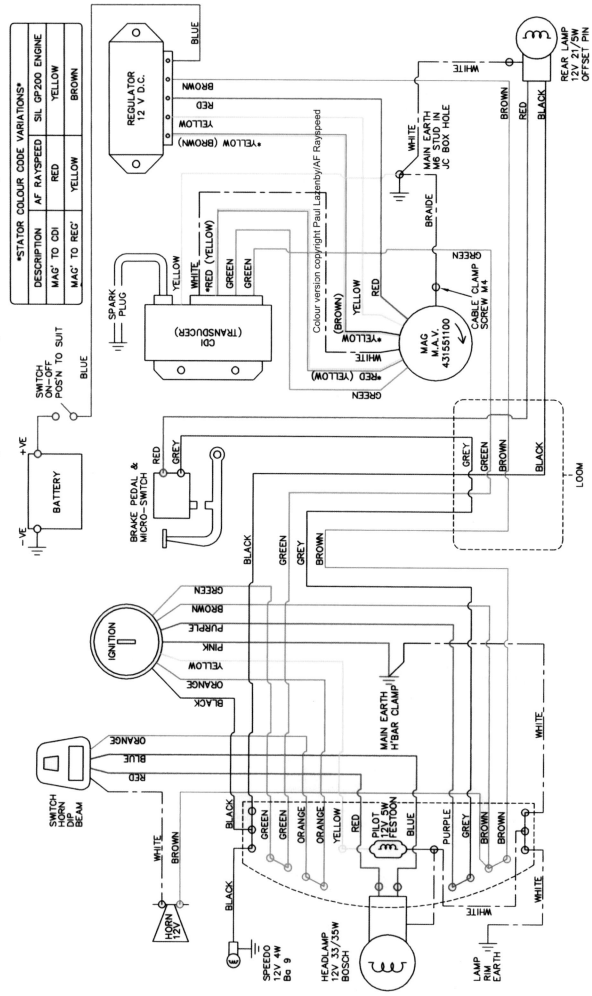

SiL Indian GP Electronic 12v DC (with battery, no indicators)

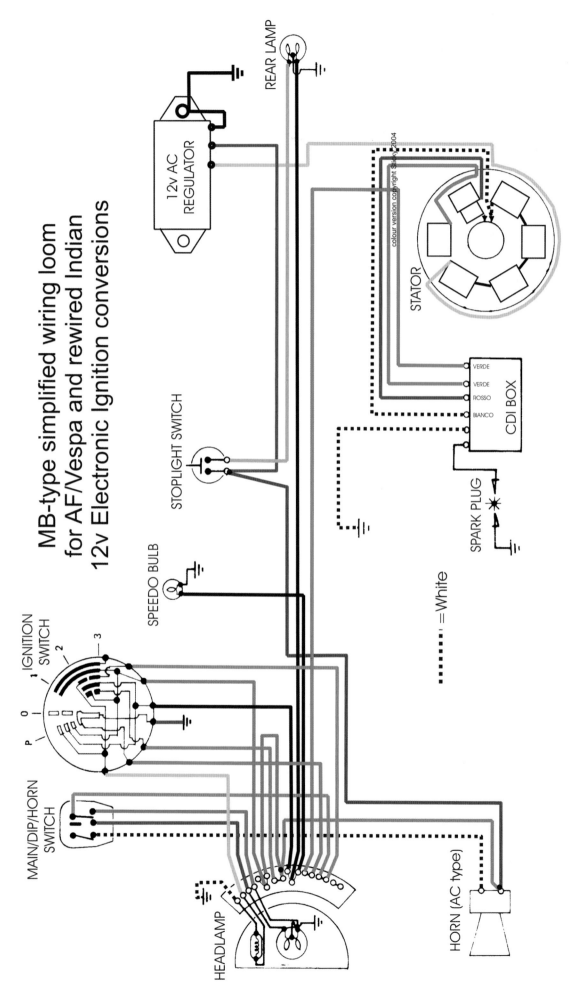

MB-type simplified wiring loom
for AF/Vespa and rewired Indian
12v Electronic Ignition conversions

REAR LAMP

12v AC REGULATOR

STATOR

colour version copyright Sticky 2004

CDI BOX

VERDE
VERDE
ROSSO
BIANCO

SPARK PLUG

STOPLIGHT SWITCH

SPEEDO BULB

IGNITION SWITCH

3
2
1
0
P

MAIN/DIP/HORN SWITCH

HEADLAMP

HORN (AC type)

········· =White

# **Lambretta** DEALER LOCATER

## UK – SOUTH WEST

### SOUTH WEST SCOOTERS
**Address:** 5 Central Road, Yeovil, Somerset, BA20 1JL
**Tel:** 01935 475574
**Fax:** 01935 432625
**Web:** www.swscooters.com

### WESTON SCOOTER PARTS
**Address:** 77 Alfred St, Weston-Super-Mare, Somerset, BS23 1PP
**Tel:** 01934 614614
**Fax:** 01934 620120
**Web:** www.westonscooterparts.co.uk

## UK – SOUTH

### ALLSTYLES SCOOTERS
**Address:** 9-10 Artillery Row, Ackworth Rd, Portsmouth, Hampshire, PO3 5HJ
**Tel:** 023 92 655565
**Fax:** 023 92 667009
**Web:** www.allstyles-scooters.com

## UK – SOUTH EAST

### CAMBRIDGE LAMBRETTA WORKSHOPS
**Address:** Stepney's Yard, Ditton Walk, Cambridge, CB5 8QD
**Tel:** 01223 516662
**Fax:** 01223 509362
**Web:** www.lambretta.co.uk

### KEGRA RACING LTD
**Address:** 91-93 Prince Avenue, Southend on Sea, Essex, SS2 6RL
**Tel:** 01702 331686
**Fax:** 01702 300017
**Web:** www.kegra.com

### KICKSTART MOTORCYCLES
**Address:** 2a Burnt Ash Hill, London, SE12 0HL
**Tel:** 020 8857 4908

### SCOOTER IN STYLE
**Address:** 34 Star La Ind. Est, Great Wakering, Southend-on-Sea, Essex SS3 0PJ
**Tel:** 01702 219244
**Fax:** 01702 219244
**Web:** www.scooterinstyle.co.uk

### SCOOTER SURGERY
**Address:** Arch 219, Trussley Road, Hammersmith, London W6 7PP
**Tel:** 020 87480882
**Fax:** 020 87480882
**Web:** www.scootersurgery.co.uk

### THE SCOOTER EMPORIUM
**Address:** 10 Dray Walk, The Old Truman Brewery, 91 Brick Lane, London, E1 6QL
**Tel:** 0208 375 2277
**Fax:** 0207 375 2277
**Web:** www.scooteremporium.com

### THANET AREA SCOOTER SERVICES (TASS)
**Address:** 114 Northdown Road, Margate, Kent, CT9 2RE
**Tel:** 01843 292440
**Fax:** 01843 223308
**Web:** www.t-a-s-s.co.uk

## UK – WALES

### TAFFSPEED RACING
*Address:* 128 Corporation Road, Newport, South Wales, NP19 0BH
**Tel:** 01633 840450
**Fax:** 01633 246175
**Web:** www.taffspeed.co.uk

## UK – MIDLANDS

### BEDLAM SCOOTERS
**Address:** 1a Edison Road, Elms Farm Industrial Estate, Bedford, MK41 0LF.
**Tel:** 01234 327555
**Fax:** 01234 340255
**Web:** www.bedlam-scooters.co.uk

### DIABLO MOTO
**Address:** Hill Farm, Tunnel Rd, Galley Common, Nuneaton, Warks, CV10 9PE
**Tel:** 02476 393988
**Fax:** 02476 393988

### GRAND PRIX SCOOTERS
**Address:** Unit 31, Boston Rd, Gorse Hill Ind. Est., Leicester, LE4 1AW
**Tel:** 0116 235 7595
**Fax:** 0116 235 7595
**Web:** www.grandprixscooters.freeserve.co.uk

### GRAN SPORT
**Address:** Birmingham, West Midlands
**Tel:** 0121 773 0706

### INTERSCOOTERS
**Address:** Unit 26, Lythalls Industrial Estate, Holbrooks, Coventry CV6 6FL
**Tel:** 024 7668 9333
**Fax:** 024 7668 9333
**Web:** www.interscooters.co.uk

### ITAL SCOOTERS
**Address:** Unit 4C, Ridgeway Farm, Powick, Worcester, WR2 4SN
**Tel:** 01905 831444
**Fax:** 01905 831444
**Web:** www.italscooters.co.uk

# Lambretta DEALER LOCATER

**JC SCOOTERS**
**Address:** Unit 1, Lamb Farm, London Road, Canwell,
Birmingham, B75 5SD
**Tel:** 0121 308 1112
**Fax:** 0121 308 1112
**Web:** www.jcscooters.co.uk

**READSPEED SCOOTERS**
**Address:** 35 Mitton Street, Stourport on Severn,
Worcestershire, DY13 9AQ
**Tel:** 01299 828037
**Fax:** 01299 827442
**Web:** www.readspeedscooters.com

**RESURRECTION SCOOTERS**
**Address:** Unit 44, Imex Business centre, Shobnall Rd,
Burton on Trent DE14 2AU.
**Tel:** 01283 517055
**Web:** www.resurrection-scooters.co.uk

**SCOOTER RESTORATIONS**
**Address:** 153-157 Commercial Road, Bulwell, Nottingham,
NG6 8HT
**Tel:** 0115 927 7277
**Fax:** 0115 976 0700
**Web:** www.scooterrestorations.com

## UK – EAST ANGLIA

**ABSOLUTE LAMBRETTA**
**Address:** Unit 8, Darrell Road, Carr Road Ind. Est.,
Felixstowe, UK, IP11 3UU
**Tel:** 01394 677488
**Fax:** 01394 674411
**Web:** absolutelambretta.co.uk

## UK – NORTH WEST

**PM TUNING**
**Address:** 5/A Major Industrial Estate, Middleton Road,
Heysham, Lancashire. LA3 3JJ
**Tel:** 01524 850800
**Fax:** 01524 850700
**Web:** www.pmtuning.co.uk

**TOTALLY SCOOTERS**
**Address:** Tower View, Lyndale. Cumbria, LA11 6LX.
**Tel:** 01539 534317
**Fax:** 01539 534317
**Web:** www.totallyscooters.com

## UK – NORTH EAST

**AF RAYSPEED LTD**
**Address:** Five Acres, East Heslerton, Nr Malton, North
Yorkshire YO17 8EN
**Tel:** 01944 710693
**Fax:** 01944 710081
**Web:** www.afrayspeed.co.uk

**MB DEVELOPMENTS**
**Address:** Unit 17, Broomhouse Lane Ind. Est., Edlington,
Doncaster, South Yorkshire, DN12 1EQ
**Tel:** 01709 869 756
**Fax:** 01709 860 576
**Web:** www.mbdevelopments.co.uk

## ITALY

**RIMINI LAMBRETTA CENTRE**
**Address:** Via Gessi 14, 47030, Borghi (FC), Italy.
**Tel:** 0039 0541 947492
**Fax:** 0039 0541 947332
**Web:** www.riminilambrettacentre.com

## GERMANY

**SCOOTER CENTRE (KÖLN)**
**Address:** Ludwig-Erhard-Straße 1, 50129 Bergheim -
Glessen
**Tel:** +49(0)2238.30 74-30
**Fax:** +49(0)2238.30 74-74
**Web:** www.scootercenter.com

**WORB 5**
**Address:** Dahlienweg 13, Arenberg - 56077 Koblenz
**Tel:** 0049 - 261 - 9639782
**Fax:** 0049 - 261 - 9637834
**Web:** www.worb5.com

## AUSTRIA

**STOFFI'S GARAGE**
**Address:** Ornetsmühl 38, A-4910 Ried/Tumeltsham
**Tel:** +43 / 7752 / 88707
**Fax:** +43 / 7752 / 88707-4
**Web:** www.stoffis.com

## USA

**(WEST COAST) LAMBRETTA WORKS**
**Address:** 6244 University Ave. San Diego, CA 92115, USA
**Tel:** 619.229.0201
**Fax:** 619.229.9157
**Web:** www.lambretta.net

## VIETNAM

**SAIGON SCOOTER CENTRE**
**Address:** K300 Cong Hoa street, Tan Binh District, Ho Chi
Minh City, Vietnam.
**Tel:** +84-(0) 903-013690
**Fax:** :+84-(8) 8118872
**Web:** saigonscootercentre.com

**SCOOTRS**
**Address:** Vietnam (internet only)
**E-mail:** info@scootRS.com
**Web:** www.scootRS.com

# INDEX

# INDEX